God Interrupted

God Interrupted

HERESY AND THE EUROPEAN IMAGINATION BETWEEN THE WORLD WARS

Benjamin Lazier

PRINCETON UNIVERSITY PRESS

PRINCETON AND OXFORD

Copyright © 2008 by Princeton University Press
Published by Princeton University Press, 41 William Street, Princeton, New Jersey 08540
In the United Kingdom: Princeton University Press, 6 Oxford Street, Woodstock,
Oxfordshire OX20 1TW

Library of Congress Cataloging-in-Publication Data

Lazier, Benjamin, 1971–
   God interrupted : heresy and the European imagination between the
world wars / Benjamin Lazier.
      p. cm.
   Includes bibliographical references (p.) and index.
   ISBN 978-0-691-15541-8
(Judaism)—History of doctrines—20th century.   2. Philosophy,
Jewish—History—20th century.   3. Jonas, Hans, 1903–1993.   4. Scholem,
Gershom Gerhard, 1897–1982.   5. Strauss, Leo.   6. Heresy—History—20th
century.   7. Pantheism—History—20th century.   8. Gnosticism—History—20th
century.   9. Europe—Intellectual life—20th century.   I. Title.
   BM610.L3935 2008
   296.3'110904–dc22   2008005405

British Library Cataloging-in-Publication Data is available

The publication of this book was made possible in part by a generous grant from the Koret
Foundation.

This book has been composed in Sabon

press.princeton.edu

Printed in the United States of America

10 9 8 7 6 5 4 3 2 1

For my parents

"And what is this God?" I asked the earth and it answered: "I am not He," and all the things that are on the earth confessed the same answer. I asked the sea and the deeps and the creeping things with living souls, and they replied, "We are not your God. Look above us." I asked the heaven, the sun, the moon, the stars, and "No," they said, "we are not the God for whom you are looking." And I said to all those things which stand about the gates of my senses: "Tell me something about my God, you who are not He. Tell me something about Him." And they cried out in a loud voice: "He made us."

—Augustine, *Confessions*

What is *the world*? The world is our whole existence, as it has been, and is, conditioned by sin. There has come into being a *cosmos* which, because we no longer know God, is not Creation. . . . In so far as this world is our world, it is the world into which sin has entered. In this world, on this earth, and under this heaven, there is no redemption, no direct life.

—Karl Barth, *The Epistle to the Romans*

Our world is truly the morphological world itself, an unending revelation of matter.

—Hans Jonas

Contents

Preface and Acknowledgments

"SHOULD THE EMANCIPATION and secularization of the modern age, which began with a turning-away, not necessarily from God, but from a God who was the Father of men in heaven, end with an even more fateful repudiation of an Earth who was the Mother of all living creatures under the sky?"[1] At first glance, the question seems simple. Man has turned his back on God the Father, his call interrupted. Will humankind now turn its back on Mother Earth as well? At second glance, it reveals itself as a series of questions in the guise of one. What are we to make of these pirouettes? Are we to celebrate the first turn as our liberation and bemoan the second as our imminent demise? Why, historically, should one follow upon the other at all? And what makes the second more fateful than the first? The philosopher and German-Jewish émigrée Hannah Arendt posed this question in a book called *The Human Condition* (1958). It is also the question, or one of them, to which this book attempts an answer.

. . .

The title of this book may risk jocularity with a subset of readers, and so a few words are in order as to why I selected it nonetheless. I once imagined I would call the book *Redemption through Sin*, as homage to Gershom Scholem, whose essay of that name I address in some detail. For a variety of reasons, not least the blank stares I encountered when I broached it with friends, I elected to leave that title behind, and settled on *God Interrupted* instead. The title certainly has a drawback: depending on your cultural vocabulary, it may echo that of a best-selling memoir (about a psychiatric patient no less), later adapted for the screen with much success. These may not be the sort of friends a work of scholarship—this book—should court. Still, *God Interrupted* is simply the most apt encapsulation I can imagine of the book's central theme: why so many Europeans between the wars thought themselves to live in a world marked by the active interruption of God's call or command, why many (believers included) found the idea so appealing, what sorts of human projects—political, theological, cultural, technological—were enabled by God's absence, and how Europeans alternatively diagnosed this absence as liberation, license, and loss.

God Interrupted appeals to me for another reason. Its power is both substantive and formal, both material and poetic. It communicates, but it also echoes and zips. In this, it points to the kind of historical writing to which I have always been most attracted, the kind that announces itself as a writerly endeavor. It is also the kind I have aspired to in this book. I tried to invest the careful exposition of a challenging set of ideas with narrative force, or more colloquially, I tried to put a bit of story into intellectual history. This meant to take a few risks with the writing. And so I wish to express thanks to my enthusiastic impresario-editor at Princeton University Press, Fred Appel, for granting me the leeway to do so.

My debts to others are both wide and deep, and I am pleased, finally, to have the chance to thank them for their help. First, a series of institutions for their material support: in rough chronological order, they include the Jacob Javits program of the U.S. Department of Education; the German Academic Exchange Service (DAAD); the Andrew Mellon Foundation; the Leo Baeck Institute; the Woodrow Wilson Foundation; the Department of History, the Doreen B. Townsend Center for the Humanities, and the program for Jewish studies—all at UC Berkeley; the Society of Fellows at the University of Chicago; Reed College; the Stanford Humanities Center; and the Koret Foundation. I thank them all.

Thanks are due also to a second series of institutions, where I was invited to present work in progress: they include the University of Virginia, the Johns Hopkins University, Arizona State University, the University of Chicago, Yale University, and most recently, the intellectual history seminar at the National Humanities Center. Deserving of special mention at these (and other) places are Allan Megill, David Nirenberg, Steven Smith, Kalman Bland, Malachi Hacohen, Steven Vincent, and Tony La Vopa. Small portions of this book have appeared elsewhere—in *New German Critique*, in the *Journal of the History of Ideas*, and in an edited volume (Hava Tirosh-Samuelson and Christian Wiese, eds., *Judaism and the Phenomenon of Life: The Legacy of Hans Jonas* [Boston: Brill Academic Publishers, 2008]), and I thank each for permission to reprint that material here.

I am also pleased to thank those who helped me access the sources I needed to complete the study: in particular, the staff at the archives of the Hebrew University and Jewish National Library, at the Department of Special Collections at the University of Chicago, at the Staatsbibliothek in Berlin, and at the Philosophisches Archiv at the Universität Konstanz (Brigitte Uhlemann, above all, for her assistance with the papers of Hans Jonas). I thank Joseph Cropsey for allowing me to consult the Leo Strauss Papers in Chicago. Tobias Blumenberg helped me with the papers of his father, Hans Blumenberg, in Ravensburg, Germany. He also allowed me to work at Blumenberg's desk—a genuine, if fleeting, thrill. I also thank Lore Jonas for meeting with me in San Francisco as she made her way west to Hawaii. The interwar scene came alive for me in her presence.

This book was born as a dissertation at UC Berkeley, where I enjoyed the aid and camaraderie of friends, fellow students, and teachers. At the time, I knew they were talented and distinguished; in retrospect, I am stunned at just how much. Jan Plamper and Amir Banbaji assisted with some of the trickier translations from the German and Hebrew, respectively. Gerard Caspary offered expert assistance with the Latin, a great joke or two about Origen (there are such jokes), an inimitable laugh, and an infectious enthusiasm for the history of religious thought. He will be missed. Susanna Elm, Erich Gruen, and Jed Parsons helped me with questions about the history and languages of late antiquity. Miryam Segal, Hamutal Tsamir, and Sheila Jelen all read early drafts of chapters, as did Robert Alter, Michael Weingrad, and the other members of the Jewish Cultures Reading Group. John Abromeit, Paul Reitter, Manuel Rota, Jennifer Greiman, Ben Wurgaft, Jonathan Sheehan, and Dirk Moses deserve my thanks. So do Andrew Jainchill, Abe Socher, the ubiquitous Azzan Yadin, and Peter Gordon. I feel elevated in their company. Ania Wertz suffered the roughest of my drafts and worst of my wit, all with neighborly cheer. Sam Moyn was my most pugnacious reader and a deeply discerning one as well. His presence makes itself felt in these pages in many ways I recognize, and, I am quite sure, in ways I do not—but all of them for the better.

I owe thanks also to a formidable group of scholar-teachers. They include Carla Hesse, who offered support and guidance for which I am grateful, a metaphor she is sure to recognize in these pages, and the example of a pedagogical charisma I could only hope to match. Tom Laqueur is possessed of a brilliant historical mind, not to mention a personality and disposition that enlivened those of us around him. As for my dissertation committee, it was second to none. Daniel Boyarin was my outside reader, and in that capacity unleashed a torrent of suggestions, about Paul and gnosticism above all. I had the good fortune to work also with David Biale, who cochaired my committee, and whose writings on Scholem have been since their inception the standard in the field. His confidence in me as a student meant much, his friendship as a colleague still more. Last, I thank Martin Jay. The standard he sets with his learning is simply astonishing. It is also matched, as those who have worked with him can attest, by a generosity and a graciousness that are equally, if not more, impressive. I count myself lucky as the beneficiary of both, during my time in Berkeley and after. In short, I was privileged to have so many conscientious and capable readers. As for whatever factual errors, omissions, commissions, infelicities of style, or other gross lapses remain, the fault of course is mine. Still, I cannot help but hope what every author must wish at this point—that readers will pardon me these defects (or blame them on someone else).

I left Berkeley (it is hard to leave Berkeley) for a three-year stint as a postdoctoral fellow at the University of Chicago, which styles itself both the center of the academic universe and "the place where fun comes to die." If my experience was typical, there is a semi-serious argument to be made on behalf of the first. I learned much there—a serious understatement—from a group of friends and interlocutors: above all, Gary Herrigel, Devin Pendas, Debbie Gould, Paul Mendes-Flohr, Rochona Majumdar, Zarena Aslami, Moishe Postone, Andrew Sartori, Andrew Sloin, and Jonathan Lear. I owe special thanks to Julia Kindt and Paul Cheney, partners in talk both high and low at the "Cove"—an improbable tropical beachhead on the shores of Lake Michigan, and proof that the U of C is neither a place where fun dies (it's just hibernating) nor "the circle of hell Dante forgot" (as a favored T-shirt gloats).

A book is nourished by more than its community of readers, as anyone who has undertaken to write one can attest. I extend thanks and deep admiration to Robert Jackler. Marc and Lise Howard, Melody Ng, Gillian Weiss, Arianne Chernock, Michael Frankenstein, Kyra Caspary, Mark Feldman, and Tamara Metz graced me with their friendship. So did Iana Dikidjieva, one of the most talented persons I know. My fellow travelers in the Olet Studies Working Group—Norman and Charlotte Sissman, Max Leva, sister Yoni and brother Ari—likewise deserve my thanks, as do Paula Pafumi, Willie Hulce, and the team of Trisha Kyner and David Friedheim at grendelsmother.org. In Portland, I thank my new colleagues at Reed College for providing me with a congenial academic home. I thank Jeanine Leva in Mulhouse, who gave me a real home I didn't know I had. In Freiburg, I thank Reinhard Flessner and Annette Pehnt for plying me with Christmas goose, *Pflaumenmuss*, and more varieties of drink than I knew—not to mention the heady conversation and new-old, easy friendship all this bounty fueled.

There is thanks and then there is thanks. The first takes the form of well-meant words, the second a yelp of the soul. I am bound by the first, but it is with the second in mind that I dedicate this book to my parents. They created me as lovers and they sustain me still as friends. For that I cannot thank them enough.

Stanford, California
Thanksgiving 2007

God Interrupted

Introduction

"NOTHING WILL HAPPEN to you if you don't eat pork," opined Shimon Peres, at the time the prime minister of Israel, in 1985. Peres meant to justify his concessions to the ultra-orthodox, whose support he required to advance negotiations with Israel's adversaries. Israelis could do without swine, he reasoned, "but things will be very bad if we don't renew the peace process."[1] Peres was right about peace, but he was wrong about pig. He was wrong, that is, to think that Israel's geopolitics had nothing to do with how Israelis defined themselves as Jews. To concede to the ultra-orthodox on the right to pork may have seemed a worthwhile forfeiture. Its greasy delights pale in comparison, certainly, with the return on a comprehensive settlement in the Middle East. But Peres conceded more than he had realized. To the ultra-orthodox he had given in, but he had also given something up. He had given up on the heretical ideal.

This ideal was born of Europe between the world wars. To its interwar advocates, however, it had seventeenth-century roots, and in one episode above all. In 1665, a twenty-three-year-old named Abraham Nathan ben Elisha Hayyim Ashkenazi—Nathan of Gaza for short—identified as the messiah a sometime Jerusalemite called Sabbatai Sevi, and roused Jews on three continents who proved eager to heed his call. Sevi was an improbable candidate for the job. He was blessed with noble looks and a mellifluous voice, but he was a second-rate intellect, haunted by demons (which he called "the sons of whoredom"), and given to "strange acts" in fits of manic activity. Some of these acts were decidedly odd—he married himself to a Torah scroll, refused to consummate his marriages to women, and once swaddled a large fish in infant's clothes. But some of these acts were antinomian—open transgressions of Jewish law.

The untruth of his messianic pretensions did not, of course, distinguish him. With one possible exception, the erstwhile messiahs of Western history have to this day been proved false. But Sabbatai Sevi was no mere false messiah. He was an apostate messiah, and his apostasy was understood as part and parcel of his mission. To his detractors, he converted to Islam on pain of death at the hands of the Ottoman sultan. His was an act of craven capitulation, with the salutary effect of exposing him for what he was: a charlatan and a fraud. But to the more radical of his supporters, he had entered the realm of evil to defeat it from within. He had announced by example a full-fledged doctrine of the holiness of sin, and many felt enjoined to do the same. His apologists developed a theology out of the sources of Jewish tradition that turned that tradition on its head. Not the pious observance of law, but its oddly and equally pious transgression would usher in the messianic age.

The upheaval that ensued engulfed the Jewish world. Further installments of the controversies—some fantastic, others frankly bizarre—lasted well over a century. They also left lasting wounds. The upshot, or one of them: successive generations of Jews, whether proponents of rabbinic creed or the Enlightenment project, for various reasons did their utmost to efface the phenomenon from Jewish historical memory. This, at least, is how a man named Gershom Scholem was to speak of their fate.

In 1973, Scholem published his masterpiece, his biography of Sabbatai Sevi. Here is what the literary critic Cynthia Ozick had to say about it:

> There are certain magisterial works of the human mind that alter ordinary comprehension so unpredictably and on so prodigious a scale that culture itself is set awry, and nothing can ever be seen again except in the strange light of that new knowledge. Obviously it is not possible to "review" such a work, any more than one can review a mountain range: an accretion of fundamental insight takes on the power of a natural force. Gershom Scholem's corpus has such a force and its massive keystone, *Sabbatai Sevi*, presses down on the grasping consciousness with the strength not simply of its invulnerable, almost tidal, scholarship, but of its singular instruction in the nature of man.[2]

Ozick's is heady stuff, but her sentiment is not without warrant. In the years since Mt. Scholem erupted—smoking, raining ash, belching fire, and for those who knew him, making a lot of noise—it has lost none of its grandeur and little of its capacity to induce awe and wonder among those who behold it. But it no longer strikes the witness dumb, at least not permanently. Its fires have cooled. Its peak has weathered. The scholarship remains tidal, as Ozick put it, but navigable. And its singular instruction, if still in the nature of man, appears now to speak just as much, if not more, to the nature of Scholem and his peers.

The English revision of the book came toward the end of a life that began in Berlin and would end in Jerusalem. The span of time (1897-1982) saw Scholem catapulted from modest beginnings—fourth son to a typical family of assimilated German Jews—to a position inside and outside the academy bordering on apostlehood. His fame came on the strength of researches in the history of kabbalah, or Jewish mysticism. These did not break new ground so much as create it. As the theologian Martin Buber once put it, Scholem did not merely found a school, but established a discipline. The tenor of his writings on kabbalah owed much to his work on Sabbatai Sevi, the final fruit of which Ozick rightly celebrated. But Scholem's massive keystone had its more humble origins in an essay of 1936, called "Mitzva ha-ba'a ba-avera." The phrase is a rabbinic category and refers to a divine command fulfilled through transgression. More colloquially, it is translated "Redemption through Sin."[3]

Scholem's essay charts the adventures of the apostate messiah and the series of movements he spawned. Its great achievement was to rescue the Sabbatian controversies and kabbalah itself from the dustbin of Jewish history, and to grant them pride of place in a story about the rise of the modern Jewish world. As Scholem saw it, contemporary Jewish indifference to the law followed upon the Sabbatian program of its deliberate and studied violation. His argument had its problems. Still, it made claims about the relation of heresy to modern Jewish identity that merit notice and regard. It also incorporated a full-fledged theory of secularization that reversed the reigning approach, for which secularization—whatever it meant—proceeded against and beyond religion rather than through it.[4] Scholem argued for secularization from within rather than without. Judaism, it turns out, secularized itself. His essay proved to be the single most important piece of Jewish historical scholarship written in the twentieth century. It proved also to be one of the most important in twentieth-century religious thought, period. Some of what follows explains why.

But this book has more fundamental aims. Simply stated, it is an intellectual history of Europe between the world wars, the Weimar period above all, and some of its important afterlives, approached by means of revisions in theological thinking that were also much more. The study asks that we take theology seriously as a cultural and intellectual practice. It asks that we appreciate theology as a vehicle for commentary on the political, aesthetic, and philosophical present common to us all, and not merely as the parochial pursuit of like-minded, if fractious believers. Throughout, the work foregrounds the relation between the ways in which Europeans in this period spoke of the divine with the ways in which they spoke also of themselves and of the natural and human-built worlds in which they lived. It stresses the capacity of theological language to assert itself in apparently unrelated domains—in talk of art, for example, or politics, or natural science, or philosophy. In short, the study describes a theological dimension to interwar life—it is easy to detect it in many of the major cultural undertakings of the early twentieth century—and for a variety of reasons, the study privileges the problem of heresy to address it.

In part, these reasons are formal. The "logic" of heresy makes the category a useful one for anyone concerned with the displacement and diffusion of God-talk. On its face, the mark distinguishes and excludes. It names a person or a position as other. It is no accident, for example, that in rabbinic Hebrew the term *acher*, other, is a euphemism for the heretic. But to apply the mark of heresy is also to assert a claim to ownership. It is an exclusion that also includes, since heretical deviation is intelligible only in terms of the norms it reworks or disputes. Applied to persons, the label comments on the inside and outside of human communities. Applied to ideas, it begs the question of the limits and the beyonds of our thoughts about God.

But the reasons for attending to heresy are not only formal. They are also—first—historical. The interwar era witnessed a resurgence of interest in the heretic as both object and inspiration. As Scholem unearthed the Sabbatians of old as a resource for Jewish identity in the present, his friend, the philosopher Hans Jonas, was goaded by the spirit of the times to retrieve a much older group of heretics. Jonas discovered in the gnostic spirit of late antiquity an early avatar of the alienation and estrangement from the world that dominated leading currents of interwar thought. The diagnosis, and Jonas's efforts to overcome that spirit, would produce a philosophical biology and environmental ethics of real consequence: in Germany, Jonas became a "guru" to the Green movement as it developed over the 1980s; in the United States and Europe, he helped set the direction of bioethical inquiry and practice. Meanwhile, the philosopher Leo Strauss, another close friend of Scholem, devoted the bulk of his intellectual effort in the 1920s to the arch Jewish heretic Baruch (or Benedict) Spinoza. Strauss undertook to decipher the mysteries at the heart of Spinoza's critique of religion and the stakes of his heresy for the modern era. The consequences: Strauss would set out to recover a natural standard by which to judge the rightfulness of human action—a kind of worldly surrogate for a lost God. Whether he found it is up for debate, but the importance of his quest is not. It has inspired several generations of students and disciples, and by some accounts has made him the intellectual touchstone for a neoconservative revolt in American politics and culture.

Strauss was only one of hundreds of interwar observers for whom Spinoza's example had something timely to convey. Ernst Bloch, a Marxist philosopher of great renown and another of Scholem's familiars, would sum up this sentiment nicely: "The best thing about religion," he wrote in 1968, "is that it gives birth to heretics."[5] For the generation that came of age between the world wars, heresy had again become a problem. For many it also became a model. But why then? A model for what? And above all, why should we care? What were the implications for Judaism, for theology, for modern Western thought? These are the basic questions this study undertakes to pose and, I hope, to answer.

RELIGION AFTER LIBERALISM

Begin with the death of an ideal. For many Europeans, the First World War drove a stake through the heart of liberal civilization. At first glance, the claim appears odd. After all, the war's end marked the end also for four of Europe's imperial powers, and saw the spread of republican governments across the continent. Before the war there were three; after, eighteen. Parliaments ruled where once potentates reigned. With some notable exceptions the liberal agenda of constitutional rule was the order, literally, of the day. But the recasting of bourgeois Europe proved short-lived. By the end of the decade the center was besieged and in some places had collapsed altogether. Support for the German experiment in democracy in particular had never been more than tepid, indicated by the name for those who had made it possible in the first place. The regime of the *Vernunftrepublikaner*, republicans of reason or pragmatism, gave way to radicals of right and left unafraid to back conviction with force.[6]

A typical liberal wish list looked like this: a constitution, rule of law, individual liberties, a market society, property rights, and an expanded, if not universal suffrage. But liberalism was no exclusively political or economic program, and its demise was in part prepared by the demise of its cultural and intellectual forms. The liberal project—at least in the nineteenth century—had derived much of its impetus from a confidence in the capacity for human progress, and could not help but falter as the trust proved folly. The war in particular dealt a deathblow to a faith in the progressive moral perfection of man, and in its wake came a post-liberal ethos more at home in crisis than calm. This was the case in politics, in cultural circles, in philosophy, and not least in theology.[7] The crisis in relations among men, it turns out, had much to do with innovations in the ways Europeans thought about God.

Post-liberal theology was not born of the postwar period. Its roots tunnel deep into the nineteenth century, and as a discernible movement or mood, albeit a minority one, it commenced before the advent of war. But its rise accelerated in the spirit of existential dislocation that prevailed in its wake. In Protestant circles, it went by the name of "crisis theology" and referred to the circle of thinkers grouped around Karl Barth, Friedrich Gogarten, and Eduard Thurneysen. The name of their journal, *Zwischen den Zeiten* (Between the Times), summed up their message well. They thought themselves to live in the theological breach: unmoored, cast adrift, dislocated. They undid a liberal Protestant tradition that had reigned in the latter half of the nineteenth century by hacking away at its roots. These roots extended deep into the eighteenth century, when biblical scholars first transformed the Bible from a record of God's word into a cultural treasure.[8] In philosophical terms, however, they meant to unearth and overturn the thought of the theologian Friedrich Daniel Ernst Schleiermacher.

Over a century before, Schleiermacher had made man's subjective experience of the divine the foundation of his theology, and as a corollary had stressed the presence of the godly in the worldly. In the more optimistic of its incarnations, the Protestant-liberal synthesis discovered in human history the progressive unfolding of religious truth. Barth and his followers would have none of this. It was hard, after all, to find God in an experience of the world defined by man-made mass death, and the attempts of some liberal theologians to justify the war as a part—even the apotheosis—of their endeavor only aggravated their opponents all the more. Post-liberal Protestants rid God of his worldly corruptions, so much so that they threatened to exile him from his creation altogether. To contemporaries, this recalled the gnostic idea of an absent God or *deus absconditus*. In order to save God, they banished him from a world soaked in sin.

Judaism and Jewish thought underwent a similar transformation, if with different and more far-reaching consequences.[9] In the nineteenth century, especially, German Jews had thrown in their lot with liberalism. Their legal equality hinged on the success of liberal politics. They voted for liberal parties and supported constitutional government. They favored free trade. They argued for individual liberty and for more ecumenical versions of religious belief and ritual. Above all, they pursued a metamorphosis: from a religious community into "German citizens of the Mosaic persuasion."[10]

The legacy of the war and its aftermath was twofold. On the one hand, the war's end and the advent of the Weimar Republic marked the apparent completion of the emancipatory project begun 150 years before. For the first time, Jews became full participants in German civic life. Yet the war had eroded the enlightened, liberal foundation that made this emancipation possible in the first place. All this left Jews in a precarious position. The world they had long sought to enter, a world whose threshold they had crossed and whose ideals they had done much to uphold—for many interwar observers this world had vanished. The irony was this: Jews became full participants at a moment when the ground for their participation no longer seemed so stable. Whether a salvage operation might have saved this foundation is difficult to know, but to know its fate is not. Fifteen years later, it collapsed.

This political predicament of German Jewry had a theological corollary. The era witnessed a renewal of Jewish life, a renaissance of a peculiar sort. If diverse, the new cultural and religious forms Judaism took on in this period were united in their thrust: they were all post-liberal and, with a few exceptions, post-assimilatory as well. This holds true for German-Jewish Zionism, for Jewish anarchists like Gershom Scholem, for newfangled forms of Jewish mysticism, and for neo-orthodoxy as well. All styled themselves a return of sorts, and all repudiated the model for modern Jewish identity that had until then reigned in Germany—the nineteenth-century Jewish-liberal synthesis.

The synthesis shared much with its Protestant cousin, so much so that its champions (such as the philosopher Hermann Cohen) could speak of a spiritual affinity joining Protestant to Jew. The undoing of this synthesis also shared much with its Protestant analogue. Its repudiation typically took the form of an Oedipal revolt, a reaction of the sons against the fathers. Franz Kafka's reproach against his father's "bourgeois Judaism" was only the most famous example of a transconfessional symptom. By the end of this period, in 1933, Kafka's generation had done much to sever the Jewish-liberal synthesis. As Franz Rosenzweig, the most important Jewish theologian of the time, put it: "The Liberal German-Jewish standpoint on which almost all of German Judaism had enough room for nearly a century has become so tiny that apparently only one person—I myself—can live there."[11] Not even Rosenzweig would remain there for long.

Even the proponents of liberal Judaism undertook to redefine their liberalism in line with the spirit of the age. Liberal Jews had once celebrated the philosopher Moses Mendelssohn as their model and hero. In the late eighteenth century, Mendelssohn had reconciled orthodoxy with Enlightenment. He had made Judaism safe for Europe and Europe safe for the Jews. But those whose lives he had enabled now disparaged him as unoriginal and of little consequence. In the course of a generation, he and his successors were transformed: from the founders of modern Judaism to "Protestants in Jewish garb." Before, liberal Jews had disavowed Hasidim (eastern European Jewish mystics) as retrograde enthusiasts. They banished these "daughters of darkness" from sight. But in the interwar era, they stressed the affinities of Hasidism for liberal Judaism, and in a complicated operation—better described as casuistry—declared it born in the spirit of liberalism. Earlier, German Jews had welcomed the replacement *of* Hebrew *by* German as the language of prayer. But they now came to realize that it was precisely the opacity of the Hebrew, the fact that it was not understood as it was enunciated, that lent the act of prayer a nonrational and deep-seated emotional appeal.[12]

There is an irony here. The innovations introduced to liberal Jewish culture and theology represented a partial reversal of Enlightenment traditions that emphasized the common elements of all monotheistic religions and culminated in a single, nonsectarian faith. The partial retrieval of nonrational elements in the Jewish tradition was therefore enacted in the name of Jewish difference and distinction. Yet this very move—to recover the irrational—was just as definitive an inclination in European culture of the 1920s as its converse had been in the age of Enlightenment.

Martin Heidegger, Ernst Jünger, Carl Schmitt: names like these make the point abundantly clear. In other words, even as they once again discovered their distinction, Jews did so in an idiom they shared with their non-Jewish neighbors, an idiom that therefore marked them at once as distinct and as same. In every act to assert their difference, they had in part already erased it.

Ultimately, these innovations were holding patterns, last-ditch or stopgap measures by the generation of the fathers to stave off a reversal of the theological-political order. Neither could a mere appreciation for the irrational elements of the Jewish tradition on the part of change-minded liberals compete with the wholesale revival of a heretical ideal among the sons. In some instances, this revival was lived out without much sense for its fact. In others, it was paradoxically and knowingly calculated to revitalize Jewish life in the modern age.

The arrival of this ideal marked the definitive end to a chapter in German-Jewish history that began with Moses Mendelssohn. Mendelssohn had ushered Judaism into the modern age, or so the story proceeds, by defining it as a religion of revealed law alongside the universal religious truths available to all. The rise of heretical forms of Jewish return signaled the demise of Mendelssohn's gambit, as it undid both aspects of his legacy. This was first an antinomian Judaism that rejected revelation and law. It was happy to acknowledge itself as deviant. But it contested the other half of Mendelssohn's bequest no less. It reversed the universalism introduced by Mendelssohn himself, and developed in unexpected ways in the nineteenth century by Mendelssohn's liberal heirs. Jews in the interwar period invoked heresy not to assert their sameness but to reassert their difference. To describe the advent of this ideal is one of the aims of this study.

This is a Jewish story. It is also a European one. To this end, I redescribe the Weimar milieu in general from the view afforded by the concern of its inhabitants with the divine. The problem of heresy turns out to have been of special concern across confessions, and so I lay bare the grammar of the two leading languages of heresy in the period, which I call, as a kind of shorthand, the gnostic and the pantheist. Though associated with epochs long past, each enjoyed a heady revival in the interwar years. The first expressed hope for salvation from a sinful world by the grace of an absent God, and was linked in the interwar period with the Protestant representatives of crisis theology. But those who spoke the pantheist language of heresy contested the gnostic spirit. They insisted that God (understood as the impersonal, creative force in nature) was anything but absent. Indeed, God was everywhere: pan-theism. They divinized the world, and they were abetted in this endeavor by the spectacular revival of Baruch Spinoza, the seventeenth-century philosopher and most consequential of

Jewish heretics after Jesus. These languages were theological innovations, but also much more. They resonated beyond their theological chamber of origin. They echoed among jurists, philosophers, artists, and astrophysicists. To consider what this group thought about God opens up a new perspective on their generation as a whole.

The final aim of the study is to trace exfoliations of the encounter with these languages of heresy down to the present day. I want to show how interwar theological debates lie at the root of important and apparently unrelated chapters in the history of ideas. The work of Hans Jonas, Leo Strauss, and Gershom Scholem, for example, lives on in the environmental movement and bioethics, in a political philosophy sometimes marshaled on behalf of neoconservative politics, and in a radical rethinking of what it means to be a Jew, but all had common origins in arguments about heresy between the world wars. Undoubtedly there are other, similar stories to be told. But these examples ought to suffice to demonstrate the abiding salience of the divine to cultural and political life between the wars and beyond. If nothing else, the stories presented here should alert us to the ways in which talk about God could be adapted for talk about nature, or politics, or art, to the ways in which discourses of the divine not only persist as an alternative to this worldly world of ours, but also flourish in the midst of our most secular of pursuits. Thinking about heresy between the world wars enables us to think with greater care about what has happened to religion in the modern age.

THREE THINKERS

Hans Jonas, Leo Strauss, Gershom Scholem: they were German Jews, titans of scholarship, émigrés, and friends. Each deserves attention. The study begins with Jonas, who first made his name as a masterful interpreter of religion. His dissertation, written under the philosopher Martin Heidegger and the Protestant theologian Rudolf Bultmann, followed on the heels of a concise but neglected study on Paul and Augustine, and eventually became the first volume of *Gnosis und spätantiker Geist* (Gnosis and the Spirit of Late Antiquity, 1934). The book endures to this day as a monument in the field of religious thought. Jonas arrived in Palestine in 1935, joined the British Army's Jewish Brigade in the Second World War, and fought in the Israeli war for independence in 1948. Some years later he arrived at the New School for Social Research in New York. There he produced a series of important studies in philosophical biology, on the history of the technological ethos, and in biological and environmental ethics. On the strength of the last, especially, Jonas earned wild applause. His foremost book on the theme,

Prinzip Verantwortung (The Imperative of Responsibility, 1979), sold over two hundred thousand copies in German alone. This was a stunning achievement for a work of philosophy, all the more so given the manifest oddity of some of its claims.[13] Jonas also wrote a series of essays in post-Holocaust theology that have made him a minor star in the Jewish theological firmament.

But the diversity of his corpus has worked to the detriment of its grasp. To some, he is a maverick scholar of religion. To others, he is an environmentalist. To some, he is a Jewish theologian. To others, he is a phenomenologist, or one of Martin Heidegger's conflicted Jewish "children."[14] All are right. But to the extent that they are right, these accounts are also local in outlook. They tend to pass over what I take as the most salient aspect of his work. Beneath the apparent diversity there lies also a deep historical and philosophical unity. This story I tell in part 1, and I describe it as an "overcoming" of gnosticism.

I borrow the phrase from Hans Blumenberg, the eminent German philosopher and historian of ideas. Blumenberg described the birth of the medieval and modern epochs as first and second overcomings of gnosticism. What Blumenberg meant by this is complicated. But to simplify: he thought that early medievals and early moderns invested a modicum of dignity in the world and in human endeavor that the gnostics—who thought the world sinful and irredeemably so—were at pains to deny. The twentieth century witnessed a third return of gnosticism in the form of crisis theology, and also its third overcoming, in the person of Jonas above all (he was not alone, only the most accomplished). His philosophical biology and environmental ethics ought to be understood not as some post-Hiroshima anxiety about technological excess. Rather, they were born of a hostile Jewish response to Barth's theology and the gnostic return in general. To overcome gnosticism meant to overcome the forces, both religious *and* technological, that alienated man from the natural world. Jonas helps us see how the ways in which we relate to our planet have much to do with the ways in which we relate to the divine, even (or especially) when the divine is nowhere to be found.

But what if the divine were not nowhere but everywhere? In our world? In our blood? In our love? Many interwar observers—some silly, most serious—thought just that. I address them in part 2 ("The Pantheism Controversy") by canvassing the reception of the philosopher Baruch Spinoza, the arch Jewish heretic who thought he could prove that God—what he called God—was everywhere. Spinoza enjoyed his second great renaissance in this period, comparable only to his first in the wake of the so-called pantheism controversy in late eighteenth-century Germany. It was no accident that Spinoza arrived when he did. The gnostics had rid the world of God in order to save him; Spinoza had divinized the world, but in order to destroy him—to destroy, that is, belief in a providential deity personally invested in our doings. Those dismayed by the revival of gnostic heresies turned to Spinoza for help in banishing them, once and for all, from the face of the earth.

Their number was great and their kind, diverse. Occultists approved of Spinoza's karmic consequences. Catholics revived him as an antidote to the Protestant theologians of crisis. Jews, meanwhile, revoked his excommunication and recovered him for the Jewish people not despite his heresy but because of it. This last story is important in its own right, as a chapter in the advent of Judaism's heretical ideal, and I treat it at some length. But it also helps to set the stage for the bulk of the discussion: a reinterpretation of the philosophical career of Leo Strauss (1897-1973).

Our understanding of Strauss has suffered the same difficulties as our understanding of Jonas, only more so. There is first the formidable bulk and diversity of his work: a dissertation on Friedrich Heinrich Jacobi, the bête noire of the German Enlightenment, a first book and a series of essays on Spinoza, writings on Moses Mendelssohn, a book on Maimonides, several treatments of Hobbes, and of course his masterpiece, *Natural Right and History* (1953). This takes us only through the first half of a career celebrated just as much for what came next, a series of studies in political philosophy from the Greeks to Machiavelli to Nietzsche.

There is also the problem of his legacy. Strauss has inspired veneration among several generations of students and interested observers who agree on the greatness of the man, but not on his message. To some he is the champion of the ancients against the moderns. To others he is a Nietzschean in disguise. To some he is illiberal kin to Carl Schmitt, for a time the "crown jurist" of the Third Reich. To others, he is a defender of American liberal democracy. To some he is the founding father of a neoconservative revolt in American politics and culture, and as such to be venerated. To others he is that same father, and so to be vilified. For my part, I feel the need neither to apologize (Strauss can defend himself) nor to condemn. I want to question instead.[15]

All this is compounded by another division: Strauss the philosopher versus Strauss the Jew. At their most egregious, his philosophical champions have dismissed his work on Jewish topics as a smoke screen designed to blind the uninitiated to the philosopher's dangerous truths. His Jewish champions have, for the most part, left the interpretation of his apparently philosophical works to others. Both impulses are understandable, as they proceed out of fidelity to Strauss himself, or to one of the hallmarks of Straussian thought: that philosophy and religion are at odds, and defy genuine reconciliation.[16]

But devotion can also be blind, and to understand Strauss we would in fact do well to betray him—sort of. Strauss developed an antihistoricist approach to reading; he insisted on the timelessness of questions posed by Paul or by Plato, thought it possible, crucial, to read them as contemporaries. He identified historicism as the root of much that was wrong in his world, of Nazism and nihilism not least, because he thought it to leave us without an enduring, timeless standard by which to decide whether what we do is right. Rather than approach Strauss philosophically, however, I suggest we do so historically. I trace how Strauss, following both Spinoza and Hobbes, came to identify the relation between theology and politics as *the* problem of the modern age. His approach was both idiosyncratic and complicated. But for now, in a sentence: man had seized the prerogative to master the world as he saw fit by doing away with two traditional sources of authority—divine revelation and nature—that once had specified the right way for man to live. Strauss hoped to revive a version of the latter to temper the political and technological excesses of his age.

But *how* did Strauss arrive at this point? By what provocation? And to what ends? Posing the question this way promises a new perspective on the problem of Strauss and his legacy. It also resolves many of the antinomies that attend his reception. For one, it enables us to see how Strauss's formulation of the theological-political predicament evolved in the context of a contest: between competing idioms on the relation of God, man, and world—the gnostic and pantheist languages of heresy— and between their principal exponents on the interwar scene. It also enables us to understand the great shift in Strauss's thought: from the question of God to the question of nature. It enables us to understand Strauss's quest for natural right as akin to a search for a lost or absent God, and his option for philosophy as a form of heresy. It enables us to understand the most "secular" formulation of his message as more involved with the divine than his philosophical champions will admit, but not in the way those who have attended to his writings on religion have claimed. It may even enable us to make sense of a peculiar rapprochement: the one that has led neoconservatives, many of them ethnic but secular Jews, to make common cause with millenarian Christians on a range of issues, from scientific experimentation to foreign policy in the Middle East. Whatever the explanatory return, the story begins with Strauss's early interest in Jacobi, Spinoza, and Mendelssohn. These were the personalities at issue in the pantheism controversy of old, and so I cast Strauss as the pugilist most intent on fighting a "second round" of the pantheism controversy, a rematch which transpired in the arena of interwar Europe.

Some in this fight were impressed by God's absence—the world was too debased to accommodate him. Others were more impressed by his presence—the world was too wondrous to exclude him. But could God be both present and absent at once? Some argued no, absolutely no. They were a minority, but they are useful as ideal-types. They exemplify the revivals of gnosticism and pantheism in their purest form. The closer we look, however, the more obvious it becomes that they were just that: ideals, not realities (even absolutists like Barth were not exempt, and in some of his moods he was forthright enough to admit it). These heretical options, after all, were not philosophical systems. I call them "languages" instead, the spoken expressions of more fundamental, felt sensibilities. Each had a "logic" or physiognomy, a typical set of concepts or traits at work in both their popular and philosophical expressions. But if the gnostic and pantheist options in their pure form were logically powerful (and this is debatable), they were historically fallible, never quite lived out. And so most interwar observers, whether they knew it or not, balanced divine absence with divine presence. Like the philosopher Franz Rosenzweig, they allowed that God was far, yet near. Impressed by the depredations of man, they nonetheless sought—and claimed—the consolations of the divine.

But there was at least one man for whom none of these sensibilities quite sufficed. There was at least one man so convinced of God's absence, yet so desperate for his presence, and so suspicious of indulging just that want—a man of a mind so schizoid, perhaps—that he could imagine only one way out. God, this man reasoned, must be nowhere and everywhere, nothing and everything—and all at once! That man was Gershom Scholem.

Scholem's idea was strange, but not unprecedented. Some kabbalists, for example, thought that God manifested himself in the world as nothingness, albeit of a special kind. They imagined creation as shot through by the nothingness of an otherwise absent God. Scholem was not a kabbalist. Their era was not his own. Still, he did discover through them ways to think about problems that flummoxed him in his time—in fact, the same problems and anxieties afflicting all those in the interwar period who made recourse to the gnostic and pantheist languages of heresy. Scholem felt them at fever pitch, and in his person is exemplified a generation. He described every major episode in the history of kabbalah either as a form of Jewish gnosticism or as a Jewish flirtation with pantheism. And so the great expanse of his scholarship, his history of Jewish mysticism, his life's work—all this ought to be understood as an attempt to speak Jewish revisions of both these languages, but together, at the same time. Scholem's options for Jewish gnosticism and Jewish pantheism were the most obvious and willful of his choices for the Jewish past. As it turns out, they underwrote also the most obvious and willful of his choices for the Jewish present: Zionism. In part 3 ("Redemption through Sin"), I try to show how.

Just how he did it is fascinating. Scholem's story is an odyssey though time, space, and ideas. With him we travel from Berlin to Jerusalem, from nihilism to nothingness, from gnosticism to pantheism and back. Along the way we encounter angels and golems, sinners and apostates. We also meet puppies and kittens. It is a story of homecoming and exile, megalomania and despair, clairvoyance and feigned insanity. It is a story of forbidden love, divine love, self-love, unrequited love, and love triangles. Scholem was an outrageous and imaginative man—for a short time he thought he was the messiah—and we might as well face up to the fact. We serve him ill to ignore it.

Scholem had a story to tell about himself, and it is related to the stories he had to tell about the Jews. Scholem was frank about the fact, but frankly a tease about how. This raises a problem that has long vexed those who have listened to what he has to say. It is difficult to distinguish between his life and work, to know where Scholem ends and scholarship begins. Was Scholem secretly a kabbalist? A Sabbatian? A gnostic? There is no end to the speculation. Scholem's genre of choice—history—makes the task still more intractable. Historical inquiry enabled him to hold in suspension a variety of inclinations within and about himself, without forcing him to choose between them or resolve their inner tensions. It did so by offering up a host of figures from the past through which to explore his commitments in the present. Friedrich Nietzsche once wrote that every philosophy resolves itself into autobiography in the end. Nietzsche was for some time an inspiration to Scholem, and if his maxim has any truth to it, then surely it is here. One question is how.

Nietzsche's dictum also raises two related questions. Does what Scholem did count as philosophy at all? Does it matter? In this respect, the problems Scholem poses differ considerably from those posed by Jonas and Strauss. They are nearly the inverse. With his friends, the challenge is to specify the theology at the heart of the philosophy for which each is better known. The challenge is to specify the Jewish, as it were, in the Greek. It is to recount the story of the philosophers they had become and the Jews they wished to remain. With Scholem, the Judaism is obvious (even if his commitments remain elusive), but the philosophy, if any, is hidden from view. Scholem opted for history and philology as best suited to his aims. The result: it is difficult to appreciate his writings as interventions in the history of Western thought, rather than as historical arguments about a particular religious tradition. But they are as much the former as the latter.

They are also—they are precisely—an instance of what Nietzsche wanted from philosophy. Nietzsche once declared that he had no desire to replace the great error of Judeo-Christian morality with its ugly truth—that it was merely a weapon used by hypocrites and weaklings in their war against the strong. Truth did not interest him all that much. He wanted to destroy an error he thought inimical to life as it ought to be lived with a splendid and affirmative error instead. He wanted to overcome one myth with another.

Something of the same ought to be said of Scholem. Something, but not everything—Scholem, after all, was a historian, and he did not hesitate to appeal to the historical record to trounce his foes. Still, his relation to the norms of the profession was ambivalent at best. He practiced philology, but he also joked that God resided in the textual details. There was a myth in there waiting to be discovered, or made. In other words, Scholem's work is both history and myth, both social science and a passionate, creative, glorious *error*. It is an error in the finest Nietzschean tradition, an interpretation that has eclipsed all others in its beauty and its will. It is why I also think that those who reject Scholem by casting doubt on his historical project miss the point in part. It is why I hold to a thesis once advanced by a reader of Hannah Arendt: that even if every historical claim in her monumental book on the origins of totalitarianism were proved false, the whole of her work would endure as an indispensable truth—an indispensable error—for our time.[17]

THE TWIN EXCLUSION

What Scholem's truth was and what it is good for will come later. But the aim of his truth, or his error, was simply this: Jews ought to affirm the world, not the beyond, in whatever form such an elsewhere or otherwhen might assume. Jonas and Strauss had much the same to say, not just about Jews but about human beings, and for them all, it was the encounter with the gnostic and pantheist languages of heresy that led them to say what they did.

Their affirmation probably sounds banal. After all, where else is meaningful life to be lived? Their conclusion may also sound vague. After all, there are many ways to be in the world. Jonas asked after the biological dimensions of worldliness—the living world. Strauss asked after its political dimensions—the world as the cities and states we inhabit. Scholem was interested in both. But above all, he wanted to secure the world as a historical arena for human action unaided and unmolested by God. To say they affirmed the "world" is to say several things at once, or perhaps nothing at all.

But perhaps not. The conclusion is neither as banal nor as vague as it might at first appear. It is not banal because it runs against one of the common estimations of their generation of German-Jewish thinkers— that this was a group obsessed with the prospect of messianic redemption. It is certainly true that Scholem and his peers repudiated the milquetoast

God offered up by liberal theology. It is true that they devoted great energy to deciphering the mysteries of the messianic impulse. But it is also true that many of them came to repudiate that impulse, Scholem among them. Equally if not more impressive were their efforts to root man in the world, in this world, whatever its deficiencies or its wonders. In other words, the story of their generation does not end in the interwar period; the international exfoliations of interwar thought—among them diverse withdrawals from messianism—are just as much a part of its history. Neither is the conclusion vague, or at least it does not need to be. That is because all three made recourse to the same, specific vocabulary to voice variations on a common theme. All three revived an ancient Greek distinction: they set law and convention (*nomos*) against teleological notions of nature (*physis*), and for the most part they adjudicated this contest in favor of the latter.

This requires some explanation. Physis is a slippery term with multiple dimensions. In Aristotelian biology (or more precisely, physics), it entailed the idea that organisms possess within themselves the source of their own movement. Organisms are not mechanistic assemblages of matter, but have lives and trajectories of their own, and are in this sense autonomous. Twentieth-century intellectuals dismayed by the mindless pursuit of technological advance sometimes revived and revised this notion of nature as an antidote. They used it to question the modern equation of human freedom with the fabrication of our world and ourselves. Physis also has political dimensions. Embedded in both physis and nomos, after all, are claims about how to live. Those who prefer physis hold up nature as a standard by which to measure the rightfulness of human law or convention, and by extension our cities and states. Those who prefer nomos hold that nature, human or otherwise, has little to say about the matter, and if it did would lack the voice to say it.

But what does any of this have to do with God? As it turns out, a great deal. The appeal to a natural standard prior to human design only makes sense as a corrective to the perceived excesses of human creativity, or to the waywardness of human will. Atom bombs, transgenic rabbits that glow in the dark, and not least our political experiments with totalitarianism and the industrial slaughter of human beings—different animals to be sure, but all in their way have generated a felt need for limits, moral limits to the license men have arrogated to themselves to do with the world and one another whatever they see fit. There are any number of stories about how this situation arose. The ones advanced by mid-century intellectuals were complicated and diverse, but many shared a sense that the evaporation of limits had something to do with the evaporation of God's authority over man. They worried that modern man had set himself up as God. Even worse, the apparent rebellion against God dovetailed with a rebellion against teleological nature. This, many emphasized, was precisely the aim of leading early-modern thinkers. Francis Bacon, for example, inaugurated modern learning by submitting the Aristotelian cosmology to ridicule, and recommended that man re-create Eden on earth by "wresting from nature her secrets." Nature was not to be an object of idle contemplation; it was a resource to be exploited and mastered. Hobbes thought appeals to nature as spurious as appeals to God as a foundation for the state. The state was not natural, but artifactual, and the human act of making that brought it into being was akin to God's creative act at the beginning of time, his *fiat lux*. Let there be light.

The light may have driven God and teleological nature into the shadows, but it has not managed to eradicate them. Moderns remain haunted by their twin exclusion. Sometimes it produces vigorous counterreactions. Modern religious fundamentalisms, for example, are an obvious instance of a response to the exclusion of God. But the haunting applies just as much to the most committed of atheists. They protest too much, and in their dispute with religion inadvertently sustain it. Karl Marx once wrote of atheism as the active negation of God. Active negation, however, makes sense only as a reaction to a position it disputes, and so atheism accords to God both longevity and the legitimacy of an opponent. Marx called for a "negation of the negation" instead: a negation of atheism that would supersede antagonism to God and culminate in simple indifference. But Marx's hope for man's relation to the divine has not come to pass. Perhaps that is because appeals to God are a permanent, transhistorical option—even the default option—for how humans conduct their lives.[18] Perhaps it is because God is one of the names we have for a "something more" without which we cannot live. Perhaps the need for something more is a part of the human condition. All this is open to question. But whatever the case, the anti-godly is not yet the ungodly. We fear this shadow still.

We are haunted also by the exclusion of teleological nature. Sometimes this produces redoubled labors to banish it—by erecting an artificial planet fit to displace the earth. Sometimes it elicits an intuitive (as opposed to reasoned) disgust for technological novelty or planetary vandalism. It is easy to understand how teleological nature still exerts its pull. We open our eyes and appear confronted with its overwhelming fact. The world *lives*. It moves. It grows. It undulates, sways, and swells. From metabolism to the very quaking of the earth, the world appears to the precritical mind as invested with unconscious will. It is self-organizing and self-regulating, its own cause and effect. It appears also replete with design, which has naturally generated a search for its designer. In other words, teleology can spawn theology. The converse can hold as well, its exclusion linked intimately to the exclusion of God.[19]

These are some of the basic intellectual problems that confront the modern age. In the interwar period, however, they were pursued through the gnostic and pantheist languages of heresy. For all their apparent opposition, both languages perpetuated the twin exclusion that inaugurated the modern era. For all their apparent animosity, they in fact shared much. To the neo-gnostic mind, God was absent and "totally other." To the pantheist, he was everywhere, but no longer a personal God invested in our doings. He (or it) was a natural force instead. Those invested with the gnostic spirit were also immune to the charms of teleological nature. Or as one sympathizer put it, the neo-gnostics had assembled a worship "that practices, or executes, the end of the world."[20] As for pantheism, it does not reject teleology as a matter of course, but it can, and in Baruch Spinoza (if he was indeed a pantheist), it did. As a consequence, these languages of heresy were perfect vehicles for thinkers anxious about the modern age to revisit the twin exclusion that enabled it in the first place. They discovered that the crisis of religion in the modern world was also a crisis of nature, the crisis of nature a crisis of art or artifice, and the crisis of them all a crisis of what it meant to be a modern man.

It was also a crisis of what it meant to be a Jew, and Hans Jonas helps to show us how.

PART ONE

Overcoming Gnosticism

IN 1984, about a decade before his own murder, the Romanian scholar of religion Ioan Culianu complained of a more widespread, if decidedly less grisly form of assault.[1] The gnostics had "taken hold of the whole world," he declared, "and we were not aware of it. It is a mixed feeling of anxiety and admiration, since I cannot refrain myself from thinking that these alien body-snatchers have done a remarkable job indeed." Culianu referred here to the proliferation of meanings associated with the term, which had outstripped polysemy and had attained the right to a more dubious designation: hypersemy, a term invented by the Yiddishist Uriel Weinreich to describe a concept overly promiscuous about the meanings with which it coupled. Not only had gnosis lost its identity; it had come to confuse it with those of its numerous partners. Gnosis, Culianu declared, was a "sick sign":

> Once I believed that Gnosticism was a well-defined phenomenon belonging to the religious history of Late Antiquity. . . . I was to learn soon, however, that I was a *naif* indeed. Not only Gnosis was gnostic, but the catholic authors were gnostic, the neoplatonic too. Reformation was gnostic, Communism was gnostic, Nazism was gnostic, liberalism, existentialism and psychoanalysis were gnostic too, modern biology was gnostic, Blake, Yeats, Kafka, Rilke, Proust, Joyce, Musil, Hesse and Thomas Mann were gnostic. From very authoritative interpreters of Gnosis, I learned further that science is gnostic and superstition is gnostic; power, counter-power and lack of power are gnostic; left is gnostic and right is gnostic; Hegel is gnostic and Marx is gnostic; Freud is gnostic and Jung is gnostic; all things and their opposite are equally gnostic.
>
> Once I had believed that Gnosis was a chapter in the history of Western thinking; now, after having read so many fascinating studies on this subject, I finally reached illumination: I understood that the opposite is true, i.e., that Western thinking and acting form a chapter in the history of Gnosis.[2]

Though offered in jest, Culianu's expression "alien body-snatchers" accurately describes what has remained since 1934 a leading view of gnosticism as an identifiable phenomenon. In that year appeared the first monumental volume of *Gnosis und spätantiker Geist* (Gnosis and the Spirit of Late Antiquity) by the young Jewish philosopher Hans Jonas.[3] Over the next sixty years, Jonas returned to the theme again and again. The gnostic spirit was guided by a feeling for *das Fremde*, a term that refers not only to "the alien," by which it is usually translated, but to its cognates as well: the strange, the foreign, the other, the unknown, the uncanny, and the like. All suggest a sense of being not at home in the world. Alienation is wildly overdetermined in gnostic theology: man is alienated from himself, from an absent, transcendent God, and above all from the material, sensuous universe in which he lives, created as it was by an evil, malicious demiurge. Such "anti-cosmism" or hostility to the world usually prompted ascetic retreat—celibacy, for example—but it could also license an antinomian and libertine descent into the carnal abyss, if with the intent to defeat the world of flesh from within. The gnostics were therefore "body snatchers": gnostic theology made impossible any positive appraisal of the physical body, or of the physical at all for that matter. As the political philosopher Leo Strauss would later put it in a letter to Jonas, gnosticism may well have been the most radical rebellion in Western history against the Greek notion of physis.[4] But more about this later.

The sickness of the sign of gnosticism as outlined by Culianu is of recent origin. Nearly all those in his rogue's gallery arrived there sometime this century. For some reason, the term and its associations echo with us late moderns. Somehow "gnosticism" has provided us with a convenient diagnosis for modernity's most riotous movements, its ills and contradictions.[5] All this suggests that the term became unmoored in recent decades. In part revived, in part invented for the first time in the seventeenth century, the term was definitively cast adrift only in the second and third decades of the twentieth. Ironically perhaps, its final untethering was unintended, the inadvertent product of Hans Jonas's most concentrated efforts to curb its conceptual wanderings.

In more stylized terms, Jonas's efforts represent what I would like to call a third "overcoming of gnosticism." I borrow the expression from the German philosopher Hans Blumenberg, who coined it in a book called *The Legitimacy of the Modern Age* (1966), among the most ambitious revisions of Western intellectual history ever ventured. Against a rash of attacks on the modern West as an ill-concealed, secularized, and "illegitimate" derivative of an earlier Christian era, Blumenberg stepped up in its defense. He linked the modern age—defined by man's need for self-assertion, to act in the world—to a second overcoming of gnosticism at the end of the Middle Ages. Blumenberg's story went something like this. The inability to account for evil in a world created by a benevolent and omnipotent God had first left Christianity vulnerable to the gnostic thesis of two powers in heaven, which Augustine "overcame" by discovering the origins of evil not in God but in man. Even as Augustine did battle with the gnostic threat, however, he unwittingly enabled its return. His stress on man's insufficiency before God, his powerlessness, appeared later in the form of nominalism and voluntarism, a loose confluence of thought in late-medieval scholastic theology centripetally bound by the black hole of the *deus absconditus* or hidden god. God may have absconded from the world, but this only accentuated the threat of his arbitrary intervention. Man was left denuded of power. And so overcoming gnosticism a second, final time meant that man would have to assert himself in the world—an attitude Blumenberg thought best exemplified in the scientific program of Francis Bacon. In sum: modern Western man defeated the caprice of the hidden god by arrogating to himself both the power and right to master the natural world.

To suggest that gnosticism returned for a third time in the 1920s and '30s is therefore to take leave of Blumenberg's account, if also to extend it. Gnosticism (or a host of phenomena going by the name and understood as such) was revived with a vengeance in this period—on the occult scene, in philosophy, in theology of all persuasions, even in the natural sciences. Its revival dovetailed with the breakdown of a triumphalist story of the modern West—a story of progressive secularization and technological advance. This story had it that modern Europe had transformed Christian eschatology into the pursuit of moral and technical "progress." It had made immanent in the historical process Christian hopes for human completion associated with the *eschaton* or end-time. Gnosticism's return posed a threat to this narrative. It signaled the resurgence of the existential anxiety and dread that had prompted modern man to assert himself in the first place.

This period also witnessed the return of *the* theological dilemma attending the birth, on Blumenberg's account, of both the Middle and modern ages: that of *coram deo*, or man's sufficiency before God. In the 1920s, Karl Barth resuscitated the problem with his commentary on Paul's Epistle to the Romans and in the form of "crisis theology." It is difficult to overstate the importance of Barth's *Romans*. In the interwar period, it did most to systematize a gnostic language of heresy spoken well beyond confessional boundaries, and it set the terms—whether embraced or disputed—for much of Christian and Jewish thought in the wake of Versailles.[6]

The return of gnosticism staked a challenge to the reigning ideas about knowledge as well. Gnosis translates as knowledge, though of a peculiar sort, with little resemblance to what most today would understand by the term. It does not refer to something man attains by his own devices, whether by experiment or contemplation. It describes instead a revelation in the world issued from a transcendent beyond, a revelation *in* the world that ensures salvation *from* the world. It posed a particular threat to systems of knowledge that conceived of the world as an enclosure and of themselves as sovereign within it. In the years before 1918 these were neo-Kantian epistemology and a scientific approach to nature informed by Bacon's bequest. "Baconian science"—or knowledge as technology—appeared especially perverse when pressed in the service of military mass death, as it was during the First World War. No longer a solution, man's technical mastery over the world had instead become a problem. To wrest from nature her secrets, as Bacon had suggested, produced a kind of knowledge repudiated by a gnosis described as trans-mundane and revelatory. Meanwhile, the gnostic view of the world as soaked in sin could make inquiry into the world's workings a suspect enterprise at best.[7]

Asked toward the end of his life what it was about gnosticism that would have interested a philosopher at the time, Jonas answered simply. With gnosticism, knowledge had attained "an entirely new role."[8] His answer is worth taking seriously. His own age contended no less with tumult in the rules by which knowledge was produced and authorized, turmoil prompted in part by his teachers Edmund Husserl and Martin Heidegger, in part by the theologians of crisis. To all this we will return. Suffice it to say for now that the problems apparently resolved at the end of the Middle Ages surfaced again in interwar Europe, their earlier solutions undone.

To refer to the story that follows as a third overcoming of gnosticism has several drawbacks. These deserve mention at the outset. First, it assumes that there *was* a historically specifiable phenomenon called gnosticism, that this phenomenon could return periodically, and that all this remains open to historical review. Such conjectures seemed relatively safe for Jonas and his immediate predecessors, but they do not seem so today. Recent writing on the history of late antiquity has taken aim at the term—and for a variety of reasons has declared it incoherent.[9] This line of argument foregrounds the contingency of the term as we use it, a use perhaps indebted more to Jonas than anyone else. As much as Jonas discovered the unity of the gnostic spirit, so too did he invent it. This underwrites a story that finds in the 1920s a spirit of alienation—Jewish and otherwise—partially retrojected on to the gnostic era. But it also gives rise to the curious fact that Jonas invented the phenomenon (or a version of it) he then sought to overcome. The question is why.

The answer is in part bound up with a second drawback: to call this story an overcoming of gnosticism obscures the fact that Jonas's attack on gnostic thought had its precedent and complement in his attack on Paul. Like the gnostics, Paul enjoyed a renaissance in this period, prompted not least by the theologians of crisis. Many associated Paul with gnostic theology, and in this Jonas was no exception. He in fact advanced a strong version of the thesis, describing Paul as the most perfect incarnation of the gnostic spirit. This equation proved fateful, and helps account for the deep coherence of his diverse investigations. Not only an overcoming of gnosticism, Jonas's philosophical career reveals itself also as a profoundly hostile, Jewish response to the Pauline condition as he (following Barth) understood it. His work on the gnostics and Paul were inseparable, the two projects one. The series of concerns Jonas encountered there set the terms for the postwar writings for which he is known best: a philosophical biology and an environmental ethics that made him an inspiration to environmentalists across Europe.[10] It also gave rise to the sensibility at work in the writings for which he is known least: his essays in post-Holocaust theology. There he developed his own myth of the hidden God—elaborated to empower man to live a mortal, finite life in a wondrous, if mysterious world. They were written with the conviction that after Auschwitz must come neither Jerusalem nor Israel, but Earth.

CHAPTER ONE

The Gnostic Return

BY MOST ACCOUNTS, gnosticism—as a related set of phenomena if not yet as a name—had its first lasting invention in the work of the early church heresimachs, or heresy hunters. Until 1945, in fact, nearly all access to gnostic texts had come refracted through their preservation in church polemic. In that year a group of Egyptian peasants avenging a blood feud accidentally unearthed at Nag Hammadi an entire library of gnostic writings.[1] Until then, however, tracts such as the *Exposure and Refutation of Knowledge (Gnosis) Falsely So-Called*, authored in the year 180 by Irenaeus, bishop of Lyon, provided the primary means by which the gnostic heresies survived. Here we need only register the dominant associations of the terminology, associations bequeathed by the church orthodox. Gnosticism demanded their attention insofar as its heretical views were identifiably Christian in derivation. For the most part, these either had sprouted from Christian soil or had made unlicensed use of the figure of Jesus.[2] The orthodox equated such sects with a threat to church hegemony, a menace made all the more frightening by the quiet sense that the gnostics possessed an interpretation of scripture more internally coherent than the church's own. This discomfort was nowhere more evident than in efforts to account for the origin and continued presence of evil in the world. No matter the explanations offered, they could hardly compete in imaginative force with the gnostic solution: two powers in heaven, one the evil creator, the other an absent, unknown, and transcendent god of salvation.

Even as they feared the cogency of gnostic exegesis, the early heresy hunters complained of gnosticism's prodigious capacity for invention, its penchant for spontaneous mythmaking. They contended—or so they claimed—less with codified dogma than with more elusive prey: pseudo-spiritual fictions, theological hobgoblins, and metaphysical bugbears. Though the sects themselves generally disappeared by the end of the fourth century, to name them ironically ensured their survival, at least as an idea available to others. This survival came at a price, certainly more to the church than to the gnostics and their legacy, who, had they been around to witness it, would likely have reveled in their lasting and doctrinal alienation from normative religion. The church had in effect created for posterity a primordial heresy, one that could—and would—return intermittently to haunt it, if always in modified form.

"Gnosis" has its equivalent in ancient Greek, and later, in Latin. "Gnosticism" does not. The latter was born just as much of religious polemic, however, if fourteen centuries later. The Cambridge Platonist Henry More was the first, in 1669, to affix its fateful suffix, fateful insofar as it carried with it the latent potential for a certain slippage in meaning. In an anti-Catholic treatise instructively titled *Antidote Against Idolatry*, More complained of those who accepted the plurality of religious doctrine, blind as they were to the fact that such plurality was "but a spice of the old abhorred Gnosticism." More's use of the term is extraordinary. In its very invention, he managed to both expand and circumscribe the term's capacity to refer. He destabilized the term's relation to its putative historical referent (identifying Catholicism's foundational heresy with a version of Catholicism itself). At the same time, he preserved and amplified gnosticism's association with moral depravity and with the heretical, broadly construed.

The nineteenth century, however, brought with it the first sweeping evaluations of the gnostic phenomenon of direct relevance to the figures under consideration here. The Protestant theologian and Tübingen professor Ferdinand Christian Baur provided the reigning interpretation in his work of 1835, *Die christliche Gnosis*. Baur approached gnosticism in part as Jonas would a century later. He aimed to grasp the gnostic phenomenon not only in its "mere outer appearance" but in the "internal movement" and in the "totality of moments" unique to its *Begriff*, its concept—something about gnosticism transcended any of its distinct historical episodes. The result was a sprawling ramble through nearly two millennia of intellectual history: from gnostic beginnings in the confluence of Judaism, Christianity, and paganism, to its concretions in the likes of Basilides and Marcion, then to the attacks it suffered at the hands of Neoplatonist critics like Plotinus and Christian ones such as Irenaeus and Tertullian, and finally to the return of gnostic questions in the theosophy of Jakob Böhme and in Friedrich Schelling, their modification in Schleiermacher, and their eventual resolution in Hegel.[3]

Debates over gnosticism raged among nineteenth-century Jews also. Heinrich Graetz, doyen of modern Jewish historical writing, penned a dissertation called *Gnosticismus und Judentum* (1846), intended in part as scholarship, in part as a salvo in his dispute with a nascent German-Jewish Reform movement. Graetz understood some of the gnostic sects as heretical deviations from a Jewish norm, and characterized his Reform contemporaries in similar terms: the ancient epoch presented an "undeniable analogy with our own time; for gnostic dualism one need only substitute modern pantheism."[4] Fifty years later, Moriz Friedländer reversed the terms of Graetz's argument. He also reversed the terms of Jewish orthodoxy, convinced as he was that pharisaic Judaism represented a reactionary deviation from a Hellenistic norm. Against Baur, he located gnostic beginnings in pre-Christian Diasporic Judaism, and hence the title of his study: *Der vorchristliche jüdische Gnosticismus.*[5]

By the 1920s gnosticism (the term) had hardly a vestige of an agreed-upon meaning. That gnosticism had returned in some form was a sentiment shared by many, but what that meant was up for debate. Some, notably those on the occult scene inspired by the maverick educator Rudolf Steiner, greeted the new age with enthusiasm. Much of Steiner's literary production from the first decade of the twentieth century appeared under the mark "Lucifer-Gnosis."[6] Salvation, he argued, meant to liberate a germ of spirit from its earthly bonds, a process set in motion by a knowledge of self or gnosis.[7]

The gnostic revival exercised thinkers in more mainstream circles also. Those attracted to the concept or called gnostic by detractors generally had a distinct theological-political physiognomy. They tended to be exponents of a "new religiosity" opposed to the nineteenth-century synthesis of religious belief and liberalism. They identified "culture" as their primary enemy, either *Kulturprotestantismus*, or in the Jewish case, hostility to the bourgeois fetish for *Bildung*, or self-cultivation. They harbored a deep animus toward the reigning conception of religious experience, the subjective human experience of the divine, inaugurated more than a century earlier in the Protestant theology of F.D.E. Schleiermacher. In German-Jewish circles, they would include many of those recognized as prominent intellectuals following the First World War: Gershom Scholem, Walter Benjamin, Franz Rosenzweig, Leo Strauss, and Ernst Bloch come immediately to mind. In Protestant circles, this movement would include the "crisis theologians" Karl Barth, Friedrich Gogarten, and Eduard Thurneysen, and in certain of his moods more prominent toward the very end of his life, the great liberal theologian Adolf von Harnack.

To grasp what was at stake in this revival, it helps to focus on the representation of a single, crucial figure: Marcion of Sinope (110-160 C.E.). Marcion had undertaken to emancipate early Christian teaching from its Jewish corruptions. If Christianity evolved out of Judaism, it nonetheless ought to be understood as its strictest opposition. The God of the Old Testament he described as an evil demiurge and all creation his malicious work. The God of the new dispensation, incarnated by Christ and best described by Paul, was in turn the God of salvation, love, and mercy. His teaching of the two Gods made him persona non grata with the fledgling church, which dismissed and persecuted him as a heretic in the gnostic mold.

In the interwar period, the name Marcion had Adolf von Harnack to thank for its remarkable currency.[8] The first edition of Harnack's study of Marcion appeared in 1921, a revision of his dissertation written fifty years earlier. It came at the end of a career that had seen him rise to the pinnacle of Protestant thought at the fin de siècle. Harnack's statement was and remains the most forceful in favor of a non-gnostic Marcion. Although Marcion had reproduced and even radicalized the gnostic distinction between an inferior and oppressive creator of the world and the God of salvation, he had also reversed the gnostic "logic" of home. He refused to define the world as the site of alienation—for on Marcion's account, man remains until the advent of Christ through and through of this world. God does not gather lost children, but extracts miserable strangers from their native land and receives them in a new father's house. Men do not return from exile. On the contrary: "a magnificent foreign land is disclosed and becomes their homeland."[9] Nor did Marcion reproduce the grand theoretical aspirations of the gnostic thinkers, a pursuit linked intimately to the elaboration of a gnosis. Having rejected Hellenic notions of gnosis and having thrown in his lot with Pauline faith, Marcion could not, on Harnack's view, belong integrally to gnosticism, understood by him as the acute "Hellenization" of Christianity.

If not a gnostic per se, Marcion was nonetheless easily assimilated to the neo-gnostic spirit of interwar Europe. Harnack asked after Marcion's relevance for the modern age. "Was not Marcion right in his relationship to Christianity at large, both then and in the present time?" "Is it not always a failed undertaking when one strives to harmonize the essence and nature of faith, its ground and its hope, with the 'world'—that is, to comprehend faith from the perspective of reason?"[10] His questions reveal deep ambivalence about the liberal synthesis of reason with faith, of confidence in progress with a providential theology. In the more Marcionite of his moods, Harnack appeared to endorse the heretic outright. Marcion ought to be understood as the culmination of a course that runs from the prophets through Jesus to Paul and beyond. Paul's antinomian turn, instigated but not supported by Jesus, remained unintelligible without Marcion as its telos, a telos newly revealed as such by the neo-Marcionite spirit of the day. Still, Harnack hardly offered an unqualified endorsement. He rebuked Marcion for his attack on the first tenet of churchly faith: "I believe in God the Father Almighty." Harnack's concluding exhortation—that "one can only wish that in the chaotic chorus of those who seek after God [even] Marcionites might once again be found today"—came with the reservation, often ignored by his more ardent contemporaries, that truth reveals itself more easily through error.[11]

Harnack's book ignited a firestorm of controversy among his Protestant colleagues (not to mention Jews such as Martin Buber, Franz Rosenzweig, Hans Jonas, and Gershom Scholem).[12] For many the book induced disquiet, if not outright alarm. "I am certainly not the only one of [Harnack's] students," wrote Erich Foerster, "for whom this book has prepared difficult days." Harnack's sympathy for Marcion's critique of the world, this "world-cockroach" as Foerster put it, led him to describe the book as "nothing other than an attack against German Protestantism."[13] The theologian Arnold Hein likewise reacted with dismay to Harnack's conclusion, and took it upon himself to shield his flock from "early Christian agitation, precisely because our time so dangerously resembles theirs."[14] Above all, however, Marcion functioned as a conduit for debate on a new development within the realm of Protestant thought, a development that would, however, reverberate far beyond its boundaries. This was the advent of "crisis theology," its challenge to the Protestant-liberal synthesis, and the rise to theological stardom of its champions, Friedrich Gogarten and Karl Barth above all.

Barth and Gogarten argued for what Harnack had for the most part only described, a Christianity whose touchstone resembled Marcion's: *das Evangelium vom fremden Gott*, or the gospel of the alien God. Their contemporaries thought of them as latter-day gnostics. Adolf Jülicher, a prominent liberal theologian and for a time a teacher to Barth, likened Gogarten to a "Basilides wandering among the aeons." And he attacked his one-time pupil as a "half-gnostic Marcion with his radical dualism of all or nothing and with his wrath against all that is half." Hein also called Barth a Marcionite, given the otherness of his God and distaste for the world. Against him, Hein insisted in a high Disney moment that "the father Jesus Christ will always be the creator of this great big wonderful garden of men and animals." He thought that Luther's "naive joy in nature and art, in man and the world" (!) provided a more salutary example for the Protestants of his day.[15] Foerster, too, recognized in the theologians of crisis the "renewal of Marcionitism," even if they refused Marcion's teaching of the two gods.[16]

Barth admitted to his critic's equations. He first encountered Harnack's book as he composed the second edition of his commentary to Paul's Epistle. "I was puzzled," he wrote thereafter, "by the remarkable parallels between what Marcion had said and what I was actually writing." Barth echoed gnostic ideas about gnosis, of a message from beyond. "The truth has encountered us from beyond a frontier we have never crossed," he wrote. "It is as though we had been transfixed by an arrow launched at us from beyond an impassable river. . . . We speak as prisoners at liberty, as blind seeing, as dead and behold we live." Barth was attracted also to the gnostic and Marcionite critique of Christianity, that its representatives failed to separate the finite from the infinite, the human from the divine. "Transforming time into eternity, and therefore eternity into time," Barth wrote, "they stretch themselves beyond the boundary of death, rob the Unknown God of what is His, push themselves into His domain, and depress Him to their own level. Forgetting the awful gulf by which they are separated from Him, they enter upon a relation with Him which would be possible only if He were not God. They make Him a thing in this world."[17]

Still, Barth thought that the parallels warranted little cause for concern. "At the crucial points," he felt, "these agreements break down." He noted the slew of heretics with which others had associated him. With a mix of amusement and scorn, he suggested that his critics, these "learned theologians," would have done better to agree upon their choice before "they made up their minds to throw me to some ancient and venerable heresiarch." "As it is," he announced, "I remain unscathed."[18]

Barth was indeed correct. The analogy does fail. This should hardly have given cause for celebration, however, neither for him nor his critics. For in his *departures* from gnostic theology lurks the true and terrible fright of Barth's universe. Barth reversed the logic of the gnostic notion of gnosis. Gnosis no longer rescues; it bears no providential tidings. "All we know is that the union between God and man has been changed from divine pre-supposition to human supposition, and that, consequently, every human position has suffered dislocation. On the very brink of human possibility there has, moreover, appeared a final human capacity—the capacity of knowing God to be unknowable and wholly Other." Barth's gnosis can do nothing, then, but open man's eyes to his loneliness. The pessimism and alienation of Barth's theology far outstrip its gnostic equivalent. Whereas the gnostics could exult in the love extended them by the transcendent divine—and for some scholars, love supersedes alienation as the primary gnostic mood—Barth had little truck with such fluffy niceties. "Religion is an abyss," he wrote. "It is terror."[19]

All told, confusion reigned among both the lay and the learned in the gnostic name game of the 1920s. Both Barth and Harnack called Steiner a gnostic. Harnack thought of Barth as gnostic, even as Harnack elicited suspicions among his liberal colleagues about his own sympathies. Barth at times considered himself Marcion's heir, and at times he did not. Gnosticism managed to include them all under a single semantic canopy, though at the price of precision and consistency. It had become, as Culianu later put it, a sick sign. Into this confusion Jonas stepped, and with lasting consequences.

To begin, Jonas recognized in his age—and in Barth—a recrudescence of gnosticism. In a draft of his dissertation, in a passage marked through with a large leaden *X* (and therefore of special importance!), Jonas drew the parallel: "What the Church fought down with the entire array of its forces . . . is today on the other hand conscripted, if less defiant and more tacit (and naturally also without the notion of two gods) into Christian and especially Protestant theology, this time as a quasi-official *opinio communis*, even if not formulated as such. It no longer proffers, if it does not *e silentio* negate, a realist, worldly notion of God's providence, or even the world as the domain of his power." To this extent, Jonas felt, "one could well speak of *all* recent theology as Marcionite through and through."[20]

This passage indicates a crucial fact: Jonas discovered in his age not only a parallel to the gnostic era, but also a proximate cause or stimulus to his researches. These transformed scholarly debates about gnosticism also, which suffered from just as debilitating a confusion as that which reigned in cultural circles. The preceding twenty years had witnessed a slew of attempts to specify gnosticism's historical origins. Before the nineteenth century, the sects later sheltered by Jonas under the gnostic umbrella were generally understood as post-Christian heresies and perversions. Heterodoxy was a reaction to orthodoxy, derivative and inferior. Late in the nineteenth century, however, a series of scholars turned east, toward ancient Persia especially, in the search for gnosticism's pre-Christian origins. Known collectively as the *religionsgeschichtliche Schule*, the group included acclaimed figures like Wilhelm Bousset and Richard Reitzenstein.[21]

Jonas approved of the turn to the Orient as a corrective to those, like Harnack, blinded by their commitment to Hellenic origins. Represented in the 1920s by Hans Leisegang, the latter position denied the otherness of the gnostic phenomenon, domesticated it, by situating it in the continuum of Western thought—of the gnostic beast was made an amiable puppy.[22] (As Jonas saw it, the Greek language in which the gnostic sources were clothed masked gnostic alterity.) The gnostic impulse was not merely otherworldly but antiworldly, characterized above all by an *Entweltlichungstendenz*, a tendency toward "de-worldification" (or a making-absent-from-the-world). But Bousset, too, came in for criticism. Though useful as counterpoint to the advocates of the Panhellenic thesis, he conceived of gnosticism as little more than a hodgepodge of extant ideas, a mealy mush, an open shelter for the conceptual freaks and sociopaths of late antiquity.[23]

Jonas shifted the terms of discussion entirely. He declined to forward his own account of gnostic origins, one that might compete with Harnack's "acute hellenization of Christianity," with Friedländer's Jewish, Baur's Christian, or Bousset's Persian gnosis. Instead, he disavowed the search for origins altogether. Gnosticism he defined as a *Daseinshaltung*, an attitude or stance toward human being. The gnostic spirit was irreducible to its historical origins, whether Iranian, Jewish, Christian, or Greek. As a "fundamental" category, it was irreducible to anything but itself. "It is the genuineness, the underivative nature, of this substance [underlying gnosticism]," Jonas would later write, "that defeats all attempts at derivation that concern more than the outer shell of expression." One might well specify the origins of the intellectual detritus of which the gnostic spirit made use. But its organizing principle was nothing less than the deep structure of human being, or at least one of its possibilities. Jonas thought himself to speak not of gnosticism per se, but of "Dasein as such."[24]

The wild proliferation of meanings associated with gnosis and its cognates, the legion of competing historical accounts—all became epiphenomena. With the publication of *Gnosis und spätantiker Geist*, the swift expansion of the gnostic semantic universe abruptly slowed, stopped, reversed itself, and raced back to collapse at its indeterminable point of origin. One contemporary called it no less than the advent of a new intellectual epoch.[25] Leo Strauss wrote shortly after that even one (like himself) unfamiliar with the gnostic texts could feel justified in saying: "only so *can* it be, only so is [gnosticism] at all intelligible."[26] Astonished, Hans Blumenberg later said much the same.[27]

But Jonas's efforts to contain one big bang of meanings only ignited an explosion of even greater magnitude. By associating gnosticism most closely with alienation and otherness, he at once limited its scope and prompted its radical expansion. Distilled to a sensibility so crucial to the modern temper, gnosticism gathered into itself the concerns of an entire epoch. As a mood or disposition, it was divorced also from its original historical context. This happened despite Jonas's best efforts to counteract this tendency—with one significant exception—throughout his scholarly career.[28] The exception was Heidegger, whose existentialist "nihilism" Jonas later recognized as the first true eruption of the gnostic spirit in two thousand years.

This repudiation of Heidegger was first occasioned by Heidegger's infamous rectoral address of 1933. Heidegger had assumed leadership at the university in Freiburg, and as part of the process of *Gleichschaltung* or ideological coordination had thrown in his lot—and evidently the lot of philosophy itself—with the Nazi cause.[29] The move confounded both his students and colleagues, not least the circle of brilliant Jewish acolytes who had gathered around him. The devotion of his students led Jonas to liken them in retrospect to followers of the Lubavitcher Rebbe—"as if Heidegger was a Tzadik, a miracle-rabbi or a guru"—and in such a light the intensity of incredulity and betrayal is not difficult to fathom:[30]

> The falling into line of the deepest thinker of the time with the thundering lockstep of the brown batallions appeared to me as a catastrophic debacle for philosophy, as a world-historical disgrace, as the bankruptcy of philosophical thought. I held then to the notion that philosophy should guard against something like that. . . . It could not be. All collaboration, all ideological "coordination"—everywhere

one could posit stupidity, blindness, weakness, cowardice as explanations. That the most important, most original philosophical thinker of my time went along, however—that was a monstrous blow for me, not only personally, but in the sense of an event to be taken seriously in the history of philosophy itself.[31]

If Heidegger's decision continues to confound—how after all are we to account for the alliance of the century's most important thinker with its most horrific regime?—it is also in retrospect intelligible.[32] Heidegger's rhetoric of "decision" and "resolve" in the face of terrible anxiety (as elaborated in *Being and Time*, his 1927 masterpiece) could be shoehorned into a Nazi program that counseled much the same.

This insight and the attack it occasioned first achieved written form in 1952, when Jonas published what remains his most widely read essay, "Gnosticism and Modern Nihilism."[33] Looking back, Jonas attributed the astonishing fit of the gnostic phenomenon to Heideggerian categories—a fit that in no small part accounted for the force of his interpretation—to the ways in which Heidegger's existentialism replicated and radicalized gnostic nihilism. Above all they shared a dualism that set man over and against the world, abetted for them both by God's absence. Accordingly, accounts of Jonas's philosophical work tend to link his postwar writings in philosophical biology and environmental ethics to this renunciation of Heideggerian and gnostic nihilism. To overcome Heidegger meant also to overcome gnosticism.[34]

No doubt this was true, but only in a secondary sense. His attack on Heidegger was in fact not one, but two. Its second iteration exploded on to the world scene in 1964, twelve years after the first. It was then that Jonas addressed a conference of Protestant theologians gathered to honor Heidegger, and revealed to them the face of the pagan obscured by the mask of Heidegger's surface piety. And it was the paganism, not first the nihilism, that Jonas identified at the heart of Heidegger's receptivity to the Nazi call. The speech was a sensation. It received prominent coverage in the *New York Times*, provoked a series of disputes, and in Germany earned Jonas the fame reserved for the most celebrated of academic stars.

But the attack therein proceeded in curious fashion. It *affirmed* the notions of divine absence and transcendence Jonas had earlier identified and opposed as the core of gnostic nihilism, and which he associated in his own day with both the theologians of crisis and the natural-scientific spirit. His twofold attack on Heidegger thus reveals a great deal. Jonas must be understood both as one who opposed a dualism that set man over and against the world and as one who hoped to save enough of the dualistic insight to make human life meaningful in the first place. The balance was perforce a delicate one. It was also, in my view, the hallmark of his philosophical career—and the philosophical expression of his most basic sentiments about human life on this planet. In the pages that follow, I would like to offer an account that discovers the kernel of this stance in an early and fundamental confrontation—not with Heidegger and not with the gnostics (or not merely with them), but in a Jewish encounter with Paul.

CHAPTER TWO

Romans in Weimar

IN THE WORLD of the academy, one line of reasoning goes, it is better to be despised than ignored, since at the very least someone has taken notice. Sometime in 1930, such platitudes must have crossed the mind of the twenty-seven-year-old Hans Jonas. For it was then that a reviewer for the *Theologische Literaturzeitung*, Hugo Koch, irritably dismissed a recently published book, Jonas's first, in its initial review.[1] The text in question, a concise study of the Pauline problem of freedom in the work of Augustine, stoked the ire of the well-regarded historian not on account of what Jonas said but on account of how he said it. "Had I but a suspicion" that the text perpetrated linguistic crimes such as "phenomenological," "existential-ontological structure," and worst of all, "the objectified reality of the act," he wrote, "I would have refused to review it." Another referee belittled the idiom as *Kauderwelsch*, as insufferable, unintelligible jabber.[2] Koch himself called it *einen groben Unfug*, a resonant phrase for disorderly conduct "through which German scholarship makes itself ridiculous before the rest of the world." For such brazen impunity against the Holy Ghost of the German language, Koch condemned the latter-day Jonas to three days captivity in the belly of a great fish.[3]

Koch was not without warrant. Even Jonas's teacher Rudolf Bultmann, on whose assurances the house of Vandenhoeck and Ruprecht published the piece in the first place, later felt compelled to apologize for the linguistic temerity of his talented protégé, and Jonas himself came to rue the "overburdened jargon" he once embraced.[4] The difficulties of the text's language derived in part from the novelty of Heideggerian categories, though by 1930, three years after the publication of *Being and Time*, such rhetoric was hardly unknown in the philosophical world. Jonas apprenticed with Heidegger in the mid-1920s in Marburg, and his essay had origins in Heidegger's seminar. To risk anachronism, Jonas might be likened to a precocious graduate student in today's academy dazzled by the latest philosophical innovations, agog to assimilate and apply them (though to be sure, both Jonas and his teacher outstripped in acumen their generic, latter-day counterparts).

Still, the judgment of Koch and others was premature. The self-reflexivity Jonas brought to his inquiry indeed bordered on the maddening. But it also bore considerable fruit, specifically in an outline for the program of "demythologization"—an innovation of lasting consequence in the history of theological thinking—later developed and applied by Rudolf Bultmann above all.[5] The Augustine text also marks the origins of a comprehensive intellectual project, even if it does not do so alone. It has as its indispensable complement—its completion, really—the plan for an "existential analysis" of Paul, which Jonas first outlined in a letter to Bultmann in 1929. Jonas thought the letter important enough to return to it thirty-five years later. With several crucial emendations, it became an essay, a 1964 contribution to a *Festschrift* for his teacher. Historically speaking, this letter and essay contain *in nuce* the whole of his philosophical career, the unfolding of which discloses itself as a profoundly hostile, Jewish response to the Pauline condition. This understanding of Paul was in many ways Barth's understanding, yet translated (and thereby transformed) into a Heideggerian idiom. Jonas referred to this move as a *Rückübersetzung*: both a *re*-translation and a translation *back* into the more fundamental categories he thought adequate to the question of Being as such.[6]

This move was enabled in part by the fact that Heidegger, though born and reared a Catholic, had by the early 1920s imbibed at Barth's well.[7] Barth, the crisis theologians, and their theological inspiration Franz Overbeck became important for Heidegger at just the time Jonas arrived to apprentice with him. Forty years later, Hans Georg Gadamer, another of Heidegger's students, would recall Heidegger's enthusiastic reception of Thurneysen, whose lecture before the Marburg theologians "was for us young people a first missive from the dialectical theology." The early form of *Being and Time* was in fact a lecture delivered in 1924 to the department of theology.[8] In that same year, Bultmann openly repudiated liberal in favor of dialectical theology, a move no doubt noted by Heidegger, a regular participant in Bultmann's seminar.[9] This rare intellectual alliance with Barth at its helm, one that would last for half a decade at best, left its mark on Jonas's thought, but did not determine it. For without naming him as an interlocutor, Jonas also contested Barth, and in ways that set the terms for his confrontation with Heidegger.

The story begins with his book on Augustine. There Jonas described the shift in Augustine's thought provoked by his dispute with the Pelagians, who had taken issue with Paul's insistence on man's inherent sinfulness, the intrinsic concupiscence of his will and its result: that in the act of willing to do good, man sins. Not only, the Pelagians argued, was it possible to adhere to the law, but precisely on that account morally required. Jesus did not do away with the law, but brought its completion and a guide to its fulfillment, and was as a consequence "demoted" from savior to prophet. The Pelagians had in effect denied the necessity of Christ's intervention *as* Christ. The controversy itself centered on the doctrines of original sin and predestination, of which the former, Jonas tells us, was for Augustine by far the more important.[10] Augustine developed his ideas through his reading of Paul's Epistle to the Romans—especially its seventh chapter, in which Paul distinguished most forcefully between flesh and spirit, law and grace. Not coincidentally, this chapter elicited some of the most explosive rhetoric in Barth's commentary also: no coincidence, in part, because Paul does no less in this chapter than elaborate a philosophical anthropology predicated on the unresolvable antinomies of law as such—at least as Jonas was to see it.

Before his encounter with the Pelagian heresy, Augustine sometimes made appeal to the logic of forbidden candy to describe the sinfulness attached to law: that which is taboo entices, that which is prohibited tempts. Jonas relegated this thinking to the realm of child psychology. Augustine's other texts, however, provided a more plausible alternative. On this view, vanity falsifies the willful act from within, since taking pride in our works converts an ethical obedience of the law into its opposite. This failure is no coincidence: it is intrinsic to Augustinian man, as the purity of will tends to decay into *amor sui*, or love of self.[11]

To defeat the Pelagian heresy, however, Augustine abandoned a dialectical view of the relation of law to grace. On this new account, in the dialectic of willing and incapacity the latter had finally triumphed. *Homo sub lege*, or man under law, was divested of all capacity to will or do good. His freedom consisted only in the *delectatio peccati*, the lust for the sinful. No longer did Augustine speak of a serious fight against temptation. As man was emasculated and the sphere of his capacity abridged, grace became all the more decisive as a saving power. This move served Augustine well in his battle with the Pelagians, who contested man's principal insufficiency, and thought of grace as taught and attained rather than granted. Though inferior, because heteronomous, the old law was a stage and an impulse toward grace, understood by the Pelagians as the "full, autonomous sufficiency of man."[12] As men on their way to grace, the Pelagians could ignore those passages of Romans that were for Augustine most vital. In response, Augustine severed, completely and absolutely, the state of grace from the state of law. Where the Pelagians found law and grace on a continuum, and where the early Augustine could at least imagine them as permeable, the later Augustine imagined them as separate realms altogether. From this perspective, the Pelagians inhabited a space that simply could not be, suspended somewhere between the two.

Jonas thought Augustine's scramble to protect grace from impurity an abject failure. The Augustinian strategy worked only so long as man under grace need not describe his condition with reference to his debased predecessor. Wittingly or not, he otherwise acknowledged a deeper ground upon which their differences became intelligible, a degree of identity that denied the incommensurability upon which the state of grace had first been predicated. The pertinent passages in Paul's Epistle referred obviously to the status of man under law—articulated, however, from the standpoint of man under grace. The passage "does not concern two different men, categories of men, phases of development, or historical epochs, but essentially a single existence: as soon as the man under grace wishes to speak of himself as man, of his human situation, he can see himself only *sub lege*." The state of grace thus lost the essential autonomy that Augustine hoped to grant it. It was instead merely the "current cancellation of the state of law." Paul's Epistle therefore both required and made it "unthinkable" that grace might be freed from the demands of law, independent that is, "from that which man quite simply is before God." On the contrary, any account of grace inevitably "consists in admitting one's actual imprisonment under the law," as grace was in fact constituted through its "dark and secret underground" and "primordial condition," the state of law to which it remained dialectically bound.[13] Confronted with the Pelagian threat, Augustine had rent this dialectic asunder—for Jonas an indivisible "existential unity"—and hypostatized its moods into separate realms of experience, its stages into unrelated moments in time.

Such speculation may at first appear far removed from its interwar context. But it spoke to some of the more pressing existential questions of the day. Not by chance had Barth explored this issue at length in his own commentary on Paul. Barth described the relation of sin to grace as one of nonlogical difference, as a relationless relation. "Sin and grace," he wrote, "cannot be placed side by side, or arranged in series, or treated as of like importance, any more than death and life can be so treated. There is no bridge across the gulf which separates them. They have no blurred edges which might be run together."[14] That the recognition of this cleft eludes most of those who inhabit the dim world of men does nothing to alter its fact. Barth imagined grace as a realm of purity beyond purity, in which law and grace cease to function as intelligible words. Grace was for him a "realm where there is no law."[15]

All this seems to reveal Barth as an antinomian in its most resolute and obstinate guise. Consider: "The law—sin? It seems obvious that we are almost compelled to the judgment that the law is sin." Or: "How enticing to us some semi-antinomianism, or indeed, complete antinomianism!" Or again: "Why should we not enrol ourselves as disciples of Marcion, and proclaim a new God, quite distinct from the old God of the law?" Alternatively, and for Barth this amounted to the same, one might dissolve God's law into the immanence of the world, and "set forth the secret of a true supernatural religion running at all points parallel to natural religion." Others in his time, preeminently the champions of Spinoza, appeared to do just that. Yet all these Barth repudiated as illusory. He poured scorn, for example, on the desire to "advance out of the realm of sin into the realm of grace simply by some complete or partial abrogation of the law."[16] Why? "The answer," he wrote, citing Paul, "is simply—God forbid!"[17]

Paul's words notwithstanding, the answer was in fact not so simple. To an antinomian position and to Marcionite theology too, Barth could not in the end grant his blessing. He considered both false alternatives, "pseudo-radicalism," for both were born and remained of this world. On Barth's logic, escape remained impossible "as long as a man liveth," which is to say, as long as man lives as man under law, and not as quasi-divine under grace, as long as man remains confined to his human possibilities and excluded from his godly ones.

Barth had left man in a difficult position. Following Paul, he thought of will as infected with sin. The will simply had no role to play except as that from which to be freed. What, then, was a man to do? Barth's answer: to stand fast. Like so many of his contemporaries, he counseled simple resolve. "At whatever cost," he wrote, "we must remain at our post and drain the cup to its dregs. . . . We must submit to the full paradox of our situation." This situation he described as a "condition of shattering confusion" from which man might never escape.[18] (Curiously, Barth did not comment on the willfulness implicit in such resolution. Logically, his position should have led to a kind of withdrawal or ataraxia, a calm disavowal of human initiative regarding ultimate things and a wait for grace from beyond. But this it did not do.)

Paul and the gnostics (both ancient and modern) had for various reasons denigrated the world and imagined some otherworldly realm of escape. They located true freedom elsewhere, often in death metaphorically construed. Here, for example, is Barth: "Through the slain body of Christ, we are what we are not. Observed from this scene of death 'we' live no more; we are dead to the law, dead to the possibility and necessity of religion, dead to every human possibility; we are removed, set free, unfettered."[19] Likewise, the gnostics had anticipated what Jonas called an *erlösende Vernichtung*, a redeeming annihilation.[20] They too felt compelled to denigrate what Barth, following Paul, called the flesh, understood as "unqualified, and finally unqualifiable worldliness." Since for Barth "the passions of sin spring ultimately from the 'vitality of mortality,'" their vigorous energy can—apart from the final word 'Resurrection'—produce only—fruit unto death."[21]

All of this Jonas came to abhor. Whereas Barth found freedom in metaphorical death, Jonas would locate it in the phenomenon of life. This, not incidentally, was the title of his first book to follow *Gnosis*. There he developed a philosophy of the organism that could hardly oppose the Pauline denigration of the flesh in terms any more emphatic than it did. The guiding impulse of his philosophical biology, to revalue the world in the face of the absent God and to reinsert man into the continuum of biological life, turned both gnostic and Pauline theology on its head. Barth bemoaned human vitality, which after all had its origins in man's fall. Jonas evinced none of this nostalgia for prelapsarian grace and discovered in flesh the source of freedom, human and otherwise. Barth's antinomianism was underwritten by an association of slavery to the law with a "psycho-physical occurrence."[22] His hostility to human as opposed to godly life he conflated with his hostility to law, and located in the human body their shared origin. Meanwhile, Jonas came to find freedom, not servitude, in the very fact of metabolism, in the unconscious, cellular, all-pervading *willfulness* of the organism. At times, Jonas pushed the threshold of freedom even further back, and claimed to hear its dim echoes in the muted call of the inorganic. The mystery of origins may remain ultimately closed, he admitted, but that could not dissuade him from his preferred hypothesis: "that even the transition from inanimate to animate substance, the first feat of matter's organizing itself for life, was actuated by a tendency in the depth of being toward the very modes of freedom to which this transition opened the gate."[23] Whereas Barth erected entirely distinct realms for transcendence and immanence, for the divine and the worldly, Jonas thought even the lowliest amoeba endowed with the horizons of both. His philosophical biology, it should now be clear, developed out of an early encounter with Paul.

The traces of this encounter are preserved for us—in his letter of 1929 to Bultmann and in the essay of 1964 in which the letter was reproduced. We would do well not to dispatch the letter to the collective trash heap of philosophical *Jugendschriften*, for Jonas identified his analysis of *Paul* as the foundation of his work on gnosis. He called it the "kernel of the whole," the "normative position," and the "rare high point" of the gnostic *Daseinshaltung*. Paul "cast light on all other cases" and enabled an "understanding of all the appearances in the entire [gnostic] realm." The Pauline Epistle contained the "most original and unclouded" statements of the gnostic spirit. Even when left unspecified, Jonas instructed the reader to assume Paul's presence in the explication of every last detail of the gnostic phenomenon. This, because Paul was the "locus classicus" of gnostic thought.[24]

In his correspondence with Bultmann, Jonas redescribed in the language of phenomenology what Paul had accomplished in Romans. He wrote of Paul as a philosophical anthropologist whose touchstone was primal sin "inevitably committed and constantly renewed."[25] Jonas hoped to prove here what remained an assumption in his essay on Augustine, that the statements of Romans 7 referred not to Paul the person, not to a psychological type, and not to any notion of historical mankind that must pass through temporally successive stages from law to grace. They referred, rather, to man as such. Only so could they have comprised an argument for the Christian alternative to Judaism and paganism. Bereft of chance and accident, Romans spoke the universal and necessary.

But who was this "man as such"? *What* was he? He was pharisaic man, and a conflicted creature, to say the least. Jonas's analysis focused on the acts of thinking and willing. Thinking, he observed, is always also thought about the act of thinking itself. "I think" is always also "I think that I think," or in the Latin, *cogito me cogitare*. Something similar, he thought, happens in the will: "willing" is also "willing to will," a process that Jonas described as the exercise of freedom. The difference is that thinking is "self-conscious" about itself in a way that willing is not. Or not necessarily: Jonas described the transformation from "willing to will" into "I think that I will" as freedom's own dispossession: "instead of living within the execution of its self-chosen action, [freedom] looks at it from without as its own observer and so has already become a stranger to it—has at bottom forsaken and betrayed it."[26] In other words, unconscious willing has come to be displaced by a self that observes itself as an actor. It is akin to the difference between Adam before and after the Fall, now conscious and ashamed of his nakedness.

Paul, Jonas thought, had a similar story to tell about God's law. Only through its revelation did we become aware of our insufficiency, and in a way, aware of ourselves at all. This new awareness, this "I think that I will," Jonas described as the fall of freedom—prompted, it turns out, by the "trap in the Law," a trap "not only consistent with its holiness but even directly caused by it, since the Law as such enjoins self-consciousness." That is to say, law elicits the will's self-objectification. "As the Law through its Ought first makes freedom reflective and thereby morality possible, so through its compulsion to self-scrutiny it creates at the same time the condition for the plight of subjectivity," and more to the point, the condition for "the perversion of purpose."[27] This is the case whether one has in mind heteronomous, Pauline law or autonomous, Kantian law. Utilitarian calculations of reward and punishment in the former and vanity in the latter dirty the will's strivings toward holiness, or in the Kantian scheme, toward dutifulness.[28]

Either way, law created a new kind of self. It was a self compelled to scrutinize itself for the waywardness of its inherently wayward will. It was a self compelled to condemn itself even as it willed itself to holiness—and not only, as Augustine had worried, because the will to do good works decays into self-love. Here is how Jonas described it:

Freedom, even when successful in abstaining from unethical outward "work," encounters in the own most sphere of its self-grounding this inward possibility of itself which always lies in wait and claims its mental enactment; and the fact that here, within the mind, the mere thought is the act, and the possibility to think it is necessity to think it, and willing not to think it means to have already thought it, and not-having-thought-it may be concealing it, and concealing it may be its most suspicious presence: this labyrinthine structure of subjectivity per se makes the self-temptation irresistible to freedom in its helpless dealing with itself. Prior to any explicit counter-resolve, even in the heart of any counter-exertion itself, it has already succumbed to it in some subtle way.[29]

This, then, was the lot Paul and Augustine had left to pharisaic man: a "ceaseless, self-mirroring back-and-forth," a dialectic of freedom and its undoing, of the will to holiness as sin, a dialectic that might be interrupted only from "somewhere else"—that is, from God. But about this last possibility, Jonas wrote, "philosophy has nothing to say."[30]

If in Paul's world *homo pharisaius* predominated, he can hardly be said to have reigned. All in all, as Jonas described him, he was a miserable, pitiful creature. Constitutionally deficient, unable to fulfill the demands of God, the law or even his own, he could do little more than skulk through life aware of the fact, and wait for a grace that might well never come. How, Jonas thought, he must have wished to abandon Paul's world for that of his teacher Jesus. The difference between them was their anthropological premise. Whereas Jesus exposed a wanting form of law-ful piety, Paul denied its very possibility. Whereas Jesus attacked from within a "false and corrigible attitude," Paul described from without a "true and unavoidable experience." For Jesus, *pharisaius* was an inferior but empirical type among others. For Paul, his was "the ultimate position before grace" and his defeat the "defeat of man as such."[31]

In sum, Jesus had not "summoned away from the law," but called from its superficial to its serious compliance, from letter to spirit. "Where that call leads, there the real experience of the Law waits." Thus corrected, however, pharisaic man would only then find himself in the Pauline predicament, "still unredeemed but aware of it." He would find himself in the Barthian situation, in which knowledge of God's absence counts as man's matchless triumph.[32] Only the man made aware of his incapacity and led to despair by law's demand finds himself primed for the reception of grace. For all its hostility to law, Paul's scheme cannot do without it, and it is here that he helps us see the conservative (or nomocentric) moment in the consistently antinomian position.

In 1964, in published form, Jonas was content to end the analysis there. In 1929, in a more private medium, he was not. In the letter to Bultmann, he adverted in conclusion for the only time to the first person voice, and offered "an entirely personal argument, but for myself the decisive one." "As a Jew," he wrote, "I feel myself attacked by Jesus' critique not essentially, but only in a particular expression of Jewish piety. By Paul, however, I feel myself essentially and basically struck, so that neither as a Jew nor a man would I have something to defend myself against [him]."[33]

Jonas might have substituted Barth's name in this announcement for Paul's—and with some justice. Jonas's story of the will repeated in Heidegger's terms Barth's commentary on Paul's Epistle.[34] The similarities do not, however, end there. In his adieu to Bultmann, Jonas declared Paul guilty of the deepest metaphysical anti-Semitism. By attacking lawful piety as such, Paul had made it impossible for a Jew to *be* a Jew, made impossible any sort of authentic, Jewish being-in-the-world. Barth did the same. "The 'peculiarity' of the Jew," he wrote, "is occasioned by his occupation of a position so perilously near the edge of a precipice that its sheer drop may be taken as bearing witness to the sharp edge of that wholly other precipice, by which all human achievements, all concrete occurrences, are bounded; the precipice which separates men from God."[35]

Barth had translated into anti-liberal theology the anti-Semitism at work in liberal theology also. Take Adolph von Harnack as an example, who thought Jews impudent for their stubborn refusal to integrate into the universalist liberal state.[36] Harnack envisioned a historical resolution to the "Jewish problem," but Barth repudiated both liberalism and its solutions. He reiterated (albeit in modified form) an old Christian argument that requires a Jewish presence in the world, if only as a reminder of Jewish abjection and of the rightness of the new dispensation. In Barth's scheme, Jewish peculiarity continued to "bear witness": no longer to the rectitude of Christianity, but to a lack of relation between man and God more akin to Marcionite doctrine. Where the former scheme contested Jewish belief in Israel's chosenness, the latter extended the Christian retraction of providence from Israel to man as such, and adduced the status of the Jew as its proof.

It is here, occulted and occluded, that the "Jewish" sources of Jonas's philosophy are disclosed. Quotation marks seem required, first, to recall the general permeability of the category, and second, to indicate the quality of that porousness in this case: the link Jonas forged between authentic Jewish being and authentic human being. "Neither as a Jew nor a man" did Jonas have something to say to Paul. At least this was the case insofar as a response need be couched in Pauline terms. For Jonas did indeed have something to say, and he said it by disavowing the Pauline view altogether, first in the form of a philosophical biology and later in a naturalized ethics. That is to say, he took issue with Paul's hostility to the flesh and to the law, which on Barth's account were one and the same.

His analysis of Paul may now appear as that which it is: a prism through which the early, theological projects became refracted into his later ones.

It also set the terms for his confrontation with Heidegger. The Pauline mode of thought Jonas associated deeply with that of his teacher. He did not consider them equivalents. But he imagined that the forced encounter of Heidegger with Paul in the elemental conditions of his hermeneutic crucible disclosed the true meanings of both.[37] Jonas would later use similar terms to describe his Heideggerian reading of the gnostics. In his 1952 essay, "Gnosticism and Modern Nihilism," he wrote of the reversal and reciprocity of the hermeneutic functions. "Lock turns into key and key into lock; the 'existentialist' reading of Gnosticism, so well vindicated by its hermeneutic success, invites as its natural complement the trial of a 'gnostic' reading of Existentialism."[38] By most accounts, this very phrase marks the point at which Jonas turned (philosophically) on the master from Germany, the moment he linked gnostic to Heideggerian nihilism in order to reject them both. This turn can now be seen to have had its origins—its precedent, really—in a time even before Heidegger declared his allegiance to the Nazi cause. As Jonas turned on Paul, so did he sow the seeds for the turn on his teacher.

These seeds took root and first flowered in 1952. But in the speech that brought worldwide attention to the fact and extent of Heidegger's Nazism, those same flowers threatened to wither, and at Jonas's hand no less. In 1964 Jonas delivered an address to a group of Christian theologians gathered at Drew University to discuss "Non-Objectifying Thinking and Speaking in Contemporary Theology." To the layperson, the title must have promised little. But to those gathered it referred to the attempt of recent Protestant theology to adapt for its own use Heidegger's later philosophy. Theologians had long sought a way around the thorny problem of objectification—in their case, speech or thought that threatened to make an object of God, calculable, knowable, available for human manipulation—in other words, an object of what could only be subject. Precisely this issue had fueled the theologizing of Barth & Co. God ought not be reduced to an object of cognition.[39] The problem also lay at the heart of demythologization, the procedure that Jonas and Bultmann developed as a means to approach the "primal" and "existential" core of the religious phenomena obscured by the myths in which they were clothed. Some of Heidegger's later work promised a way beyond this series of problems, and Heinrich Ott, Barth's successor at Basel, convened a group of Heidegger's theological admirers to ask after whether and how.[40]

These theologians hoped to discover in Heidegger—paragon of the "most recent and modish" trends in philosophy—a language adequate to the task of theology. "So as it once had been with Hegel," Jonas later

recalled, "so it should now be with Heidegger."[41] Though scheduled to
deliver the keynote address, Heidegger bowed out on account of illness. The conference organizers invited Jonas to step to the fore, under
the impression they could expect of this one-time pupil of both Heidegger and Bultmann an affirmation of the gathering's guiding postu-
late. They could hardly have expected what was to come. "It was one
of the few times in which admittedly I was not altogether upstanding,"
Jonas later remarked, for he did nothing upon accepting the invitation
to dispel their false impressions. Instead, he thought to himself: "This is
my hour, the moment of reckoning." The expectations of Heidegger's
admirers, above all those from Germany and Switzerland, were turned on
their head. It was a "sensation," as Jonas recalled it, "and a Heidegger-
disaster."[42]

Jonas admonished his theological friends against a too-ready assimilation of Heidegger's philosophy. Heidegger's position of piety over and
against human self-assertion seemed to accord nicely with Christian
tenets, he admitted. But their apparent affinity worked only to mask all
the better Heidegger's paganism, the thoroughgoing immanence of his
scheme. At times, Jonas sounded a downright Barthian note in his attack:
"The being whose fate Heidegger ponders is the quintessence of this
world," he argued. "It is *saeculum*. Against this, theology should guard
the radical transcendence of its God, whose voice comes not out of being
but breaks into the kingdom of being from without." The similarity
Being's self-unveiling shared with Christian revelation Jonas dismissed
as superficial. The revelation in Heidegger's scheme originated not in the
beyond but in the immanent realm of being-in-the-world. "Quite consistently do the gods appear again in Heidegger's philosophy," he observed.
"But where the gods are, God cannot be."[43] To rescue divine transcendence from oblivion, Jonas could use Barth against Heidegger; in so doing,
however, he courted the loss of the world, and in the midst of a broader
project whose intent was to save it.

In other words, Jonas now *affirmed* aspects of an approach to theology
he had earlier assailed, and as a means to save Heidegger's theological
champions from themselves. His inquiries into Paul enabled him to point
to the limits of Heideggerian phenomenology, and to inoculate Heidegger's would-be epigones against a fatal contagion. The domain of the
existential concept, he pointed out, extends only to the "self-experience
of man '*before*' God, *coram deo*, not *in* God, or: *homo sub lege*, not
homo sub gratia."[44] "Where the divine itself is said to enter," he argued,
"phenomenology ceases to have a say." On this Jonas insisted, despite
some of Heidegger's recent statements to the contrary; to wit, that his
thought brought into an uneasy dependence philosophy and theology,
Being and God.[45]

Jonas had in fact developed two critiques of Heidegger, even if he did not specify them as such. He opposed the early Heidegger and the formalist, decisionist ethics of *Being and Time*. He also opposed the later, "theological" and oracular Heidegger, against whom he adduced Barthian arguments, and in so doing came perilously close to reversing his earlier position. The early Heidegger Jonas found objectionable because he offered no ground for the content of decision, only the imperative to decide. This meant trouble for ethics. But to contest this position did not demand a partial rescue of Barth. The recovery of Barth was made necessary only when Heidegger's so-called paganism became the source of his ire. The early Heidegger had elaborated an imperative to decide, the later Heidegger a counsel to wait and listen. But neither imperative had offered a means by which to distinguish—not between decisions on the one hand, not between calls on the other.

The same piety over and against human self-assertion that made Heidegger attractive to this latest generation of Protestant theologians now made him deeply suspect. Whatever its seductions to those (like Jonas) who counseled against an unbounded sense of human prerogative, it masked a failing deeper still. Heidegger had once heeded his own imperative to decide. He decided for fascism. Jonas worried that Heidegger's more recent approach was still worse. Under the guise of piety he had eschewed decisionism but had done away with a standard by which to distinguish between calls, of which Hitler, also, had been one. The result: Heidegger would leave theology without means by which to discriminate between "the inspirations of the Holy Ghost and the demons." Whatever its justice—and its justice is certainly debatable—the line worked rhetorical wonders with the theologians gathered to hear him. "That there are demons" Jonas begged of them still further, "I [only] hope you agree."[46]

CHAPTER THREE

Overcoming Gnosticism

ONE NIGHT with darkness long since fallen, in the few years between the death of Hans Jonas in 1993 and his own in 1996, Hans Blumenberg sat at his desk to remember his friend and colleague. He ratcheted a sheet of paper into his typewriter and aligned its edges. "Philosophy is no discipline of triumphant moments," he tapped out, "in which discoveries or inventions, or even new formulas" might suddenly be revealed to a world of conversant fellow men. "Rarely does applause thunder up for something unexpected." In all but the most unusual of cases, "only the long overdue is received with favor." Blumenberg had in fact known such resounding success a single time—"to be sure only as a spectator and witness," he hastily added. This rarity came to pass on the twentieth of October 1959, in a context most would sooner associate with the spittle of hoary churchmen than with philosophical supernovae: the Third International Congress for Patristics at Trinity College in Oxford. There the experts had convened to discuss, among other things, gnosticism after the recent finds in upper Egypt at Nag Hammadi. "Astonishing," Blumenberg thought, "was the extent to which one of those present could rejoice in the specialists' reluctant applause: Hans Jonas." Blumenberg linked their reluctance to the "mistrust which specialists have for all times held for the generalists of philosophy." Though no coptologue and certainly no decoder of ancient manuscripts, Jonas the philosopher had managed to do what the specialists had not—to describe with stunning accuracy the gnostic *Grundmythos* (foundational myth) a full two decades before Nag Hammadi, and this, Blumenberg gleefully noted, from a collection of sources paltry by comparison. "It was almost embarrassing," he wrote, to see these authorities of gnosis damned to skepticism by their own rigidity, and still forced to applaud in Oxford no less than "the result of prophecy."[1]

Why had Blumenberg recounted this memory at all, not to mention in such "roundabout" and "long-winded" fashion (as he put it)? Blumenberg wished not only to recall the fate of *Gnosis und spätantiker Geist*, of which forty years earlier he had spoken with a "stunned reverence."[2] He hoped also to correct or adjust the tenor of comments sounded in the wake of Jonas's death. In Germany, these referred above all to his later work, in particular *Prinzip Verantwortung* (The Imperative of Responsibility), published in 1979. The book had tapped and refined the spirit of the age.

It appeared at just the time that the threat of environmental apocalypse took on a nightmarish reality. Germans watched acid rain decimate architectural and natural treasures, from the Black Forest to the Cologne Cathedral. They watched as their country came to rely on nuclear power, and as their government stationed an arsenal of ballistic missiles on German soil. If atomic apocalypse were to happen, western Germany was to be its ground zero. In this atmosphere, Jonas's effort to delineate a responsibility mankind had to the world it inhabited and the generations it would bear had considerable resonance. Technology amok he identified as the sickness; an anti-utopian ethic based on the purposiveness of the natural organism he recommended as its cure. Blumenberg himself did not always approve. He had little use for Jonas's creative misreading of Kant's categorical imperative, even less for his so-called heuristics of fear. But as far as *Gnosis* was concerned, "that is not reason enough . . . " he began to say—and stopped.[3] There ended this fragment of a text and for that evening at least Blumenberg's recollection, with the promissory note of a dot dot dot.

Blumenberg had good reasons for recalling Jonas. The two had enjoyed (and sometimes suffered) a friendship of forty years. They met for the first time in August 1953.[4] Jonas was fifty years of age, Blumenberg thirty-three. Even before their face-to-face encounter, however, Blumenberg had entertained hopes of convincing Jonas to return to German soil permanently. He did so, as he wrote to Jonas, with the conviction that "this old and, despite everything, honorable ground" would prove in the end more congenial and fecund than any other. He did so also with the conviction, derived from his own experience, that "it is easier to be finished with the past here than abroad," where the radical changes in German life, the "successful overcoming of the [Nazi] ideological resid-uum" went unregistered. It is surprising that one as immersed in the historical as Blumenberg, and of Jewish descent no less, could speak of being finished with the past only a decade after it could be named such. Whatever the case, Blumenberg's renewed engagement with *Gnosis* made him wish all the more to see Jonas again established in the circles of German intellectual life.[5] For his part, Jonas considered Blumenberg's book, *The Legitimacy of the Modern Age*, the most important work of German philosophy to appear in some time, and could think of no reader of his own writings more treasured than Blumenberg. "Of all the philo-sophical contemporaries in Germany," Jonas wrote in 1976, it is "you I esteem most highly."[6]

Blumenberg had good reasons for recalling Jonas's early work. Its affinities with *Legitimacy* are startling. On the face of it, perhaps, the concern with secularization that powered Blumenberg's argument has little to link it with a loose group of ancient sects. Yet a concern with secularization becomes an integral part of the gnostic conceptual universe when we consider the word's literal meaning: to make something of this world. In fact, the secularizing impulse might be understood as the opposite of the gnostic. Gnosticism privileged *Entweltlichung*, literally a de-worldification, an evacuation or making-absent from the world. "To come loose from the world" or "an annihilation of that which binds to the world" Jonas repeatedly cited as the fundamental gnostic tendency, a move enabled by a trans-mundane God conceived as the "absolutely other."[7] Against gnostic *Entweltlichung*, to secularize involves a *Verweltlichung*, a making-of-this-world for which "secularization" is the only English equivalent.[8]

Like Jonas, Blumenberg's interest in the question of worldliness was prompted in part by the crisis theology of Karl Barth. This is hardly evident at first glance. An index that cites Augustine on eighty occasions, Aristotle on eighty-five, that takes note of Adrastus and Aenesidemus, Archesilaus and Aristoxenos, Callipus, Chrysippus, and E. C. Corti mentions Barth not once. That Blumenberg would ignore the evidence of gnosticism's rebirth a mere forty years before would be odd, to say the least. It seems more plausible to think of his book as a monumental but occulted response to the crisis theologians of the 1920s, and to crisis thought more generally. This reading has its license in a crucial addition to the book's second edition. In the newer version, and at its very outset, Blumenberg clarified the intentions that had earlier gone unwritten with a reference to Barth & Co., even if he declined to name them:

> The very people who were attempting to restore the radicalness of the original religious distance from the world and to renew theology's declarations of transcendence "dialectically" could see in the massive evidence of the manifestation of the world as "worldliness" the advantage of its unmistakable character of immanence. What is foreign to the world, and appears to it as the paradoxical demand that it give itself up, was supposed to withdraw itself, in a new distinctness, from the entanglement and camouflage in which, perhaps for the sake of demonstrable success, it had become falsely familiar and acceptable. A theology of "division," of crisis, had to be interested in making clear the worldliness of the world rather than in overlaying it with the sacred. That is what gave the use of the term "secularization" its specific theological pathos.[9]

Blumenberg evidently understood Barth and Gogarten as indebted to secularization in its most extreme and wrongful guise.[10] The question, then, is whether a theology or a thinking divested of crisis would suffer similarly. As Blumenberg saw it, the answer was no, in part because such thinking would have no use for the notion of secularization at all.

That, at any rate, is what he set out to show over the course of the next 591 pages.

Jonas and Blumenberg's shared concerns become evident when we consider the substance and logic of their narratives. Though not elaborated systematically or on the same scale, all the salient elements of Blumenberg's story appear first in Jonas: the original gnostic threat to the Greek cosmos and then to Christianity, Augustine's failed attempt to reign it in, the enlistment of curiosity in the catalog of vices and its revindication at the birth of the modern age, the role of natural science in that transformation. Even the mechanisms they developed to account for this series of events—the formal, narrative logic that powered their stories—attest to this affinity. Their fit is hardly coincidental. In many of its most essential aspects, Blumenberg's scheme had its model in Jonas's earlier example. But they also differ, and in ways that allow us to call Jonas's efforts, with Blumenberg but against him, a "third overcoming" of gnosticism.

The full two-thousand-year sweep of their stories need not be recounted here. It suffices to limit attention to their flash points, the moments of epochal shift elicited by the gnostic threat. The first of these, the birth of the Middle Ages, had origins in Augustine, whose crucial move came for Blumenberg in a radicalized reading of Romans in response to the Pelagian threat. To man had been ascribed a new concept of freedom "expressly in order to let the whole of an enormous responsibility and guilt be imputed to it." This innovation, which Blumenberg called a "crudity," served Augustine well in his efforts to contain both the Pelagian and gnostic heresies, especially in the form of Marcionite dogmatics.[11] Here Augustine contended not with a position that denied man's insufficiency, but with a view that imputed guilt for the world's debasement to some malicious godlike creature. Where Jonas emphasized the former threat, Blumenberg stressed the latter.

But Augustine had faltered for them both. For Jonas, Augustine fell to the Pelagian argument in his failure to preserve a purified realm of grace, separated absolutely from the state of law; it was a failed attempt at dualism, misguided from the outset. For Blumenberg, Augustine failed to overcome gnosticism because he displaced the gnostic dualism of worldly and transcendent into the dualism of damned and saved, the "absolute separation of the elect from the rejected." That this dualism proved unworkable did nothing to demote the Augustinian "solution" from its status as the foundation of the medieval theological-political order. Augustine's efforts did, however, ensure that man would renounce any volitional attempt to change his lot. As Blumenberg put it, "The senselessness of self-assertion was the heritage of the gnosticism that was not overcome but only 'translated.' "[12] In less technical terms, Blumenberg referred to this phenomenon as the enlistment of curiosity in the catalog of vices. By this, he meant the animus to theoretical curiosity about the world evident in Augustine's mature stance. Dormant for a millennium, *curiositas* enjoyed its revival and triumph with Bacon. Jonas, too, had spoken of curiosity's protracted slumber, had located in Augustine and the gnostics its soporific, and like Blumenberg, but before him, had cast Bacon and the tradition of natural science he inaugurated as the stimulus to its revival.[13]

If they share a story of the birth of the medieval age, their accounts begin to diverge at the birth of the modern. The characters are the same; so are their deeds. But where Blumenberg found his hero in the figure and program of Francis Bacon, there Jonas found his unwitting villain. For them both, Bacon stood for a knowledge wrested from nature and put in the service of man, a knowledge subordinated to power. He stood for mankind's technical mastery over the world, underwritten by an attempt to reestablish paradise—not in some transcendent beyond but on Earth. Man should live again as Adam had, with the natural world at his service. Bacon's notion of knowledge, then, had associated with it a powerful teleology. But a teleological interpretation of knowledge tends to exclude a teleological understanding of its objects. Bacon homogenized the world of objects, valued them not for what they are but for what they make possible in the journey toward paradise and in the means to that end, the working out of the scientific method. For this reason, Blumenberg found in Bacon the unwitting father of modern science. The upshot of all this was a radical challenge to the Greek notion of physis. Or as Blumenberg put it, Bacon's sense that the ancients had placed false trust in the world led directly to his "momentous exclusion of the teleological view of nature."[14]

Precisely this view of nature Jonas hoped to resurrect. Shortly after the publication of *The Gnostic Religion* in 1958, Jonas received a letter from his fellow émigré Leo Strauss. Jonas had remitted to him a copy. Strauss wrote in thanks and with praise:

I should not be surprised if the Introduction is the best thing you ever wrote. You paint a magnificent picture of an historical epoch in a way which I cannot help calling *genialisch*. This picture carries its own evidence within itself. When reading the bulk of the work I noted that you and I are attracted by very different human phenomena and this is as it should be. I was waiting for the moment when my more than aesthetic interest would be awakened, my philosophic interest. I was by no means immune to the silent appeal of your introduction, to the appeal of the non-Greek or Oriental in me. But from this point of view I prefer Hannibal to your friends. Things changed radically when . . .

you made abundantly clear that the historical phenomenon discussed by you must be of concern to every thinking man. In other words . . . I saw for the first time the connection between this fundamentally earlier study of yours and your present preoccupations. I would state it as follows: gnosticism is the most radical rebellion against physis. Our problem now is to recover physis.[15]

For his part, Jonas thought Strauss on the mark. With physis he thought Strauss to have characterized the link between his projects with a "wonderful exactitude."[16]

The term has a host of connotations. Though equated with nature, physis specifically links notions of growth with being. This coupling was likely the work of the pre-Socratics, whose "hylozoism" entailed a view of the world as a kind of organism with a life and trajectory of its own. Later, Aristotle defined physis as "the essence of things which have in themselves as such a source of movement." The Greeks also discovered in physis a natural standard by which man should live. They often opposed it to nomos, human convention or law, whenever nomos deviated from its natural model.[17]

Whereas the Greeks ordinarily privileged physis over nomos, Bacon as a rule did the reverse. Bacon the statesman spoke of his scientific program in the language of legalism—the human spirit was thought to "exercise its right with respect to nature."[18] For this reason, Blumenberg spoke of Baconian science in terms of its legitimacy. Derived from *lex*, law, legitimacy has its home in a language of entitlement, the consciousness of which arose in response to its denial, even if Bacon thought it granted to Adam by God. To assert oneself, *sich durchsetzen*, resonates with *Gesetz*, law: it is to lay down the law, to order chaos, to posit oneself over and against the world. If the gnostics diminished man, Bacon empowered him, returned to him his due. Jonas thought this empowerment excessive, the mirror image of the gnostic enervation. He therefore contested the legitimacy of Baconian science—not only the coercive violence of its methods, but also the sense of entitlement that abetted them. Bacon and the gnostics had disposed of the teleological view of nature. Jonas would set out to recover it.[19]

This became patently obvious with one of his first essays composed after the war, "Life, Death and the Body in the Theory of Being." First published in 1965, the essay served as flagship for his collection *The Phenomenon of Life* (1966), the book Jonas considered *the* statement of his philosophical enterprise. He revisited the notion of teleology, and linked its rejection to a distrust of final causes as explanations for natural phenomena, a sensibility central to the anti-Aristotelian animus of modern science.[20] But he thought its case suspect. "We must observe," he wrote, "that [the] rejection [of final causes] is a methodological principle guiding inquiry rather than a statement of ascertained fact." He thought modern science's exclusion of teleology "not an inductive result but an a priori prohibition." Science not only failed to make its case, it had in fact "never been argued." Jonas contested also the modern bias against teleology as far-fetched, abstruse, or unnatural. "On the contrary," he asserted: "nothing is more cognate to the human mind and more familiar to the basic experience of man." "That the world is alive is really the most natural view, and largely supported by prima facie evidence." Precisely this, however, was what "in the new scientific attitude counted against it." Chief among its opponents, Jonas said, was Bacon.[21]

The recovery of purposive nature attained systematic expression not with this essay, however, but with his work of 1979, *Prinzip Verantwortung*. There Jonas sought nothing less than to develop a modern ontology rooted in the idea of physis. He wanted, as he put it, to "expand the ontological locus of purpose as such from what is apparent at the subjective peak to what is hidden in the breadth of being." One way to do this was to locate purposiveness (or willfulness) in unconscious organism. From an etymological perspective, he had excellent grounds for doing so. "Organ" means "tool," something brought into being expressly to perform a "work." For this reason Aristotle called the living body organic, a *soma organikon*, and the human hand the tool of tools. The limit case for his argument Jonas found in that most apparently unwilled of bodily processes—digestion. Even here he thought it meaningful, not metaphorical, to speak of its "immanent, if entirely unconscious and involuntary *purpose*." As a corollary, Jonas took aim at the supposed incompatibility of modern science with teleological notions of nature. "It is simply not true," he insisted, "that an 'Aristotelian' understanding of being contradicts the modern causal explanation of nature or is inconsistent with it, let alone that it has been refuted by it." Though science might prove adequate to the measurable universe, it could in no way claim to account for nature in its totality, and by definition, Jonas thought, could never do so. If the power of Baconian science to account for the world had its limits, however, the power it unleashed to master the world in artful fashion did not. This power had become self-sufficient, its promise turned to threat, "its prospect of salvation into apocalypse." From its first pages, the book announced an aim at odds with Blumenberg's. Far from the celebration of self-assertion, there Jonas likened it to a "rape," to an "invasion" of nature's domain, to a "violent and violating irruption into the cosmic order."[22]

We need not, however, locate the origins of this project in 1958, the year Strauss pointed out its hidden implications. Most accounts have it that Jonas turned to philosophical biology during the six years he spent under arms, first in the Second World War, and later in Israel's 1948 war for independence. The immediacy of life and death on the front led him to depart from his earlier theological interests. Jonas himself licensed this story, invented it in fact, and in most dramatic terms:

> Five years of soldiering in the British army in the war against Hitler ushered in the second stage in my theoretical life. Cut off from books and all the paraphernalia of research, I had to stop work on the Gnostic project perforce. But something more substantive and essential was involved. The apocalyptic state of things, the threatening collapse of a world, the climactic crisis of civilization, the proximity of death, the stark nakedness to which all the issues of life were stripped, all these were ground enough to take a new look at the very foundations of our being and to review the principles by which we guide our thinking on them. Thus, thrown back on my own resources, I was thrown back on the philosopher's basic duty and his native business—thinking. And while living in tents and barracks, being on the move or in position, tending to the guns or firing them, all the reductive primitivism and ordered waste of the soldier's life in a long war are most unfavorable to scholarly work, they do not prevent, are even eminently conducive to thinking—and thinking to the point—when there is a will to it.[23]

This story, stirring as it may be, nonetheless clouds how Jonas's philosophy of the organism continued an earlier project by other means. That Jonas may have only then recognized the direction of his efforts does not mean they were not set well before. His animus against the technological ethos he likely derived from Heidegger.[24] His association of that ethos with gnosticism, however, was purely his own doing. In his dissertation, Jonas spoke of gnostic dualism as an attempt to elevate God as counterpoint to the debasement of the world. But in the 1920s, Jonas thought such dualism was merely a "reaction formation over and against natural-scientific thought, which in the world, *its* world, has left *no more room* for godly intervention." In the 1920s, that is, God's "otherworldliness" no longer spoke to his power and goodness, but his impotence and potential irrelevance. Transcendence is all that was "left over" to him.[25] What to many indicated the revival of the awesome and unknown stranger god, Jonas portrayed as his death rattle.

Preoccupation with the return of gnosticism in the form of crisis theology only deflected attention from its more pervasive and dangerous incarnation. Scientific thought replicated gnostic dualism. Both insisted on a world bereft of divinity, or in Jonas's terms on an *entgöttlichte Welt*. For both, God had absconded from a world figured as either hostile or indifferent to man's designs, a world without value in and of itself. Or in Blumenberg's lexicon, but against him: not only had Bacon's solution come undone, it had come to reproduce the original problem. It did not overcome gnostic dualism so much as reverse its terms. That one scheme conceived of man as impotent and the other as empowered, that one sought knowledge of the transcendent and the other the immanent, the naturally unknowable as opposed to the unnaturally known—all this worked only to disguise their complicity. Jonas entertained a relation between late-medieval nominalism and Baconian science that Blumenberg left unaddressed: that self-assertion does not overcome the terror of the hidden god so much as the hidden god opens up a space for and enables human self-assertion. Far from the overcoming of gnosticism, Baconian science was its coconspirator. Or as Jonas put it in his most widely read essay, on gnosticism and modern nihilism: "The *deus absconditus*, of whom nothing but will and power can be predicated, leaves behind as his legacy, upon leaving the scene, the *homo absconditus*, a concept of man characterized solely by will and power—the will for power, the will to will. For such a will even indifferent nature is more an occasion for its exercise than a true object."[26]

This anti-Nietzschean note deserves consideration: in part, because Blumenberg drew on Nietzsche's critique of teleology in his efforts to distinguish self-assertion, an existential program, from self-preservation, a biological one; and in part because Blumenberg's subject, the modern "I" or "we" that asserts itself, resembles its Nietzschean counterpart. For Nietzsche, the notion of self-preservation worked as false teleology. Self-preservation Nietzsche described not as the "cardinal instinct of an organic being," but as merely a result, if one of the most frequent, of the will to power. Self-preservation cannot have the status of teleology, it is not innate, since it emerges only as a belated reaction to a world viewed as indifferent to the well-being of life.[27] This Nietzsche rejected, Blumenberg pointed out, since the model of man's relation to reality should depend not at all on any quality actually inhering in the world. "There is neither order nor disorder in nature," as Nietzsche wrote in one essay, on the notion of teleology in Kant. "How can anyone presume to speak of a destiny of the earth? . . . Mankind must be able to stand without leaning on anything like that."[28]

Will to power reverses the terms of self-preservation: the latter thinks the world indifferent to life, the former thinks life—construed as art—indifferent to the world. This artful mastery of the world Jonas identified as the natural ally of the absent god. The same sort of mastery, if weaker in intensity, Blumenberg identified as the heart of self-assertion. In the most succinct definition of the term offered in all of *Legitimacy*, and as if in direct rejoinder to Jonas, he pointedly set it off from the "naked biological and economic preservation of the human organism by the means naturally available to it." He set it off, that is, from the foundation of Jonas's thought. He discounted the existential import of organism, within which Jonas had found the most basic stirrings of freedom. The sources of freedom Blumenberg located instead in the human capacity to metaphorize. As for existential weight, this he reserved for self-assertion: "an existential program, according to which man posits his existence in a historical situation and indicates to himself how he is going to deal with the reality surrounding him and what use he will make of the possibilities that are open to him."[29] To be sure a departure from total indifference to the world, it deviated just as much from the ground of Jonasian ethics. It divorced being from biology and wed it to art.

Blumenberg tells a story designed to help us cope. It is therapeutic. It does not command or oblige. Instead, it releases us moderns from burdens we need no longer carry. Its ethical implications inhere in the capacity for narrative—the stories we tell of ourselves, our artful redescriptions of the world—to produce freedom.[30] Whatever its seductions, and they are considerable, this view divests purposive being from nature. Only when the natural world has lost its power to command imitation, only when it is revealed as one possible world in an infinity of them, a result of blind and mechanical chance and indifferent or hostile to life, only when man stands against nature—only then can the artful redescription of contingency attain the ethical status that Blumenberg wishes to grant it.

Jonas also helps us cope. But he prescribes in a way Blumenberg does not. To specify their approaches to crisis thought helps to illustrate these differences. Blumenberg, for one, disavowed it altogether. His response to Barth, Karl Löwith, and Carl Schmitt did not so much respond as change the terms of discussion altogether. Jonas, by contrast, was an adherent of crisis thinking, even if he recognized its dangers. On the one hand, he indulged in its rhetoric. Already in his dissertation he linked the crisis of his own age to that of the gnostic era. He spoke of the crisis of Being, which gave way in his later writings to the crisis of technology and the environmental apocalypse it threatened. But Jonas declined crisis thought's usual solutions. Enough of a historicist to disavow nostalgia and enough of a pragmatist to fear utopia, Jonas counseled action in accord with a higher, if imperfect, good, a categorical imperative modified and naturalized, and designed to root man in the world, in *this* world. Jonas advanced a notion of man less differentiated from the world, rooted in it, a symbiosis of two organisms that are also one, a trust with man as its executor. He hoped for a partial, not total, reinsertion of man into the biological—and for him existential—continuum of nature. Against his mentor Heidegger, he imagined the subject-object relation God's gift to man, for it enabled human finitude and mortality.[31] He disavowed the sort of response that finds in the "new man" an answer to the dereliction of the old, a response that finds in grace, whether prelapsarian or yet to come, an answer to the debasement of the world in which we live. Herein lay his distaste for Ernst Bloch, for Barth, and in the more Nietzschean of his moods, for Scholem. As Blumenberg approvingly put it, *der Messianismus ist ihm fremd*. Messianism is foreign to him.[32] Not the transcendent alien, not the gnostic stranger god, but the impulse to take flight from the world in whatever guise, to denigrate it—for Jonas it was this which most powerfully incarnated *das Fremde*, the threat he most urgently sought to keep at bay.

For all his efforts, Jonas never managed to banish the specter of the alien. The gospel of the alien God goaded him until the very end, and in some of his moods proved victorious. One year before his death, Jonas granted an interview in Jerusalem, on the occasion of a conference convened in his honor. The words he adopted in conclusion, as to why he had not returned to live in the Jewish state he had helped to found but had shortly thereafter left—these words tell more, perhaps, than even Jonas could have known. "When I ask [myself] where [I] feel most at home, my answer, in these last years of my life," he admitted, "is that I do not feel at home in any place at all."[33]

CHAPTER FOUR

After Auschwitz, Earth

FROM THE BEGINNING, the hidden god had prompted Jonas to fascination, and even more so, to ire. In the gnostic religion, in crisis theology, and in modern natural science, God's absence underwrote attitudes that had rid the world of value. A more profoundly un-Jewish notion of God Jonas could not imagine. "Our teaching," he said once, "the Torah, rests on the premise and insists that we can understand God, not completely, to be sure, but something of him—his will, intentions, and even nature— because he has told us." Refracted, perhaps, but not entirely "veiled in dark mystery," revelation had by Jewish standards made possible an authentic being-in-the-world. Jewish norms quite simply did not admit of a completely hidden God.[1]

It is therefore surprising that Jonas uttered these words in the course of a speech, in which minutes before he had developed a reworked myth of the hidden god, his myth, one appropriate he thought to an age after Auschwitz. There Jonas imagined God as a needful being who had created the world but spent himself entirely in so doing. This was a God relegated to the back seats of the cosmic theater he had built but could not direct, for all his vital interest in the drama's outcome an impotent spectator nonetheless. This God was thought to respond to the impact on his being by worldly events "not 'with a mighty hand and outstretched arm,' as we Jews on every Passover recite in remembering the exodus from Egypt, but with the mutely insistent appeal of his unfulfilled goal." Not Exodus, but Job provided for Jonas his point of departure; not liberation from dereliction and escape into plenitude, but making do with an imperfect lot. The same problem of evil in the world that vexed his lifelong gnostic companions, and which had more recently, in Auschwitz, received the most harrowing of proofs, here inspired Jonas to theological speculation. Where Job invoked "the plenitude of God's power" as the only possible response, Jonas invoked "his chosen voidance of it." Their seeming opposition, however, belies a deeper complicity. For both solutions—if such splutterings deserve the name—praise God: the one for his omnipotence, the other for his self-renunciation, in either case "so that we, the mortals, could be."[2]

Jonas elsewhere denigrated his theological speculations as a "luxury of reason." Perhaps he thought them less valid than his ecumenical philosophy, too overtly Jewish. Earlier we witnessed an instance in which this was, indeed, the case. But they are in fact of considerable importance. It is not by accident that Jonas "returned" to theological questions toward the end of his life. It was in fact not a return at all, for he had never left them behind. His philosophical biology and environmental ethics continued by other means the itinerary he began with Augustine, Paul, and the gnostics. If his theological engagements were philosophically extraneous, if they were supplements only—and I happen to disagree with this view—they were from an intellectual-historical standpoint nonetheless crucial, because foundational.[3]

The words cited here come from a speech delivered in 1984 in Tübingen, called "The Concept of God after Auschwitz: a Jewish Voice." The myth at its core Jonas had crafted over twenty years before, at just about the time he moved from a philosophical biology that underscored man's cellular kinship with his fellow forms of life to an ethics of responsibility that stressed man's role as executor of a trust with the world he inhabited. It erects a stage upon which all the characters in the Jonasian troupe trot out for an appearance: problems of worldliness and willfulness, of knowledge and sin, law and grace, nature and man, the hidden and not-so-hidden God. The text also foregrounds the Jewish sources and ends of his philosophical interventions. By this I do not mean to reverse terms, to locate in "Judaism" rather than "Hellenism," in the "Oriental" rather than the "Greek," the true and exclusive ground of his project. For the text shows also how his philosophical commitments impelled a departure from Jewish tenets. The result is a blurring of boundaries, a jumble, a mishmash—and for all that a myth of creation, life, and history of frequently stunning beauty. Having traversed the path that brought him here, having traced its origins to Heidegger, the gnostics, Augustine, and Paul, we might now understand this myth in all its breadth.

His story of beginnings reads as much like Heidegger as Genesis: "In the beginning, for unknowable reasons, the ground of Being, or the Divine, chose to give itself over to the chance and risk and endless variety of becoming." In it echoes also the kabbalistic notion of *tzimtzum*, God's originary self-effacement or contraction, without which no space for an "other" outside God could exist at all. Jonas pushed the doctrine further; contraction for him meant the divine had abdicated the power to intervene in its own creation.[4] In kabbalah Jonas discovered a minority tradition in the history of Jewish theology that eschewed talk of total sovereignty, and so avoided the sort of speculation required to account for the failures of providence in the darkest of hours. This was a tradition that imagined a divinity "bound up with the coming-to-be of a world," upon whom the deeds of man had palpable effect. God had renounced his being in order that the world might be, in order that he might "receive it back from the odyssey of time weighted with the chance harvest of unforeseeable temporal experience," in transfigured, and perhaps disfigured form.[5]

The story continues with the first "gyrations of matter," and the advent of transcendence from the "opacity" of purist immanence. Jonas imagined the coming-to-be of an inner-worldly transcendence much like Heidegger, but with a crucial difference: it did not deny God, and still more, it discovered traces of an absent divine in the order of worldly things. This transcendence Jonas associated with "the first stirring of life, a new language of the world." With it came also a "tremendous quickening of concern in the eternal realm and a sudden leap in its growth toward recovery of its plenitude":

> It is the world-accident for which becoming deity had waited and with which its prodigal stake begins to show signs of being redeemed. From the infinite swell of feeling, sensing, striving, and acting, which ever more varied and intense rises above the mute eddyings of matter, eternity gains strength, filling with content after content of self-affirmation, and the awakening God can first pronounce creation to be good.[6]

A new principle had taken hold. The divine cause, the cause also of purposive nature, was to be vindicated by man. "The image of God, haltingly begun by the universe, for so long worked upon—and left undecided—in the wide and then narrowing spirals of prehuman life, passes man's precarious trust, to be completed, saved, or spoiled by what he will do to himself and the world. And in this awesome impact of his deeds on God's destiny, on the complexion of eternal being, lies the immortality of man." With man's appearance, in other words, the world had "awakened to itself." Through the eyes of the animal the world could look, but only through the mind of man could it also reflect. The world was not born with man, but with him became self-aware.[7]

Thereafter, the divine was thought to accompany man's doings "with the bated breath of suspense, hoping and beckoning, rejoicing and grieving, approving and frowning—and, I daresay, making itself felt to him even while not intervening in the dynamics of his worldly scene." "For can it not be," Jonas asked in conclusion, "that by the reflection of its own state as it wavers with the record of man, the transcendent casts light over the human landscape?" Jonas ended by imagining a cosmos—and a notion of man—somehow touched by a divine which could nonetheless no longer intervene in its own creation, whether to bless man, punish him, or—in the case of Auschwitz—to protect him from others of his kind.[8]

In this myth is encapsulated an intellectual and theological career. Hans Blumenberg did not say as much, though he did come close. He, too, thought this text noteworthy for its summation of a career as a philosopher and of a life as a Jew, noteworthy for the way it reversed those terms also, and he said so in a short text—this one complete but untitled—composed after Jonas's death. "It was not by accident that a self-styled 'Jewish voice'" found this conception of God necessary, he wrote. "More than Lisbon," referring to the 1755 earthquake, Auschwitz had made it impossible to ascribe to God both goodness and omnipotence. Powerlessness, partial at the very least, was from now on to be God's lot. Absolute power at any rate excludes the possibility of myth, Blumenberg went on to say, and none other than Augustine proved it. Asked why God had created the world, he had no answer but to say, *quia voluit*, because he willed it. Blumenberg therefore thought it significant that Jonas, the Jewish voice of 1984, had himself "come from the study of Augustine," when in 1930 he published "the first sample of his intentions." He thought Jonas's speculation on Auschwitz a repudiation of Paul no less, of a life in which man suffers for his failure to accord with law, a law "which could not be followed."[9]

In this, as we have seen, Blumenberg was entirely correct. Or was he? In 1993, at the age of eighty-nine, Jonas was awarded the Premio Nonino: *Prinzip Verantwortung* was to be honored as the best book translated into Italian in the previous year. "The pleasure of the surprise," Jonas recalled in his acceptance, "was for a moment dimmed by the warning voice of my recent vow of no more transatlantic travel in my ninetieth year or any still to come." But only for a moment. His eye chanced upon the donor's address—Udine—"and with the force of invincible conviction, against all counsel of prudence, I knew that *there* I *must* go!" Jonas had ended five years of soldiering in the British Army's Jewish Brigade in Udine. It was there, also, that he encountered an instance of a redeeming Christian sacrifice on behalf of the Jews tucked away in the bowels of the town, the memory of which he had carried throughout his life as a "sacred trust." The donors of the prize had requested that he speak about racism. Jonas condemned it for the scourge it had been and was, as a "blot on humankind," even as he spoke of racial diversity as a gift to the spectrum of human experience. But racial difference comes off as trivial indeed, he went on to say, under the sign of a new development in the "post-Hitler era." Questions of race had become "anachronistic, irrelevant, almost farcical" when posed on an earth threatened with ecological catastrophe. "In the grip of this challenge, mankind for the first time truly becomes one." Jonas spoke of a solidarity newly matured. "A common guilt binds us, a common interest unites us, a common fate awaits us, a common responsibility calls us. In the blinding light of this newly opening horizon, racial conflicts pale and their clamor," he believed, "should fall silent."[10]

Jonas died shortly after his return from Italy, the phenomenon of life having run in him its remarkable course. In retrospect, his speech resounds as prophecy. It does so, first, in a way he had not intended, in the uncanny presentiment of his own mortality. It may yet do so in another way, with respect to the gospel he preached in conclusion. Here are his last public words, spoken six days before his death:

> It was once religion which told us that we all are sinners, because of original sin. It is now the ecology of our planet which pronounces us all to be sinners because of the excessive exploits of human inventiveness. It was once religion which threatened us with a last judgment at the end of days. It is now our tortured planet which predicts the arrival of such a day without any heavenly intervention. The latest revelation—from no Mount Sinai, from no Mount of the Sermon, from no Bo (tree of Buddha)—is the outcry of mute things themselves that we must heed by curbing our powers over creation, lest we perish together on a wasteland.[11]

What began as a repudiation of Paul ended, curiously enough, as a second-order affirmation. Jonas embarked on his career with a Jewish refusal of a Pauline diagnosis: the abyss of the will in a benighted pharisaic man, and the claims to universality brought on his behalf. But he ended it with a Pauline universalism of a rather different sort—for there can be neither Jew nor Greek, neither slave nor free in a world made unfit for human life. The journey that began with the insufficiency of the will before God had its denouement in man's insufficiency before the natural world, the problem of original sin displaced in the end by that of ecological guilt. What began as a demythologization of the gnostic stranger God ended with a reworked myth of the *deus absconditus*. What began as a determined attempt to make him known ended with grateful praise for his absence.

• • •

Gnosticism did not reign alone in interwar Europe. It was not the only force at work in the theological politics of the time, nor was its language of heresy the only one with which Jewish thought had to grapple. That Jonas's overcoming of gnosticism came to full fruition only in the postwar period does not mean that its spirit had until then reigned unchecked. Gnosticism's antipode—though not always, as we will see, its antidote—returned as well, and in no less powerful form. It in fact makes sense to think of a twin birth, or a twin rebirth, of both gnosticism *and* its antipode in the years after Versailles. This antipode took the name—Spinoza.

PART TWO

The Pantheism Controversy

In 1932, we now know, Europe stepped fatefully in the direction of apocalypse. But not even apocalypse could put down a good party. Despite the rise of fascism, the crises of democratic politics, the failures of German constitutionalism—despite all this, Europe did have something to celebrate in 1932, an anniversary of sorts. In 1932, enthusiasts from across the continent assembled in The Hague to honor a man whose thought flashed for many as a beacon in a sea of impending darkness. In 1932, Europe had occasion to celebrate the philosopher whose "abominable doctrines and hideous errors" had earned the ire of earlier generations.[1] In 1932, Europe abandoned the tradition of infamy directed against the "Judaeus et atheista" who was arguably neither. In 1932, Europe marked the tercentenary of Baruch (or Benedict) Spinoza.

It was a big party, the party of the year, and with one or two notable exceptions, everyone who was anyone in the philosophical and theological world had made it a point to attend. Leon Brunschvicg, the leading French neo-Kantian, had arrived from his station at the Sorbonne. The German sociologist Ferdinand Toennies, Julius Ebbinghaus, the aging neo-Kantian from Freiburg, and the French historian of science Gaston Bachelard also made appearances. So did E. R. Curtius, the literary historian, from his post in Bonn, and from Munich, the Polish priest and Spinoza scholar Stanislaus von Dunin-Borkowski. But it would all have been for naught absent the irrepressible Carl Gebhardt, organizer of the congress, dapper in dress, and widely acknowledged as the foremost Spinozist of his day.

We know a good bit of what transpired there, thanks to the intrepid reporting of Hans Hartmann, who dispatched a report from the scene for the benefit of his readers in the Görres-Gesellschaft, a Catholic learned society.[2] Hartmann was well-disposed toward Spinoza, since he thought him suited to Catholic purposes: Spinoza shared the ethical implications of a mystical Catholicism impelled by a desire to pacify the inner tumult of the soul, to free man from his "disequilibrium" and from the yoke of unruly passions. But above all, Hartmann believed Spinoza to share in Catholicism's universalist ethos. By this, he meant that for both Catholicism and Spinoza the entirety of a philosophic system encompassing God, man, and world flowed from a single, leading idea. As Thomas Aquinas had derived from Aristotle the notion of a "highest and perfect Being," so, he noted, did Spinoza's system have its ground in an infinite and self-sufficient totality. Aquinas referred to a transcendent God, Spinoza to a different animal—an idiosyncratic notion of "substance" conceived as immanent in the world. Their differences notwithstanding, Hartmann persisted. He claimed to find in the high priest of scholasticism and the foundational Jewish heretic an affinity that made Spinoza palatable to Catholic sensibilities. In this assessment, as we will see, he did not stand alone.[3]

In his own age, Hartmann recognized Spinoza as a force almost without equal. "Spinozism represents today the most powerful of those philosophical movements outside the Church," he asserted, which takes as its gospel a "calm" and "intellectual" love for God. "Because it is so, that Spinozism is today the movement of the wise men and the serene men, and not that of suffering or those like Nietzsche who affirm lasting battle, for this reason we might consider it deeply symbolic that Catholics were so actively engaged and helped to lay down the basis for an encounter [with Spinoza] at the conference." In contrast to the Catholics, however, Karl Barth and his fellow travelers had declined to send their agents. With grim pleasure, Hartmann noted that the Protestants, "especially those of the theology of crisis," had chosen to emulate their God. They were "wholly absent" from the congress; they had absconded from the scene. True, these theologians had made clear their opposition to any notion of a readily intelligible divinity—so much so that by then, in 1932, Hartmann could summarily dismiss them with the offhand remark that they "essentially only repeat themselves." He nevertheless held out the hope that the champions of crisis might engage such things anew, even as he betrayed his anxiety about the results: "May their repudiation of Schleiermacher and all of his that smacks of pantheism not seduce them into rash conclusions!"[4] Once regarded as a peaceable group, the camp of the anti-Schleiermachians had since come to shelter a number of reckless hotheads.

Hartmann in fact realized only belatedly the challenge Spinoza posed to crisis theology. The fight commenced at least a decade before he announced its imminent arrival, even if the protagonists themselves remained unaware of the fact. For the most recent incarnations of Spinozism and gnosticism stepped out into the world at roughly the same time, and as competing solutions to the same set of problems. In 1920, a year before Barth's *Romans* fell upon Weimar, a group of Spinoza devotees under the leadership of the German art critic Carl Gebhardt met in the Netherlands to found the Societas Spinozana (Spinoza Society). A year later appeared the first issue of the group's literary organ, a short-lived but fascinating journal called the *Chronicon Spinozanum*, or Spinoza Chronicles. The journal's Latinate title conferred upon it a gravitas matched by the importance of its task: to resurrect Spinoza for an age in desperate need of him. The year 1926 saw in The Hague the erection of the Domus Spinozana (Spinoza House), which was to double as a seat of scholarship and a kind of halfway house for itinerant Spinozists, who traversed the continent preaching the modern imperative of Spinoza's philosophy. With 1927 came an international celebration to mark the

250 years elapsed since Spinoza's death. The year 1932 witnessed a similar celebration of the 300 years elapsed since his birth. Taken in this broader context, Hartmann helps us see what we could until now only intuit: a logic, both historical and formal, which bound interwar gnosticism with its Spinozist equivalent. Had Spinoza been absent from the scene, interwar gnosticism would have had to invent him.

First, the formal logic: Spinoza and the gnostics reappeared first as antipodes. Whereas the gnostics had rid the world of God in order to save him, Spinoza had divinized the world—but in order to destroy him. The gnostics had counseled flight from the immanence of the world to the transcendent home of the divine; Spinoza appeared to destroy philosophical transcendence altogether, and had ridiculed those who sought in it their comfort. The gnostics privileged revelation; Spinoza's *Ethics* erected a seamless and knowable universe with the express intent of denying it. "All acosmism," as Franz Rosenzweig recognized in his *Star of Redemption*, "whether Indian negation of the world or its Spinozist-Idealistic suspension"—or, we might add, its gnostic abnegation—"is nothing but a kind of pantheism in reverse."[5]

Even as they appeared in the interwar period as the most bitter of enemies, gnosticism and Spinoza nevertheless shared much, and precisely in their strongest of guises. Both, for example, lay waste to the possibility of *coram deo*, that man might stand sufficiently before God. (If God's absence made it impossible for the gnostics, since one cannot stand before something nowhere to be found, his omnipresence had the same effect in a pantheist scheme, since neither can one stand before something that is everywhere. And if willing devolved inevitably into sinfulness on Barth's account, it stood altogether beyond good and evil on Spinoza's.) Both the gnostics and Spinoza made strong claims for the category of the infinite, if in different ways. Both rejected a world understood in teleological terms. As the gnostics had challenged physis, so did Spinoza, and in no less compromising fashion. Both enjoyed from their inception hallowed status in the pantheon of religious heretics, whether Christian or Jewish or both. Above all, these languages of heresy shared in the twin exclusion that inaugurated (intellectually speaking) the modern era. For all these reasons—for what they shared and what they did not—arguments about Spinoza in this period were conducted in the same terms as those reserved for the gnostics.

Now the historical logic: on Hartmann's view—again, not alone—the rebirth of Spinoza in the 1920s and '30s was rivaled only by Spinoza's first renaissance at the turn of the nineteenth century, when Spinozist pantheism came to inspire forward-thinking German intellectuals from Goethe to Herder to Hegel.[6] This first resurrection was occasioned by the *Pantheismusstreit*, or pantheism controversy, a series of debates that

engulfed the world of German letters in the last two decades of the
eighteenth century. The controversy was born of a charge of Spinozism
levied as epithet. But the epithet quickly acquired the status of an
accolade among the leading intellectuals of the day.

Details will come later. For now it is important only to register the lines
along which the combatants split: champions of a transcendent and
extramundane deity pitted against those who privileged the immanence
of Spinoza's God; those who imagined a God who could intervene
arbitrarily and at will against those who deprived God of such voluntarist
power; those who saw Spinoza's mathematical universe as mechanistic
and arid against those who cherished it as an organism, vital and alive;
those who believed that Spinoza's rationalism devolved into nihilism
against those who found in Spinoza the very foundation of morality and
freedom. Though the positions staked out in the 1780s do not simply map
on to their interwar counterparts, the broader terms of debate—the
possibility of gnosis, the status of the infinite, the problem of revelation,
the question of teleology or physis—all returned in displaced and updated
form. On this view, the "gnostics" of the interwar period reveal themselves as one set of characters caught up in a larger drama, a drama that
included their Spinozist adversaries as well. Aspects of the philosophical
and theological configuration of the 1920s thus represent what I would
like to style a rehearsal of the 1780s and '90s, or a "second round" of the
pantheism controversy.

This conflict transcended any of its individual battles. But only through
them are its outlines to be discerned, its meaning understood. For this
reason, much of what follows tracks the efforts of Spinoza's foremost
interwar interpreters, as they navigated the waters between a pantheist
Scylla and a gnostic Charybdis. We will see how they embodied the logic
of this second installment of the pantheism controversy, how they
conformed to script—and how they also defied it. First there was Carl
Gebhardt, the doyen of Spinoza studies at the time, who mobilized
Spinoza against the neo-gnostic spirit. He did so in a fashion that
presaged a view recently popularized to acclaim: that Spinoza ought to be
understood as a Marrano, whose peculiar heritage enabled him first to
discover and then systematize a religion of immanence.[7]

More than any contemporary, however, it was Leo Strauss who seemed
to inhabit the two epochs at once, and who serves witness to the peculiar
fusion of the 1780s and '90s with the 1920s and '30s. Against Gebhardt,
the non-Jew who nonetheless counts as the greatest champion of a
Marrano Spinoza, Strauss discounted the importance of Spinoza's
converso inheritance, indeed, of Spinoza's Jewish heritage altogether.
He allied himself with the interwar exponents of divine transcendence
and revelation instead: the Jewish philosopher Franz Rosenzweig and his

Protestant "counterpart" Karl Barth.[8] Strauss singled out this twosome as the source of theology's revival in interwar Europe, and his choice to affiliate with them dovetailed with his partial animus toward Spinoza.[9]

But an iconoclast through and through, Strauss could not simply ally himself with his exemplars. Like his friend Hans Jonas, he too would find himself prompted to undertake a defense of "nature"—not only against its gnostic and Baconian detractors, but also against its erstwhile Spinozist champions—and he would adapt talk of God's radical transcendence for the job. He too would stake his claim against nomos and set out to recover a version of physis, which bloomed in his mid-century master-piece, *Natural Right and History* (1953). The book is important in part because it transformed him, after his death, from an émigré intellectual into an American icon, from an ornery and isolated German into a founding father of a neoconservative revolt (albeit at others' hands). But the project outlined in *Natural Right* had its origins in the 1920s and '30s, in round two of the pantheism controversy. Though it speaks little of heresy and not at all of Judaism, his book nonetheless attends both. As I hope to show, Strauss's intellectual career was founded, and in some ways foundered, on the problem of heresy. He wanted to nip in the bud the heretical Judaism of his contemporaries, but his option for natural right would make him a foremost example of the species.

To cast Spinoza's rebirth in this age as a single story has the unfortu-nate effect of masking one of its most salient elements. That is, the resurrection of Spinoza did not occur simply in some generalized moment of crisis. It did occur in such a context, but it occurred in other, more specific contexts as well. Spinoza's revival came to pass simultaneously in at least two camps, whose very distinction, each from the other, Spinoza himself had helped call into question. On the one hand, European Jewry, German Jews especially, had celebrated Spinoza in the nineteenth century as cosmopolitan, ecumenical, universal man—as an Enlightenment figure par excellence. They had celebrated him as the man who presaged the liberal Jewish aim of emancipation and acculturation. Spinoza had made it not only possible but also incumbent upon the Jew-in-particular to become a man-in-general.[10]

By the 1920s, however, the man-in-general had come to appear as little more than the fantasy of a European Enlightenment with universalist pre-tensions. A whole assortment of men-in-particular threatened to expose the man-in-general for the chimera he had always been. And so Spinoza came to stand for something quite different. Non-Jews could still find in him a universal exemplar, but he now came to embody two contrary impulses: as one whose existential homelessness prefigured a modern condition of alienation, and at the same time, as one whose philosophical response held out the hope for its overcoming. Jews undertook a similar recovery. They now reclaimed Spinoza not as a Jew who had superseded his Jewishness, but as an emphatically Jewish heretic. They did so, however, at a moment when a self-consciously heretical stance toward Jewish tradition had become, if not normative, then at least the position of a strong and vocal minority, and when estrangement and alienation more generally had come to define the modern temper. The idiom they adopted to express their difference marked them also as same; in their efforts to assert their distinction, they had in part already erased it.

CHAPTER FIVE

Pantheism Revisited

STRICTLY SPEAKING, pantheism identifies God with the world. The divine does not merely reside in the architectonics of orange pulp. It does not only dwell in the bubbles of your beer, or in the flies on your face. It does not simply inhabit or infuse them. It is them. The identity of world and God helps account for the heretical character of pantheist doctrine, at least for any religion that posits a breach between *deus* and *mundus*, God and world. Pantheism becomes an irresistible term of opprobrium for the defenders of monotheistic orthodoxy. That virtually none of the heresies called pantheist by their opponents have in fact espoused pantheism (strictly speaking) seems not to have checked their ardor. Referring to this tradition of the heresy hunters, Hegel perhaps put it best when he stated flatly, "It has [quite simply] never occurred to a man to say that everything, all things together in their singularity and contingency, are God." Here Hegel exaggerated. But much less, he more plausibly went on to say, has the claim been advanced by one with a rightful claim to the title of philosopher. Hegel rejected as "totally false" the assertion that "such a pantheism has been factually present in some philosophy or other."[1] But to Hegel's chagrin, those who have used the term most have rarely spoken strictly, and so pantheism has come to enjoy a referential promiscuity on a level rivaling its gnostic cousin.

The circumstances of its birth did much to secure pantheism's conceptual ambiguity, as a catchall for various and sundry doctrines of universal unity. Like gnosticism, pantheism as a term had its invention in eighteenth-century religious and philosophical polemic. The ancient world lacked the modern neologism, and with some exceptions, scholars have been just as hard-pressed to find there a functional equivalent. Though the medievals indulged in talk of a philosophy of unity, they, too, lacked the term, and by most accounts, the phenomenon. Not until the turn of the eighteenth century did pantheism as a term come into being, as discourses of philosophy, theology, and an emerging natural science competed for supremacy. The Dutch theologian J. de la Faye coined its substantive form in debate with John Toland, who had professed to share in the doctrine of the pantheists in a tract of 1705, called *Socinianism Truly Stated*. In a response, his *Origines Judaicae* of 1709, Toland returned to the term and this time bequeathed to it its classic definition: "There is no divine entity separate from matter and this world, and nature itself, that is, the entirety of things, is the only and highest God." The term spread rapidly to the continent. Leibniz wrote to Toland in criticism, while others in France made it a mainstay of the theo-philosophical vocabulary.[2] Toland's formulation also seemed to give the lie to Hegel's dictum a century before it was coined, but Toland specified his position still further a decade later, and in such a way as to avoid the nonsensical implications. In his *Pantheisticon* of 1720, Toland defined God not as the totality of the cosmos, but as the creative, intelligent force within it.[3] The esoteric code of Toland's "pantheistae" nonetheless remained vague and its time oddly out of joint, insofar as it juxtaposed ancient teachings of hylozoism and a world-soul with principles extracted from Copernican astronomy and Newtonian physics.[4]

Pantheism as a term came into its own, however, only in the eighteenth century's final decades, when the abstraction was wed to a proper name: Spinoza. It was a cosmopolitan affair. The ceremony bound an English coinage to a heretical Dutch Jew of Portuguese descent, and took place above all in the world of German letters. Though a mixed marriage on the face of it, the partners in fact had a good deal in common. Spinoza's idiosyncratic notion of "substance" came as close to a pantheism, strictly conceived, as the thought of any philosopher before him. For Aristotle, substance (his term was *ousia*, at times a synonym for *physis*) could refer to the concrete individual, to a core of essential properties, or to that which exists in its own right as an ultimate subject of predication. Descartes in part took up the theme of self-sufficiency from late-medieval Aristotelian scholastics (like Aquinas). From Descartes, Spinoza adopted the notion and made it the centerpiece of his philosophical system, concluding in his *Ethics* (ca. 1665) that there can be only a single substance, if by substance is meant "that which is in itself and is conceived through itself."[5] For this reason, Spinoza equated substance with God and nature (or the active force within nature, *natura naturans*, rather than the passive world of inert objects, *natura naturata*), terms that were for him synonymous: God, or nature. *Deus sive natura*. The phrase rejected out of hand Christian and Jewish notions of creation from nothing. It rejected also the fundamental breach between God and world posited by the monotheistic orthodoxies, since on this account God does not stand over and against the world as its transcendent (or transitive) cause. *Deus sive natura* substituted a pantheist "or" for the Judeo-Christian "and."

The byword devolved into a slogan, and has led generations of interpreters to label Spinoza, for better or worse, a pantheist. Some (like Hegel and Rosenzweig) have preferred to call Spinoza's philosophy "acosmic" in its effects. On this view, the world loses its autonomy, its distinction obliterated as it is absorbed into the greater and infinite totality that is God (whose omnipresence leaves no "room" for a world outside him).[6] Still others have called Spinoza a pan-*en*-theist. They catalog him as a latter-day Neoplatonist for whom concretions of the divinity emanate from its source, rather than as a pantheist for whom the divine suffuses even the most remote corners of the cosmos. All this remains hotly debated. But whatever the truth of the matter, one thing goes uncontested: by the end of the eighteenth century, Spinozism and pantheism had become largely synonymous and have remained so to this day, Hegel's rearguard action notwithstanding. This was the accomplishment of the pantheism controversy of old.

The notoriety of its accomplishment has endured in the English-speaking world. But that of its initial fury has not. The controversy had its origins in the censure of what posterity has come to regard, rightly or wrongly, as a "sorry, second-rate" philosopher, a man "mistrustful of human reason and burdened with missionary zeal": Friedrich Heinrich Jacobi. It began as a series of differences between Jacobi and Moses Mendelssohn over the legacy, and putative Spinozism, of Gotthold Ephraim Lessing, Mendelssohn's close friend and a leading figure of the German Enlightenment. Here is not the place to recount the debate in detail. Suffice it to say that Jacobi's attacks had the opposite of their intended effect. He had hoped to deliver a few swift kicks to the philosopher Lessing himself once dismissed as a "dead dog." But the dog had merely been sleeping, and the abuse worked only to revive him. Spinoza rose again, snarling with new life, and turned on the man who would have him dead by becoming one of German philosophy's best friends in the century that followed.[7]

German luminaries observed the spat, and decided they found more impressive the object of debate than either of the debate's protagonists. The philosopher Johann Gottfried Herder drew on Spinoza's notion of "substance" to defeat the extramundane, personalist God of traditional Christian piety in favor of a God more in consonance with an emerging natural science—God as neither mind nor machine, but as cosmic organism—and a model of piety finally shorn of anthropomorphic projection. Herder's flirtations with pantheism and a hylozoic notion of the world provided the grist, on some accounts, to Kant's mill in the third of his great critiques. Friedrich Schelling also picked up on the organism, and this despite Spinoza's explicit attack on traditional notions of teleology. Hegel read Spinoza with Schelling and Friedrich Hölderlin as students together in Tübingen, and inked into his album from the time the Greek phrase *hen kai pan*, the pantheist formula for the "one and all." Even Goethe took to carrying the *Ethics* around in his coat pocket, and felt compelled, in 1785, to tell Jacobi he had been wrong: "Spinoza does not prove the existence of God; existence is God. And if for this reason others chide him as an atheist, I should like to name him and praise him as *theissimum* and indeed *christianissimum.*"[8]

All this made Heinrich Heine feel justified in his pronouncement of 1835, that pantheism was the secret religion of Germany. "Nobody says it, but everyone knows it: pantheism is an open secret in Germany. We have in fact outgrown deism. We are free and want no thundering tyrant. We are grown up and need no fatherly care. And we are not the botchwork of a great mechanic. Deism is a religion of slaves," he announced. It is a religion "for children, for Genevans, for watchmakers."[9] The sensibility that Heine described found its way into mainstream religious speculation also. Though Goethe had little desire, in 1785, to revive Christian theology on Spinozist ground, he nonetheless demonstrated the ease with which others, a short time later, would do precisely that. In Protestant circles, this was the achievement of F.D.E. Schleiermacher. Schleiermacher famously defined religion as the "contemplation" and "feeling" of the universe. He blurred the distinction between finite and infinite, God and world, and stressed the embeddedness of one in the other. All this led directly out of his appreciation for Spinoza, whom he praised as "full of religion and of the holy spirit," and which would make of him, a century later, the prime target of Barth's drive to purity.[10] The marriage of Spinoza to pantheism played prominently in nineteenth-century Jewish circles also. Heinrich Graetz, for example, directed an attack on the "pantheism" of the nascent German-Jewish reform movement in his dissertation, on the relation in antiquity of Judaism and gnosticism.[11] Through the end of the nineteenth century, then, the union of Spinoza and pantheism had for the most part held fast. But this had done little to end the extramarital escapades of each, in part because neither term had an exceptionally stable meaning to begin with.

Spinoza between the Wars

This became obvious by the 1920s, when the name Spinoza could mean anything and everything. This was in part because the name itself had become an object of doubt. Not only could it refer to a welter of ideas. Not only could it elicit a host of insults and slurs. Maledictus, the incorrigible atheist, Satan incarnate, the leader of errant men: all these circulated widely. In the 1920s, the name Spinoza suffered a crisis of identity far deeper, since not even the name stood fast. This we learn from a curious series of articles and letters that appeared in the pages of the *Chronicon Spinozanum,* beginning with its first volume in 1921. Carl Gebhardt, the journal's editor, worried that scholars had uncritically accepted prior use of the name, and so threatened the very vocation of the society. He pointed out that the surname Spinoza had to contend with others like Spiñoza, d'Spinoza, de Spinoza, and Despinoza, all of which appeared in Spinoza's own hand. The first name had also been called into question. Was it Baruch? Benedictus? Bento? Benito? The first appeared in the text of Spinoza's excommunication. It highlighted his Jewish origins, even as it marked his alienation from them. Benedictus named the philosopher, Bento the Marrano of Portuguese descent, whereas Benito recalled the Spanish cradle of the converso phenomenon. All had their supporters. Much depended also on a recognized champion, for only with a proper name, it was thought, could the legendary unruliness of the philosophy be harnessed for the common good. Only then might the loose bands of hangers-on and fellow travelers unite.[12]

Gebhardt and other members of the Societas Spinozana left open the question of Spinoza's first name, with the result a happy ambiguity that lasts to this day. As for the surname, they settled in the end on Spinoza. But the decision was no foregone conclusion. It came only after a series of lengthy and exacting philological deliberations, and reversed the stance adopted by Spinoza's foremost fin de siècle interpreter, the Polish priest Stanislaus von Dunin-Borkowski. The exactitude of their researches betrays not pedantry so much as an anxiety about what the name stood for, about what it should mean. They were right to worry. For a variety of reasons, the interwar period witnessed an explosion of interest in Spinoza. This explosion made the Society possible. But the blast threatened also to undo it, for it ripped from the grip of any single party exclusive claim to Spinoza's legacy. Neither did Spinoza have what gnosticism had found in the work of Hans Jonas, an interpretation compelling enough to bring order to the chaos. This did not, however, stop many of Spinoza's partisans from trying. Foremost among them was Gebhardt.

"It was the world-historical mission of the Marranos to bring Spinoza forth. Out of the split in their consciousness arose the modern mind."[13] With these words Gebhardt summed up a leading motif of Spinoza interpretation in interwar Europe. Rejected by Spanish Catholics as "New Christians" tainted with Jewish blood, and often ostracized by their former coreligionists as traitors to their people, Marranos found themselves suspended in the interstices of competing legal codes. They were branded both Christian heretics and Jewish apostates, and were recuperated in the interwar period as figures who confounded classification. They lived, Gebhardt argued, in "inner contradiction to religion as such," and therefore helped account for the religious peripateticism of Spinoza's Amsterdam contemporaries, not to mention Spinoza himself.[14]

The thesis has enjoyed a renaissance, but its foremost author has lapsed into obscurity. This is a shame, since by all accounts Gebhardt reigned for twenty years as Spinoza's most vociferous champion. He was something of a polymath, and his interests ventured far afield. They led him from African languages to history of art, from drama to philosophy. He helped found a Frankfurt theater group, an institute of adult education, and most improbably, a Schopenhauer appreciation society. But his love burned for Spinoza alone. He produced the authoritative edition of Spinoza's collected writings, not to mention a series of works on Spinoza and his Marrano contemporaries.[15] In the meantime, he had founded in 1920 the Spinoza Society, together with Sir Frederick Pollock, Leon Brunschvicg, Harald Höffding, and Willem Meijer. Six years later he laid the cornerstone for the Spinoza House. As one admirer summarized the reigning sentiment about Gebhardt, "the man is himself a gospel."[16]

It is odd, perhaps, that a non-Jew counts as the greatest champion of a Marranic—and religious—Spinoza. But to refer to Spinoza as a Marrano did not at all mean to enshrine his Jewish origins. On the contrary: Gebhardt stressed that Spinoza ought not be yoked to the doctrine he repudiated and the community he defied. The thesis of his Marrano origins invalidated all attempts to make of Spinoza a Jew. And the extent to which the Spinoza of the seventeenth century had become, with time, a different figure altogether counseled even more decidedly against returning him to the fold. Even if Spinoza's problem had been Jewish in origin, his solution "belonged not to Judaism alone, but to all mankind."[17] He was the "first European and truly ecumenical man." His Marrano heritage did not set him beyond religion (as Strauss would argue), but in its midst; at the same time, it predisposed him to religious skepticism and to heresy, its result.[18]

Gebhardt deserves attention also because he exemplified the Spinoza-gnostic rivalry in one of its purest forms. Barth and his minions count as the theological expression of a sentiment that insisted man drain his cup to its dregs. This attitude counseled resolve in the face of division and crisis; it eschewed fantasy and false hope. But for many, it offered an overly bleak outlook on the world, a world rent by troubles of every stripe, but not beyond hope of repair. This very fact made Spinoza's revival important, Gebhardt thought, and almost inevitable. "Spinoza's teaching will become vital for us once again," he insisted. "It is a stroke of destiny, that the individual experience of the Marrano Spinoza, *to search for a lost God*, is also the common experience of *our* century."[19] The upshot: Spinoza was the philosopher whom the Marranos of interwar Europe had best to emulate. Those who considered the Marranic experience their own, those who felt it their lot to seek after an exiled or absconded God, those who bridled at the exile of the divine from the world—these men had only to unfurl the proud banner of Spinoza, and to march.

Many did just that. In its depth and breadth, Spinoza's revival in this period outstripped by far the gnostic recrudescence. He had become exemplary, it seemed, for just about everyone. Psychoanalysts lay claim to Spinoza's legacy, astronomers also. Lawyers and jurists called him their own, as did a smaller but still vocal group, the female cadets of Germany's teaching corps. Those looking to reanimate German national pride following the devastations of the war and the shame of its peace could, as odd as it may seem, also find in the "Jew Baruch Spinoza" a philosophical compass. Even the German dental association felt obliged to put in a few good words for the venerable Jewish heretic.[20]

The occult scene understandably mounted a concerted attempt to revive Spinoza's thought. His monism, not least his alleged pantheism, spoke powerfully to those alienated by the Cartesian bequest to Western culture: the rift between mind and body, the breach between spirit and matter too often resolved at the latter's expense. Spinoza enjoyed an especially devoted following in the circles inspired by Rudolf Steiner. Spinoza had, after all, animated the natural-scientific investigations of Goethe, himself immortalized by Steiner's "Anthroposophs" in the name of their mouthpiece, the *Goetheanum*.[21] One enthusiast, writing in Steiner's literary organ, held that Spinoza's "karmic consequences" bode well for the coming epoch.[22]

All this might seem overwrought to us today. It seemed silly to contemporaries also. But we should not underestimate Spinoza's importance in this era, nor the seriousness of purpose his votaries brought to their pursuits. Many found relief from the political and spiritual upheavals of their time in his example. Their ranks included crackpots and cranks, but also earnest spiritual seekers. Still, these were some of the lonelier prophets of Spinoza's second coming. Theirs were the voices of the plaza, largely drowned out by the din of the humdrum and the everyday. The profusion of their cries, however, testifies to a more sustained and centralized effort at Spinoza's rehabilitation—this real work took place within the temple walls.

Not all those within mainstream religious circles welcomed Spinoza's return. Some of the leading lights of interwar Protestantism, especially, could not have been overjoyed at the prospect, given the considerable effort they had expended ridding theology of its pantheist residues. Rudolf Bultmann made this emphatically clear in the most programmatic of his statements regarding the "latest movement" in Protestant thought: "It is no more possible to see divine forces or the revelation of the divine in the inter-related complex of history and in historical forces than it is in the inter-relatedness of nature and natural forces. Truly, here too it is only man that is deified." Bultmann insisted that "at every point—against both pantheism of nature and pantheism of history—the polemic of Barth and Gogarten is valid. For that polemic is aimed directly against the temptation to deify man; it is a protest against every kind of direct knowledge of God."[23] For their fellow travelers it was a call to humility, for their opponents it was cause for alarm. Whatever its intent, the effect of the move was to summon up the specter of ancient gnostic heresies, heterodox notions that the fledgling Catholic Church had failed to quash or erase from memory, and which had returned periodically to haunt it. So it should perhaps come as no surprise that interwar Catholics, German Catholics especially, would invoke Spinoza in the name of banishing once and for all the bugbear that would not go away.

Hans Hartmann was one of them.[24] In his initial report on the Spinoza Congress of 1932, as we have seen, he could not help but note the absence of his Protestant colleagues. Months later, Hartmann again evoked the challenge Spinoza posed to Barth and his followers, this time in a more thoughtful report to the *Preußische Jahrbücher*. He began with a typical evaluation of the fractious spiritual climate: "The number of movements which offer themselves as an escape from the material and spiritual emergency of today's men becomes ever greater. That most of these are themselves internally split makes the state of affairs all the less possible to overlook. Where should the man of the present, who wills to carry his fate," he asked, "derive the time and energy to orient himself, if only temporarily?" Hartmann thought such perspective best attained from atop one of those few peaks "which enable a view of the world unified in greatness, beauty and depth," and recommended in particular the vantage afforded from the summit of Mount Spinoza. It had much to recommend it: above all a view from eternity and an appreciation for the worldly infinite, or in Spinoza's terms a view *sub specie aeternitatis*. In this, Hartmann demonstrated a deep appreciation for the potential of interwar Spinozism to contest the theology of crisis. He understood liberal Protestantism as a version of—or at least in cahoots with—a Spinozism for which the natural world brims with divinity, and he recognized crisis theology as its most complete denial. Against the consolation of Spinoza's nature-god, the crisis theologians forecast disquiet as man's lot; against the unity of the divine and the natural, they insisted on a "pure opposition of creator and creation."[25]

Hartmann recommended Spinoza also as an ersatz Catholic. Like Catholicism, Spinoza appealed to those "who sublimate, spiritualize and generalize." The Catholic (and Spinozist) penchant for inclusion—its universalism—stood in sharp contrast to the demand the crisis theologians laid upon man to *decide*—either for the world or for God.[26] In this, Hartmann expressed a sentiment akin to the one that inhered in a declaration published a decade earlier, in 1923, by a fellow and more infamous Catholic intellectual: "The Marcionite either-or is answered [by the Catholic] with an as-well-as." This gnomic statement becomes all the more interesting when we consider the identity of its author—the scholar of jurisprudence Carl Schmitt, who would later stand beside Martin Heidegger as a twin pillar of the Nazi intellectual edifice.[27]

Schmitt's Catholicism was not typical for the time.[28] Nor did he expressly mobilize Spinoza to contest the gnostic spirit. He can, however, help us understand why other Catholics would. Commentary on his book of 1923, *Roman Catholicism and Political Form*, tends to identify it as a response to Max Weber's thesis on the Protestant ethic. Schmitt took his fellow Catholics to task, this argument goes, for acceding to the rule of Protestant asceticism and its economic consequences. As an antidote to "economic-technical" reason, Schmitt offered a Catholicism understood as a "political idea" and public institution.[29] This reading has much to support it: the essay's original German title, *Der katholische Gedanke*, would seem to present "the Catholic idea" as an explicit rebuttal to the "Protestant ethic" (though it also seems to identify the Protestant ethic with Lutheran inwardness rather than Calvinist predestination). But Schmitt's text dwells in a home just as much haunted by interwar gnosticism as by the maligned spirit of a tormented German mandarin. In 1923 the "Marcionite either-or" was not gnomic, but gnostic. Nor did it refer to Weber. It referred to crisis theology, and to its philosophical roots in Kierkegaard.

In their zeal to split the temporal world from spiritual grace, in their desire to save God from sin, Protestant theologians had banished him from sight. They had left the world to the devil, Schmitt thought, acquiesced to the reign of his "legality" by granting him entrance through the back. They had in effect granted him sovereignty over the world, which recalled the malicious demiurge of gnostic provenance. In an earlier essay, Schmitt worried also that Protestant hostility to the world licensed a descent into secret worship and transgression of the visible order. Protestantism would then leave to man two roles: "the 'pure' Christian who serves God in the most extreme invisibility; and, separate therefrom, the one who serves mammon in the most manifest visibility and is proud of the fact that he has liberated *spiritualia* from its logically sordid association with *temporalibus*." Schmitt concluded the essay with a series of thoughts stunning in their prescience: "The man so exacting that to him every formulation of the infinity of God appears contradictory and insincere"—the hallmark of Barth's critique—the man "who remains silent for sincere reasons because every word would be a lie if he did not simultaneously make a serious effort to destroy his own concrete visibility, would tomorrow lie in equal sincerity because only the lie would be the true expression of an untruthful nature." It was as if

Catholicism had answered Barth's *Romans* before the latter had even been penned.[30]

Schmitt also railed against Protestants for abetting the despoliation of the physical world. Like Jonas, he thought them complicit with the modern recasting of the relation between art and nature (at the latter's expense). "It appears that Catholics have a different relation to the soil than Protestants," Schmitt observed. "Compared with these indigent, dispossessed peoples, the Huguenot or the Puritan has a strength and pride that is often inhuman." The Protestant is "capable of living on any soil, because he makes himself master of nature and harnesses it to his will." By contrast, "Roman Catholic peoples appear to love the soil, mother earth, in a different way; they all have their own 'terrisme.' Nature is for them not the antithesis of art and enterprise, also not of intellect and feeling or heart; human labor and organic development, nature and reason are one."[31] Like Jonas, he opposed Protestant (or gnostic) dualisms. And he evinced a generically catholic sentiment which others like Hartmann could find buttressed in the philosophy of Spinoza.

None of this is to say that Schmitt was an acolyte of Spinoza, who had gone too far in his attempt to draw God into the world.[32] Schmitt's politics, after all, likened sovereign decisions to divine intervention from beyond. Spinoza's concerted assault on miracles argued in theological terms what Schmitt wished to dispute in jurisprudential ones.[33] Still, even in these moments of hostility toward Spinoza, Schmitt lays bare the logic of the twin rebirth out of Europe's troubled womb: gnosticism and pantheism together. Whether Marcion or Spinoza deserved the birthright depended on your point of view.

BENEDICT OR BARUCH?

Interwar Protestants found inspiration in Paul, in Marcion, in the gnostics. Interwar Catholics found inspiration in Spinoza. Interwar Jews found inspiration in them all. That they could do so says much about the heretical spirit that in certain circles ruled the day. For gnosticism and pantheism might be understood, logically if not historically, as Judaism's two most potent heretical alternatives. They certainly hold such rank if Judaism is understood as a religion of revealed law, as Moses Mendelssohn so famously defined it. Mendelssohn ushered Judaism into the modern age by casting religious truths as available to all by virtue of reason. In the end, all that distinguished Judaism from natural religion was God's revelation to the Jewish people. But this revelation included no exclusive religious truths; its exclusivity inhered only in the law granted to the Jewish people by God. What Christians understood as an imposition, a yoke, Mendelssohn cast as a revealed code of ritual conduct, granted to the end of felicity both personal and communal. Praxis trumped doxa.

Given Mendelssohn's definition, it is easy to see how gnosticism and pantheism, as ideal-types, posed the threats that they did. Gnosticism accepts revelation, indeed is predicated upon it. But gnosis reveals truths, not law, which the gnostics reviled as the work of the devil. Gnosticism favored love in law's place. As for pantheism: it does not do away with law per se, though it could sanction just as potent an antinomianism as its gnostic cousin. But pantheism does reject revelation from afar. By conflating God with nature, it does away with the sort of transcendence required by the monotheistic orthodoxies. As they ran to embrace gnostic and pantheist heresies, many Jews in interwar Europe abandoned for good Mendelssohn's ramshackle home. But how did this come to pass? And did the Jewish heretics raise a new edifice, more capacious perhaps, in its place?

The opinions elicited by the Spinoza celebrations of 1927 and 1932 offer some provisional answers. At times, the Jewish recuperation could mirror in aspect the likeness of Spinoza retrieved by Europeans more generally. An observer in the Jewish periodical *Der Morgen*, for example, proclaimed the dawn of the age of Spinoza: "That a Spinoza society was founded not long ago is itself a sign of new conviction. After the rule of materialism in the previous century, after the monstrous triumphs of the natural sciences, of historicism and of epistemological investigations— after all this, man . . . has come to demand a return to synthesis, to unity." Though still an object of scorn at the universities, "a new ethics and a new religiosity germinate . . . and group themselves ever more tightly around a name: Spinoza."[34] The drive for unity, the hunger for wholeness that fueled Spinoza's comeback among occultists and philosophers alike—here it found its Jewish equivalent.

A man named Siegfried Hessing was hungriest of them all. Hessing edited a volume dedicated to Spinoza in 1933, and made clear his reasons by waxing rhapsodic in its preface: "You, Benedict, you alone are absolute, have lived and experienced the absolute in spiritual and bodily reality. You great God! You nameless one! You are truth, you are love! You are everything! You are everything! You are the cosmos and you are Being! Everything is a path to you." Just as Christ had fashioned in his image and in the wake of his death a community of love, so too, Hessing thought, had arisen in recent years a "community in you, in Spinoza." Such a community assumed all the more importance given the way "the cosmic unity of time and eternity" had been "desacralized by progress and civilization, that is, by work and by life utterly bereft of thought and feeling." Only the desire to suture the wound rent by the "boastful achievements of the technological impulse and its harmful, mechanizing, routinizing influences, only the yearning to return to everyday life some semblance of the sublimity and magic of the supratemporal" could possibly account, Hessing insisted, for the explosion of interest in Spinoza to which he bore witness.[35]

The Jewish philosopher David Baumgardt (at the time a young assistant professor in Berlin) thought of Spinoza in similar terms: as a figure possessed at once of the greatest nugatory and affirmative powers (though Baumgardt tended to emphasize the former). In his diaries, Baumgardt had written of Spinoza as the last of the holy ones. "If one were to think to oneself the philosophy of a God," he surmised, "so would one always be compelled to choose Spinoza's."[36] In public, Baumgardt was a bit more circumspect in his praise. Still, in Baumgardt's Nietzschean interpretation, Spinoza was thought "to have returned to the world its innocence." From Nietzsche, Baumgardt continued, his own age had inherited its most vital Spinozistic problems. And it is to Spinoza that interwar Europe should turn for help with the problem of "Beyond Good and Evil."[37] Having negated boundaries inimical to life as he desired it to be lived, Spinoza then went about erecting another edifice in its place.

Both Hessing and Baumgardt were exponents of a Jewish neo-romanticism in vogue at the time. Both imagined a Spinoza who was at once philosophical and religious, if also (or for that very reason) heretical. They recuperated him, in other words, as an identifiably Jewish heretic. This tendency had no greater exponent than Joseph Klausner, who convened the Palestinian equivalents to the celebrations in The Hague, first in 1927 at the Hebrew University in Jerusalem, then in 1932, where he spoke to a packed crowd at Tel-Aviv's Beit Ha'am (Hall of the People). Klausner had made a name for himself already in 1922 with a treatment of Jesus, the other great heretic of Jewish history.[38] But it was in his speeches on Spinoza that he intervened—or sought to—in the course of Jewish history itself.

His orations dealt primarily with the status of the *herem*, of Spinoza's ban from the Amsterdam Jewish community. Klausner demoted the centrality of the writ of excommunication. It was used extensively, by no means only for Spinoza, and by no means only for those who developed philosophical systems designed to contest the transcendent and personal God of Jewish history.[39] He underscored also its inconsequence (from Spinoza's perspective). But he did so from a stance only recently made possible by the consolidations of Jewish nationalism: to depart from the synagogue or the community, on this view, did not mean to leave the Jewish nation. "Do the writings against traditional Judaism suffice to make one no longer a Jew?" No: Spinoza had not ceased to be a Jew, "only a kosher one." That such a stance was by no means accepted or even possible in Spinoza's own time, that Klausner professed to refrain from a decision either for Benedict or Baruch—this did little to check the drive to its logical conclusion. The moment had arrived to reverse two centuries of infamy and revoke Spinoza's ban. Klausner was not to be found "among the hypocrites or the cowards," as Scholem would later put it.[40] And so compunction could not suppress his announcement "from the heights of Mt. Scopus," from the halls of "our own little temple":

> The ban is revoked!
> May your punishment be gone and your sin atoned!
> You are our brother!
> You are our brother!
> You are our brother![41]

Above the chorus of yea-sayers rang out a few, if powerful, dissenting voices. Among Jews, these belonged above all to Franz Rosenzweig and to Leo Strauss. Both had little truck for the image of the philosopher "drunk with God," invented by the German romantics a century before and copied by their Jewish followers. Both found more compelling the resolve of a Karl Barth (or for that matter, a Heidegger) than Klausner's apologetic babblings. Both affiliated themselves less with the votaries of divine immanence than with the champions of philosophical and theological transcendence.[42] But above all, both harked to the call of a third from beyond the grave, *the* voice of nineteenth-century German Jewry, but a voice that had recently fallen upon deaf ears. They harked to the disembodied voice of Hermann Cohen.

"Cohen took Spinoza seriously," Rosenzweig wrote of his mentor. But with a single exception, others had failed to heed Cohen's example. The exception was Leo Strauss, whose 1924 essay ("Cohens Analyse der Bibel-Wissenschaft Spinozas") had adjudicated at length the justice of Cohen's attacks.[43] Rosenzweig was quick to distinguish this "small and valuable work" from the spirit then triumphant among Germany's Jews. "The signature of the age, and especially among Jewry," Rosenzweig averred, "became evident at the Spinoza festival of 1927: with the exception of a few orthodox voices there was unanimous enthusiasm for the 'great Jew,' from the most extreme versions of 'religious' Judaism to the most extreme versions of 'national' Judaism. How then could one expect understanding for a statement of the problem which dares to grant to the Amsterdam community 'every right' to the expulsion of the maligner and betrayer of God."[44] Cohen had insisted on precisely that right, and on the enduring historical justice of his excommunication. Spinoza's posthumous fame as the greatest of thinkers did nothing to alter the fact of his heresy. Nor, Cohen thought, could it absolve him of the malice and spite in his critique of rabbinic Judaism.

As Cohen aged, his remonstrations against Spinoza intensified in pitch. He contested the equation of right with might that seemed to follow from the identity of God and nature. Spinoza appeared not as the prophet of liberalism, but of the total (if not yet totalitarian) state, insofar as he equated the current state of affairs with the kingdom of God. A divinized world did away with messianism and man's need for redemption also, a prospect Cohen greeted with undisguised bitterness: "The peace, which the admirers of Spinozism depict as so blissful—it is a betrayal."[45] Human peace Cohen discovered not in unity with nature, but in an ideal moral world alongside the natural universe. But above all, he felt, Spinoza excluded the possibility of a religion of reason (despite the obvious objection, that his *Ethics* is precisely that, and that reason has its apotheosis in his *more geometrico*). Religion, and certainly institutionalized religion, Spinoza had cast as the provenance of the herd. For that matter, Judaism had not even the status of a real religion; it was merely a collection of statutes upon which had once been erected a state. To dispute a religion of reason in this case meant to deny the universalism of the Jewish tradition, and so it meant also to dissolve the ground of the project that had occupied Cohen in his last years. Spinoza, Cohen wrote in conclusion, had "suppressed the Noachide [commandments]," those few commands required of all persons to secure their place in the world to come, the commands that made of natural religion the "foundational idea of Jewish monotheism."[46]

Such were the gist of Cohen's theological objections to Spinoza. But as trenchant and passionately argued as they were, they could not compete, in affect at least, with the disgust elicited in him by Spinoza's simple lack of fealty to his people. Writing in 1910, Cohen declared that Jewry had yet to arrive at—or had done much to rescind—the verdict that Spinoza had rightfully earned. He thought it downright incredible. "If a Christian were to disparage the teachings of Christ, so he would have dug his own moral grave." Jewry appeared pathetic by contrast, since "even when Spinoza, with the most loveless severity, not only makes his tribe despicable (in the same days in which Rembrandt lived on his street and eternalized the ideal of the Jew!) but also mutilates the singular God, for whose sake he along with his father had fled from Portugal and the Inquisition, not a single voice cries out against this *humanly incomprehensible treason*." He bemoaned Spinoza's "canonization," first at the hands of the German romantics, then by nineteenth-century Protestant theology. He thought it no accident that in a time in which Protestant theology had made considerable advances in its investigation of Israelite prophecy, "Jew-hatred could [still] celebrate its orgies." All this would be inexplicable, he thought, had not "the evil demon of Spinoza poisoned the atmosphere. The passages in which Spinoza had let loose his vengeful hatred against the Jews are to be found still today almost verbatim in the daily newspapers [of the movement]." For all these reasons, Cohen declared Spinoza the "impediment" and "great misfortune" of modern Judaism. Mendelssohn may have unwittingly rehabilitated him at the beginning of his career, but at the very least fought till his death to undo the damage. Spinoza alone bore responsibility for his status as the singular "accuser of Judaism before the Christian world."[47]

Cohen did not mince words. His followers were a bit more careful. Rosenzweig, for instance, admitted the "deep injustice" of Cohen's critique; he nonetheless could at least append his signature to its thrust: a wholesale assault on Spinoza's nature-god. Indeed, Rosenzweig flatly declared Spinoza an idolator on this count. He echoed Cohen's "precious words" on Spinoza's "pedantic Gleichmacherei" (making all things same). As Rosenzweig saw it, Spinoza failed when he could bring himself to say only *sive* in place of "and": God *or* nature in place of God *and* nature, synonyms in place of discrete and integral entities.[48] Through the *sive*, Spinoza had denied both the God of scripture and the possibility for revelation from afar. Herein lay his fatal flaw.

Meanwhile, Strauss paid homage by devoting an essay (of 1924) to the thesis Cohen had set out at length. At first glance, the homage appears strange indeed. For of the twenty-four pages in all, Strauss spent a bit more than twenty-three of them demolishing Cohen's argument. The thesis of Spinoza's implacable hatred for his ancestral religion Strauss dismissed as unfounded; one might understand Spinoza's critique as proceeding logically and legitimately from historical and theological assumptions prevalent in his time.[49] Only in the essay's concluding paragraph did Strauss commend the "exemplary seriousness" Cohen had brought to his task.

This was hardly backhanded praise. Strauss indeed continued Cohen's project, if by other means. His argument dovetailed with Cohen's effort to reinstate, so to speak, Spinoza's ban. To claim that Spinoza's critique did not derive from the sources of Judaism meant that Spinoza's arguments had no necessary connection with his Jewish ancestry; it meant that Spinoza need not be—and perhaps should not be—considered Jewish in any way whatsoever. "The [Theological-Political] Treatise," after all, "is a Christian-European, not a Jewish event." The argument gave the lie to the efforts of interwar Jews to recuperate Spinoza as an identifiably *Jewish* heretic.[50] Not even Spinoza's heresy qualified as Jewish; not even his heresy might be invoked, in good dialectical style, in the effort to return him to the fold. Strauss's "reinstatement" of the ban thus went further, much further, than the original. The *herem* pronounced against Spinoza, even as it excluded him from the Jewish community, still purported to include him within a Jewish universe. The ban denounced and proscribed in the most unequivocal of terms. But it also held out an implicit promise of repatriation, an offer taken up by a good three hundred of Spinoza's contemporaries in seventeenth-century Amsterdam. For Strauss, however, Spinoza was gone, and for good.

Strauss composed the essay in a mood of high reaction. Cohen's "exemplary seriousness" inhered in his refusal to pay homage to "God's drunkard," a false idol erected by the German romantics and worshiped by the Jews who aped them. Strauss's reinstatement of the ban preceded by three years its quasi-official dissolution, in 1927, on the heights of Mt. Scopus. That ceremony had crystallized a shift in sensibility much longer in the making, a sea change of which Strauss took final stock in 1932, in an essay called "Spinoza's Testament" composed on the occasion of Spinoza's three hundredth birthday.[51] If Strauss's words of 1924 had been amazingly prescient, his words of 1932 came with the benefit of a more deep-seated evaluation. Strauss had engaged at length with Spinoza in the intervening years: an essay on Spinoza's predecessors in the science of biblical criticism appeared in 1926, and later, in 1930, he published his first full-length book, *Die Religionskritik Spinozas*. What, then, was Spinoza's last will and testament? What were the wishes he took to his grave?

Strauss began with a precis of Spinoza's Jewish reception. After damnation in the seventeenth century came a partial reprieve in the eighteenth at the hands of Moses Mendelssohn, then canonization thanks to Heinrich Heine and Moses Hess in the nineteenth, and finally the possibility of impartiality at the turn of the twentieth.[52] Spinoza had, in the century just past, served admirably the cause of Jewish apologetics. Who, after all, was better suited to argue the case, if posthumously, for Jewish emancipation before the bar of modern Europe? By some accounts, Spinoza ushered Europe into the modern age, insofar as he lived a secular life before it became institutionally possible to do so; and as some Jews liked to point out, for Strauss less justifiably than more, he did so in the spirit of Judaism and by Jewish means. But in Europe after Versailles, and especially in Weimar Germany, the so-called modern project no longer commanded the admiration it once did. On the contrary, that project had come under attack from every side, and so Spinoza could no longer serve in the same capacity. Judaism—or the Jewish people—had been thrown back upon itself as cosmopolitan and ecumenical languages of identity were replaced by particularized and national ones. Still, Spinoza remained exemplary. As Strauss put it, even in this time of the "Exodus out of the new Egypt," Jews felt obligated "to bring along the bones of the man who had arisen in that land to a position on par with kings, and to inter them in the pantheon of the Jewish nation."[53] Strauss's metaphor is apt to a point. For this generation had indeed rediscovered Spinoza's bones. But it had no intention of burying them, not even on the Mount of Olives. This generation had opened liberal Judaism's skeleton closet the better to dance with the ghouls.

Spinoza remained exemplary, but for new reasons. He came to be seen as the repository of a "subterranean Judaism." In him inhered a Jewish spirit repressed by the law of Sinai, itself understood as Judaism's merely externalized form. Spinoza had liberated this spirit from a slavish devotion to law, and so had paved the way for the rebirth of the Jewish nation. Spinoza's Judaism—its true if repressed teachings—thus inhered in his heresy. This view obviously presupposed a radical change in Jewry's relation to its law, and required a good bit of interpretive work. "Several centuries had to pass," Strauss observed, "before one had made Spinoza's critique of the law supple enough to be able to recognize the law without believing in its revealed character. At the end of this development stands a generation of sufficiently free spirit to take up Spinoza's critique of the law, a [generation] still more free than [Spinoza himself], insofar as it stands beyond the crude alternatives—divine or human? revealed or invented?—altogether." For this generation, Spinoza correctly understood "not only does not stand outside of Judaism, but belongs to it as one of its greatest teachers."[54] What Strauss implied in 1924, he stated explicitly in 1932: he lived among a generation of Jews who hoped to rehabilitate Spinoza not despite his heresy, but on account of it. This was not a generation "before the law" (as Kafka might have had it). It was beyond the law, and for that reason Spinozist to the core.

To ensure the exclusion of Spinoza from the Jewish pantheon thus required a still more radical excommunication. The *herem* pronounced by the Amsterdam *parnasim* no longer sufficed. It did not, could not, go far enough. They could not have envisioned a generation of Jews that would repatriate Spinoza on the terms that it did; they could not have envisioned a generation of Jews that would in all seriousness call him "our brother" (let alone three times in succession!). Strauss therefore pursued in 1932, if less equivocally and with deeper insight, the same strategy he had adopted earlier. He proposed to hand Spinoza over to the Europeans, and in this way to safeguard him from the clutches of the lawless Jews around him. For example, Strauss rid Spinoza's critique of the law of its Jewish content. Those familiar with Spinoza's critique could not fail to know that it "would not have been possible without the foundation of modern philosophy." All of Spinoza's textual criticism must go for naught absent the presupposition "of the philosophical critique of the law, which, at least in the case of Spinoza, is bound to modern philosophy." Spinoza's star must fall and rise with the fortunes of modern philosophy, and if the latter is cast in doubt, "so too does Spinoza's critique of the law get called into question; and with it, whether or not he might be seen as a teacher of Judaism."[55] The very failures of modern philosophy, of the modern project to which that heretical generation bore witness, therefore invalidated Spinoza as one of its potential leaders.

Strauss also felt compelled to discount those moments in Spinoza beloved by his Zionist champions (and this despite his lifelong commitment to political Zionism). At one point in his *Theological-Political Treatise*, Spinoza envisioned the possible restitution of national Jewish political life. If the foundations of the Jewish religion have not "emasculated their minds," he hypothesized, the Jews "may even, if occasion offers, so changeable are human affairs, raise up their empire afresh," and with this, "God may a second time elect them."[56] It is easy to see how Zionists could find in Spinoza an endorsement of their cause. But Strauss was quick to recommend that "we discount the comment about the renewed divine election of the Jews," since, in the mouth of Spinoza, "it is no more than an empty figure of speech." The interpreter is left with but the neutral consideration, dispassionately bequeathed to the world from the philosopher's lofty perch, of the "condition of possibility for the restitution of the Jewish state." And like his teacher Machiavelli, who made Christianity responsible for the decline of Roman virtue, Spinoza held Judaism responsible for the "impossibility of the Jewish state's recreation."[57] In but a moment, and at Strauss's nimble hands, Spinoza had undergone a surgical transformation. In he went as a prophet of Zionism. Out he came as one who cast doubt, in a Machiavellian spirit no less, on the very possibility of the Zionist project.

Strauss could not purge the Jewish residues in their entirety. "Spinoza was a Jew," he plainly admitted. "The fact is confirmed, that he was born and educated as a Jew." But this, in itself, meant little, since the "Jewish ancestry and education of a great man, taken in itself, grant no right [to others] to claim his greatness for Judaism." Strauss allowed for Spinoza's literary dependence on Jewish authors; one could not deny that Spinoza had familiarized himself with the philosophical tradition as mediated by medieval Jewish philosophy. Strauss thought the fact trivial, however, because "what he learned from this philosophy are insights or opinions which he might just as easily have taken up from non-Jewish (Islamic or Christian) medieval philosophy." Such thought had nothing distinctively Jewish about it—"it is the common property of the European-Mediterranean tradition." With a hint of disdain, perhaps, Strauss declared that Spinoza had been happy to take from the Jewish tradition the "common European intellectual property which that tradition supplied him—but *not more*." For this reason, Jews had no right to venerate him, at least not as a Jew:

> Spinoza did not belong to Judaism, but to that small flock of superior spirits, which Nietzsche characterized as the "good Europeans." To this

community belonged *all* philosophers of the seventeenth century; but Spinoza belonged in a special capacity: Spinoza did not remain a Jew, while Descartes, Hobbes and Leibniz remained Christians. It therefore runs counter to Spinoza's wish for him to be taken up in the pantheon of the Jewish nation. Under these circumstances it strikes us as an elementary precept of Jewish self-esteem, that we Jews finally disavow the attempt to claim Spinoza for ourselves. . . . The respect (but not the veneration) we owe Spinoza commands us to do this: respect for Spinoza demands that we take seriously his last will and testament; and his last will was neutrality over and against the Jewish nation, a neutrality based on his break with Judaism and the Jewish people.[58]

Strauss cast his intervention as an attempt to safeguard Spinoza from those who would distort his legacy. He cast it as an attempt to honor him. But his words also have about them the ring of apology. Magnified, what appears to the naked eye as a defense of Spinoza reveals itself as a defense of Judaism also—or perhaps instead.

But why? Why would Strauss feel compelled to undertake such a defense of Judaism against Spinoza, and at a moment when most of his coreligionists lived happily with both? His religious convictions argue against it. Though reared in an Orthodox home, Strauss had since renounced his faith, and had declared himself, privately if not publicly, an atheist. He did not proclaim Spinoza guilty, as did Cohen, of treason. He did not pronounce Spinoza guilty of heresy, as had the elders of Amsterdam. But neither could he join in the spirit of the day, which reclaimed Spinoza for the Jewish people. He professed instead to speak on Spinoza's behalf, and even more specifically, on behalf of his autonomy. Strauss concluded his essay in cryptic fashion, if in a recognizable mood of resignation. "If but for the blink of an eye," he implored, "let us look away from the popular principles" on whose strength Jews had felt themselves obliged either to damn Spinoza or to venerate him. "Enough, that in this moment no one can popularize him, transform him into small coins, that no one," in one of his more remarkable metaphors, "can 'blow' him [like a wad of cash]. And then let us ask again, do we owe him reverence? Spinoza will be revered as long as there are men who know to value the inscription on his signet-ring (*caute*), or, to say it in German, as long as there are men who know what is meant when one says: *Unabhängigkeit*."[59]

Independence. It is difficult to know precisely what Strauss had in mind. But in the context of the essay, the independence to which he refers is the independence of the philosopher from the rabble, the independence of Spinoza the philosopher from the Jews who would make him their own. Spinoza, so Strauss, took to his grave the wish to stand over and against his former community and religion in a mood of relaxed, uncommitted neutrality. As we will explore at length in a moment, Strauss had in the interim, between 1924 and 1932, rejected Spinoza's arguments against revelation and the monotheistic orthodoxies as untenable. By 1932 Strauss had come to a conclusion—or at least a deep-seated intuition—about the relation between philosophy and religion. He had come to see the two as mutually exclusive. To affirm one meant to deny the other. If the *Ethics* were right, the Bible was wrong. To submit to Spinoza was to disqualify Judaism: reason or revelation, Athens or Jerusalem.[60]

The Jewish language of heresy—and its Spinozist variant in particular—threatened to undo this scheme. For it made possible a stance that was at once Jewish and Spinozist, both religious and philosophical. It did so, however, only by redefining both. The grand synthesis of a Jewish Spinozism lost the most salient aspects of each of its terms.[61] It deprived Judaism of revelation and denied the transcendence of its God, even as it stripped Spinoza of his independence, ignoring the fact that Spinoza had never expressed a desire for repatriation. As Carl Schmitt had done before them, the Jewish Spinozists substituted for the either-or a version of the both-and. They resolved the tension of the decision, not in favor of one of its terms, but by denying its fact. From Strauss's perspective, of course, the Jewish Spinozists had in a single stroke despoiled both Judaism and Spinoza, both religion and philosophy. They had accepted Spinoza's arguments about revelation, but in a perverse twist, had made this constitutive of his Judaism (and more to the point, their own). For Strauss, then, to "excommunicate" Spinoza was at the same time to save him. To defeat his attacks on Judaism was of course to secure the possibility of Jewish orthodoxy. But *in the context of the heretical Jewish challenge*, to defeat them was to secure the possibility of philosophy as well. Strauss rejected Spinoza's arguments against revelation. But he did so on behalf of the freedom that enabled Spinoza to make them, a freedom which Spinoza in no small part helped to create. Only if Spinoza were wrong could he also, in a way, be right.

To defeat the Jewish Spinozists, Strauss had at his disposal the arsenal of a competing heretical discourse. This was the language of interwar gnosticism. Understood historically, it was meditation on the issues brought to the table by the "gnostics" of the interwar period—and a qualified defense of their positions—which led Strauss to contest Jewish Spinozism in the way that he did. Meditation on these issues also set the terms for his recovery of natural right. These issues—God's transcendence, his absence, his infinity, voluntarism, and providence—Strauss addressed not so much directly as through an engagement with the personalities at issue in the pantheism controversy of old. That, at least, is what I hope to show in the pages that follow.

CHAPTER SIX

The Pantheism Controversy

TOWARD THE END of January 1970, Strauss and his close friend Jacob Klein appeared together at St. John's College to "give accounts"—accounts of the genesis of their thought, and of their philosophical differences. Strauss spoke first of the influence exerted upon him by Hermann Cohen, or Cohen's spirit, at Marburg. "Cohen attracted me because he was a passionate philosopher and a Jew passionately devoted to Judaism." But Cohen had since died, and his school, that of Marburg neo-Kantianism, had fallen into disrepair. "Cohen belonged definitely to the pre–World War I world." Most characteristic of the post–World War I world, however, "was the resurgence of theology: Karl Barth. The preface to the first edition of his commentary on the Epistle to the Romans is of great importance also to nontheologians: it sets forth the principles of an interpretation that is concerned exclusively with the subject matter as distinguished from historical interpretation. Wholly independently of Barth, Jewish theology was resurrected from a deep slumber by Franz Rosenzweig, a highly gifted man whom I greatly admired to the extent to which I understood him." Strauss was well positioned to register the impact of Barth and Rosenzweig, or was at least particularly receptive to their call, given that his "predominant interest was in theology" at the time.[1]

The impact, and the context in which it was made, proved formative. The context saw a revivified Spinozism set against a gnostic spirit associated with the theologians of crisis. The conflict played out in a Jewish milieu as well: a Jewish resurrection of Spinoza set against Barth's Jewish counterpart, the philosopher Franz Rosenzweig. These, however, are but names, a convenient shorthand for broader concerns. The debates they represent ought not be dismissed as scholastic squabbles. They implicated the most serious political and existential questions of the day—the fate of the liberal project above all—and they provided a vocabulary through which to consider them.

The conceptual universe in which Strauss made his home had at least one peculiar feature. This was a kind of wormhole, to risk an analogy with cosmology, which linked Strauss's own age with the Germany of the late eighteenth century. To judge by his first two substantial works, a dissertation on Jacobi (1921) and a book on Spinoza's critique of religion (written 1925-1928), and to judge also by the essays associated with his first editorial project, the papers of Moses Mendelssohn (1926-1937), it seems Strauss opted to undertake a systematic reconsideration of the personalities at issue in the "first round" of the pantheism controversy.[2] It was Jacobi who unwittingly made palatable the pantheist ogre, domesticated him for polite company, by impugning the Spinozism of Gotthold Ephraim Lessing, a champion of enlightened sociability and Mendelssohn's treasured friend.

Strauss's aims were several. So were his accomplishments. For one, Strauss hoped to put a definitive end to the period of German-Jewish history inaugurated by Mendelssohn. This he did in intellectual terms by allying himself with Mendelssohn's arch-foe, and by holding up against Mendelssohn's view of Judaism the gnostic and pantheist alternatives in both his and Mendelssohn's day. Liberal Judaism would have to die. So would liberal theology in general, and Strauss's resurrection of the pantheism controversy would furnish him with the conceptual tools by which to put it down.

Jacobi

Begin where Strauss did, with Jacobi. Strauss apparently did not think much of his earliest academic effort, his dissertation on *Das Erkenntnisproblem in der philosophischen Lehre Fr. H. Jacobis* (The Problem of Knowledge in the Philosophical Teaching of Fr. H. Jacobi). Strauss later denigrated the work, completed as a twenty-two-year-old in 1921, as a "disgraceful performance."[3] He may have been right. The several-score pages pale in comparison with the studies on Spinoza, Hobbes, and Maimonides that would follow in short order, let alone with the wide-ranging and wildly influential corpus of his postwar years. Against them, the dissertation comes off as dry and schematic. But as the adage has it, a good dissertation is a done dissertation, and so perhaps Strauss should have eschewed his carping in favor of satisfaction for a task at least completed, if not especially well-done.[4] Flawed or not, his text lays bare the design for the conceptual universe that he and others of his time inhabited.

Strauss disinterred Jacobi both to dust off some and to bury others of his time. He did so, specifically, in ways that linked the pantheism controversy of times past with a present riven by the challenge of crisis theology. He claimed, for example, to find in the Marburg theologian Rudolf Otto a doppelgänger for Jacobi himself (albeit mediated through the figure of Jakob Friedrich Fries, a philosopher whose star rose in the decade or two after the pantheism controversy). As the first to popularize the notion of God as "wholly other," Otto had, by some accounts, laid the foundation for crisis theology (notwithstanding his neo-Kantian heritage and liberal sensibilities). Borrowing the coinage from Fries, and later, from Kierkegaard, Otto made it the mainstay of his book *Das Heilige* (The Idea of the Holy). The book's first edition—it would go through many in short order and become the most widely read work of theology in interwar Germany—appeared in 1917, just a few years before Barth's *Romans* sacked Weimar. Barth greeted the work with enthusiasm: though Otto's approach did not loose itself from Schleiermacher's stress on the experience of the divine, it did at least displace the source of that experience from the self (man) to the unknown or intuited object (God). Otto's notion of the self "has a psychological orientation," Barth wrote in criticism to a friend. But Barth appreciated those moments in which Otto's notion of religious man "points clearly across the border into the beyond with its moments of the 'numinous' which is not to be rationally conceived since it is 'wholly other,' the divine, in God." In this, Barth found "considerable delight." It presaged the turn Barth himself had made, and signaled, as a holding pattern, the death throes of the old theological order.[5]

A few years later, in 1923, Strauss published a review of Otto's book in the journal *Der Jude*. By this time the irruptions of Barth's language had become patently obvious. Strauss rehearsed Barth's take on the present task of theology: if in a premodern world "filled with the irrationality of religion" theology had to insist upon the rational aspects of religious experience, then in a modern world, one whose "spiritual reality" had its master in ratiocination, theology ought to take up an oppositional tack and stress "the irrational in the idea of the divine," not incidentally the subtitle of Otto's book. "Then the first fact was God—today: world, man, religious experience."[6]

The time had come to reverse terms and return God to the fore. Strauss therefore expressed public appreciation for those same moments Barth had praised in a more private forum. The "great importance" of Otto's book inhered in the fact that it had made the "transcendence of the religious object the wholly natural point of departure of the investigation." Not human experience, but the fact of the transcendent and unknown God was to ground all speculation. Strauss had reservations about Otto, but even here he reproduced Barth's critique of the book: Otto's investigation had made a "thoroughgoing subjectivism" impossible, but more by accident than intention; Otto had made available a "deeper understanding of the meaning which 'transcendence' has in religious contexts," but again less by design than by chance. Barth went unnamed, and it is difficult to know if Strauss had him in mind. But Barth's absence would testify all the more to an important fact: Strauss not only invoked the interwar discourse of divine transcendence, but also had declared allegiance to its precepts (or at least, had instrumentally mobilized them). In its effects the review imported into a Jewish milieu the gospel of the alien God. By 1923, Strauss had encountered the modern Marcionites, and had made their arsenal his own.[7]

But what did this have to do with Jacboi? In his dissertation, Strauss wrote of Otto as an update to Jacobi, and precisely in those moods in which Otto had come closest to Barth. For example, Jacobi was thought to be one for whom the fact of God must come before knowledge of him. A consideration of the "reality of God," Strauss had Jacobi argue, must always precede the "question of God's 'transcendental place.' " In other words, the fact of God had to take pride of place over his position in Kant's epistemology, a scheme that threatened to reduce God to an idea produced by the mind. Strauss approved of all three—Jacobi, Otto, Barth—insofar as they opposed this reduction of God to the invention of human experience.[8]

Jacobi's sense for the priority of the divine to knowledge of him made it easy for Strauss to read him in light of his interwar contemporaries. So did Jacobi's coordinated stress on God's transcendence. Strauss claimed to discern the "justification of the transcendent reality of being" as the "foundational problem" of Jacobi's teachings.[9] Faith, Strauss understood Jacobi to argue, was best defined as "the act in which the transcendence of reality is grasped." The transcendence of God in particular is "not touched by the fact that 'God must be born in men.' " On the contrary, Strauss wrote: "God is not only 'in us,' he is at the very least just as much 'over us.' "[10] In all this, Strauss echoed Barth, who had described God's relation to Paul and to all mankind in precisely the same terms, and on the very first page of his commentary to *Romans*: God does not reside "within [Paul] but above him."[11] Jacobi did not share in Barth's disavowal of hope in God's providence, nor did he go as far as Barth in exiling the divine from creation. But he did go far enough for Johann Gottfried Herder, his contemporary, to chide him as his "dear extramundane personalist," as one, that is, who wrongfully insisted on an extra-worldly and voluntarist God.[12]

But why would divine transcendence and voluntarism require a defense at all? In Jacobi's own time, both Spinozist pantheism and Enlightenment deism offered alternatives to just such a Christian God. Of the two, the latter was the more accepted, but it was the former that comprised Germany's "secret religion," as Heine later put it. Jacobi's hostility to pantheism had much to do with the way it recast the relation between God and nature. Like the deists, Jacobi believed in a God "behind" nature. Jacobi did not profess allegiance to a gnostic God opposed to nature, but he did believe in an alien God, a God beyond nature (who could, unlike the deist watchmaker, nevertheless intervene *in* nature from afar). He believed also in a concealed God, in an "absolute spiritual principle," as Hans Blumenberg put it, "Who was endowed with the highest dignity by His hiddenness and His inaccessibility for man."[13] Jacobi insisted on the transcendence and the absence of the divine for the same reasons as Barth in Strauss's time—to protect the purity of the Godhead from the pollutions of man.

Like Barth, Jacobi needed to keep the divine infinite free from worldly finitude. It was, in fact, the question of the infinite around which revolved Jacobi's quarrel with Mendelssohn. Pantheism posed a challenge to Jacobi (and also to Barth), since from his perspective, it denied this infinity, God's primary attribute. Or rather, and worse, it wrested the infinite away from an extramundane God, and in a perverse turn, accorded it instead to his finite creation.[14] On Jacobi's view, the pantheist scheme could not in the end distinguish itself from atheism. If anything, pantheism committed the greater sin. The atheist who denies God in dogmatic terms does not rule out transcendence altogether. But the pantheist does, because he absorbs and quashes God's infinite transcendence in the limitless expanse of an infinite world. Only because the pantheist *preserves* divine infinity and relocates it in the world can he (or the invention of his overwrought critics) claim to erase transcendence from the spiritual universe. Far more than the atheist, the pantheist erases the beyond, and this neither Jacobi nor Barth could abide.[15]

On a different front, deism and the tenets of a "natural religion" available to all through the exercise of reason had accorded God his transcendence from the world, but tended to deny him the power to intervene in his creation. More than a century of speculation, from Newton to Voltaire to Mendelssohn, had culminated in short shrift for divine providence (or for that matter, divine wrath). Pantheism also challenged a voluntarist and personalist God. For the pantheist, God's action in or upon the world is at the same time and no different from action in or upon himself. Pantheism must have appeared as an attractive alternative to those who could not abide a capricious and voluntarist deity, but were at the same time dismayed by the disenchantment of the world that came with an overwrought sense for divine transcendence. Jacobi contested them both, both deism and pantheism, with a voluntarist God endowed with the capacity to intervene in his creation as a subject separate from it. Strauss described Jacobi's position in straightforward terms: not only transcendent, "God is [also] personal, an Ich." This Jacobi believed to be the case "even if there is [for God] no equivalent Du," no other with whom God might engage in dialogue as an equal.[16] Neither could the danger of making God in the image of man dissuade Jacobi from his preferred hypothesis. To be sure, "man must take care not to figure God's persona in terms of his own," as Strauss had Jacobi argue.

But the threat of idolatry, in this case self-worship, was nevertheless worth courting, so long as it helped defeat the more dangerous pantheist threat.

Strauss was not alone in his appreciation for Jacobi. David Baumgardt resurrected him also, and as a harbinger of the spirit of the age. Writing in 1933, Baumgardt crowned Jacobi the philosophical founder of an ethical standpoint that had resurfaced in his time with the "widest currency." In particular, Baumgardt discerned in Jacobi a precursor to Kierkegaard, whose tortured spirit the theologians of crisis had done much to summon up. Like Kierkegaard, Jacobi had stressed the "readiness to suffer." He held up a transcendent deity against the incursions of pantheism. The consolations of an ethical monism he contested with a dualism precipitous in its breach. Against the milquetoast ethics of "experiencing" the world he unfurled an ethics of world-overcoming. Above all, Jacobi eschewed the unchecked capacity of reason toward mastery in favor of an ethics based on the darkness of ignorance.[17] All these, Baumgardt stressed, had been revived in the heady theological and philosophical scene of his time. Baumgardt refused to name names, but the hallmarks of the age as he described it—metaphysical dualism, hostility to worldliness, a divine understood (or not) as wholly other—read like a Barthian catechism.

The parallels that Strauss and Baumgardt claimed to discern were not without foundation. A brief look at Jacobi's letters shows that for him the controversy centered on issues brought to the table in Strauss's own day by Franz Rosenzweig and Karl Barth. These were issues rather different from the "fate of reason," or concerns at least not exhausted by that appellation.[18] For Jacobi, the fate of reason had already been decided. Left to its own devices, it could lead only to a denial of a personal first cause of the world. Reason rightly used outlined the limits of its potency. In terms that adumbrated Barth's, Jacobi described it this way: "Anyone who does not attempt to explain the inexplicable, but simply to know the line of demarcation where the inexplicable begins, simply to recognize its presence: such a person, I think, has created within himself the maximum space for the harbouring of human truth."[19] On this view, as on Barth's, ignorance of the divine beyond knowledge of his otherness becomes the most that man can hope to attain.

Precisely this issue Strauss had addressed in his dissertation. As its title indicates, the dissertation purports to treat the problem of knowledge in Jacobi's teachings. But the title misleads. Insofar as it fails to specify the problem of knowledge as the problem of knowledge of God, it deflects attention from Jacobi's manifest concern: gnosis. In his exchange with Mendelssohn, Jacobi had followed Kant in disavowing the ontological proofs for the existence of God, providence, and the immortality of the soul. Such arguments led reason to affairs it could not justifiably address. If knowledge were understood as the grasp of an object in terms of its most proximate causes, then for Jacobi there could be no knowledge, strictly speaking, of God. If there was to be knowledge of God, the notion of knowledge itself would have to be transformed.[20] Knowledge arrived at by deduction or demonstration inevitably devolved, Jacobi thought, into nihilism, a term he coined to describe reason's effects, the solipsistic consequences of unchecked rational inquiry.

Spinoza represented only the most accomplished form of this process. His *Ethics* purported to prove with geometrical certainty the truth of his system, a system that left no "space" from which revelation might issue, and which pretended to an adequate knowledge of God cast also as a knowledge of self. Jacobi and, much later, the theologians of crisis spoke of a knowledge not attained, but imparted by a God understood as remote and radically other. Against demonstration, Jacobi and Barth spoke of receptivity; against logic, openness to an unwilled encounter with the divine; against reason, revelation.

The problem that vexed Strauss all his life—the relation between Athens and Jerusalem, reason and revelation—*he first explored here*, in the context of the pantheism controversy young and old. To be sure, Strauss and Jacobi arrived at different solutions. Jacobi worried that reason refuted faith, and therefore rejected reason. Strauss would disengage reason from revelation, leaving each to its own. This did not keep him from declaring allegiance to one of its terms, the one Jacobi had rejected: philosophy. But he would justify his option for philosophy by appeal to that which he learned in his encounter with Jacobi and the theologians of crisis: above all an appreciation for divine transcendence, revelation, and a deep suspicion about the penchant to reduce God (and world) to a mere experience of man. He would simply put these ideas to different use.

SPINOZA

Strauss soon had occasion to apply these lessons against the object of Jacobi's ire and the touchstone of the pantheism controversy itself: Baruch Spinoza. In 1922, Strauss later recalled, he found himself compelled to reexamine the resurgence of theology, which he associated with Barth and Rosenzweig. Theirs was not an identical reproduction of a position once lost. It was a selective recovery, which Strauss later claimed to recognize as a "profound innovation."[21] Still, a way of life once rejected had become again both "possible and necessary." This was especially the case for Judaism. Jewish neo-orthodoxy as imagined by

Rosenzweig appeared not only as a raft for the Jew lost and adrift in a non-Jewish sea, but also, Strauss thought, as the "only course compatible with sheer consistency or intellectual probity." Rosenzweig's own return may have had its origin in an epiphany on one momentous Yom Kippur. Strauss nonetheless thought it a course of action justified by more than one man's most intimate and incommunicable experience. Not a leap of faith, or not exclusively so, the move had just as compelling a ground in the cold and impersonal workings of reason.

Yet even the most resolute (or rational) of returns could not banish a presentiment of troubles ahead. "Vague difficulties remained" for the *ba'al teshuva*, Strauss recollected in 1962, "like small faraway clouds on a beautiful summer sky." These clouds gathered themselves up into a storm with an alacrity that belied their apparently benign appearance. As Strauss recalled it, the innocuous white puffs of mist "soon took the [more ominous] shape of Spinoza." This was no atmospheric accident, no chaotic flap of the butterfly's wings. As the greatest man of Jewish origin who had not merely left the fold but declined all other alternatives, Spinoza had created the problem to which Rosenzweig appeared as a response. Strauss understood Spinoza's rebirth to mean that this response would not go uncontested. "Orthodoxy," and by this Strauss meant Judaism prior to Mendelssohn and, with some qualifications, after Rosenzweig, "could be returned to only if Spinoza were wrong in every respect."[22]

Some thought Strauss set out to show precisely that. The *Detroit Jewish News*, for example, ran the screaming headline "Strauss Demolishes View of Controversy with Maimonides and Shows How Renegade Spinoza Denigrated Judaism" upon the English publication of his book.[23] Strauss did undertake a critique of Spinoza, but one more circumspect than the headlines implied. Strauss dedicated *Die Religionskritik Spinozas* to Rosenzweig's memory, and for good reason. The work apparently represented an effort on Strauss's part to continue the fight begun by his friend. Strauss resolved, it would seem, to take up the cudgels of orthodoxy dropped by Rosenzweig as he succumbed to the ravages of illness (a bitter irony given Rosenzweig's attempt to heal those well-intentioned seekers paralyzed by philosophical hairsplitting, paralyzed perhaps by the *more geometrico* Spinoza made so famous). Strauss had sown the seeds of this project with a guarded appreciation for Jacobi's notion of the divine. These seeds now took root and flowered. They bloomed into a partial defense of Jewish neo-orthodoxy against orthodoxy's most implacable opponent. In the end, to defend Rosenzweig against Spinoza meant to defend the claims of divine transcendence and revelation. It meant to affiliate with Jacobi, two centuries before, and in his own era, with Barth. But it also meant to defend philosophy against them all.

This double defense played out on several fronts. First and foremost, Strauss inserted Spinoza into a tradition of religious critique identified with Epicurus. If antiquarian on the face of it, the move nonetheless spoke to the most burning theological-political issues of the day. To make of Spinoza an epicurean, in spirit if not in fact, was to cast him also as the most potent eradicator of the gnostic spirit as defined by Barth and his followers. Second, Strauss buttressed Rosenzweig's qualified defense of miracles. Neither was this as odd as it may sound. The discourse of the miracle flourished in interwar Europe, and served as conduit for discussion on the topics—God's transcendence and providence, his distinction from the natural—brought to the table by the theologians of crisis on the one hand, by the Spinozist champions of *deus sive natura* on the other. Third and finally, Strauss developed here for the first time an argument he would rehearse again and again: that the claims of revelation and reason were both mutually exclusive and philosophically undecidable.[24] Strauss had much invested in the claim. Only so could both Rosenzweig *and* Spinoza emerge from battle, if not victorious, then at least unvanquished. And only so could Strauss defeat the Jewish idolaters who had made of Spinoza their God.

To call Spinoza an epicurean may sound innocuous on its face. But the label is in fact an instance of sharpest polemic. That is because the name of the Greek atomist has endured among Jews for two thousand years as a stand-in for heresy more generally. Even if Epicurus himself had little, if anything at all, to do with Judaism, his name was inscribed in the term *apikorus*, one of the Hebrew words for heretic, and in a label for heresy itself, *apikorsut*. The Greek origins of the term receded into the dim haze of forgetfulness; the rabbis, and Maimonides after them, thought it derived from an Aramaic word, *hefker*, used to signify abandonment. Against the *min* (or sectarian, an acronym for *ma'aminei yeshu ha-nozri*, "believers in Jesus of Nazareth"), the disbeliever and the apostate, Maimonides granted the *apikorus* a more precise definition: as one who denies prophecy, and with it, the possibility of communication between man and God, as one who disavows revelation (or the prophecy of Moses), or as one who declares God ignorant of man's deeds.[25]

Spinoza's was an easy case to adjudicate. He qualified under all three. But Strauss began with the spirit of the last, by inserting Spinoza into a tradition of religious critique designed above all to rid man of fear—fear of the intervention of the gods, whether arbitrary or appropriate, malicious or justified. Epicurus had set out in a series of propositions a scientific theory that could account in natural terms for the sort of events—earthquakes, thunderbolts, floods—otherwise attributed to the caprice of the gods, to their unpredictable malevolence toward man. "That is the very intent and meaning of science," Strauss observed. "Were we not harassed by apprehensions regarding Olympus and death, there would be no need for a science of physics." Epicurus replaced gods liable to intervene in the world with gods indifferent to its human inhabitants. Meanwhile, his atomist physics ascribed a consistency to nature that made recourse to supernatural explanations superfluous. "A soothing regularity and necessity" had to prevail. Science, then, served deeper needs: to defeat fear of the divine required a hedonist ethics whose only standard was pleasure, and whose only goal, happiness (eudaimonia).[26]

It is easy to see how Spinoza could be understood to continue the epicurean tradition. He too had set out a system in propositional style, the *Ethics*, designed to account for the cosmos and man's place in it without recourse to an inscrutable and supernatural will. He too had posited a kind of necessity that did not deny human freedom so much as redefine it. He too could be understood as the founder of an ethical hedonism—not only could, but was, in interwar Europe, by the German-Jewish philosopher David Baumgardt. Spinoza, however, did not take issue with the gods of Greek mythology. He contested the biblical God of creation and revelation. Nor did he undertake his critique in the name of freedom from fear. He undertook it, if surreptitiously, in the name of the freedom to philosophize. Strauss therefore had to exert considerable effort to justify the parallel. Strauss believed the epicurean critique could endure in an era in which biblical fear had replaced pagan fear only because it overlooked the distinction between a genuine (biblical) and a superstitious (pagan) fear of God. The critique therefore endured, but only by dismissing the true character of its object. Its motive had also transformed. Epicurus waged war against religion by means of theory; his modern successors waged war against revealed religion for the sake of theory. Nonetheless, Strauss thought it justified to shelter Spinoza in the epicurean camp.

Strauss's investment in the argument becomes intelligible when we consider the figure Epicurus must have cut on the interwar scene. The epicurean motives spoke directly to interwar theological debates, especially the ones of concern to Strauss. Epicurus might well have agreed with Karl Barth that religion is "an abyss." He might well have agreed that religion is "terror."[27] Religion as Barth described it had made dubious the prospect of God's providence (even if Barth never stressed the occasional corollary—the likelihood of his malice). But Barth's was precisely the sort of hellfire that the epicurean temper hoped to snuff. To ascribe this temper to Spinoza made of him, in the interwar context, an antidote to the peddlers of theological fright.

The apathy of the epicurean gods had a corollary. It meant also to abandon what Rosenzweig (following Goethe) identified as the "favorite child of belief," a child who had since lost its birthright. This child was the miracle. "For at least a hundred years," Rosenzweig wrote in 1921, "the child has been nothing but a source of embarrassment to the nurse which [his father] had ordered for it—to theology. She would have gladly been rid of it if only—well, if only a degree of consideration for the father had not forbidden it during his lifetime." But such consideration had its limits, and was anyway soon to fall prey to the poisons of unchecked resentment, since "the old man cannot live forever." And with his death, theology "will know what she must do with this poor little worm which can neither live nor die under its own power." Indeed, "she has already made the preparations."[28] The miracle—theology's little worm—was soon to meet its quick and messy end.

In retrospect, Rosenzweig's concern for the invertebrates of the theological kingdom seems misplaced, or at least premature. For the miracle made a remarkable comeback in interwar Europe, and from the very brink of extinction. If it did not regain its former status as theology's "most effective and reliable confederate," it at least did not go the way of other theological dinosaurs like the animal sacrifice, known for two thousand years to the Judeo-Christian tradition in fossil form only. By contrast, the miracle served as conduit for a panoply of controversies, theological and otherwise, and its survival was in this sense overdetermined.[29]

Strauss did not believe in the miracles of the Bible. Neither, he thought, did Rosenzweig. But that was not the issue. What mattered was the modern possibility of their experience. This was the question posed by Rosenzweig in the *Star*, and it was the question that Strauss, following him, had Spinoza ask of Maimonides (in *Spinoza's Critique*). Historically the miracle had been taken as a sign, as proof, if not of God's providence then at least of his agency. But could it compel belief in those who lacked it? For Strauss the answer was clear. It could not. But neither could the philosopher, in this case Spinoza, compel unbelief in the believer. Spinoza's efforts to prove the impossibility of miracles ended in failure. His critique had been predestined to defeat, since, as Strauss concluded, "miracles are not recognizable as such by the truly unbelieving mind which does not openly assume—or surreptitiously smuggle in—an element of faith." Faith and philosophy shared no common ground upon which to decide the question. The most that could be said: that miracles occur for a mind incapable of scientific inquiry and unfamiliar with the experience that comes with it. So, Strauss argued, "it is not the advancing positive method, proceeding from point to point, but only the reflection of the positive mind on itself, the recognition by the positive mind that it represents a progress . . . which creates a position impregnable to proof by miracles."[30] The critique had therefore lost (or won) before it had even begun. It was a blind and affirmative story of origins.

But this did not mean that the proponents of miracles had emerged victorious. Spinoza's defeat was not total. On the contrary: the upshot was that miracles might well confirm faith, but could not establish it. Miracles might convince idolators. The idolator, after all, admits divine action upon the world from beyond it. But the preternatural light of the miracle, which so animates the man of faith, reflects not at all in the dark and uncomprehending eyes of the atheist. Nor does it flicker in the eyes of the pantheist, the proponent of *deus sive natura*, for whom *all* of nature is infused with the godly. Idolators may fear and tremble. But atheists, pantheists—and philosophers—do not. Fright is only for those who have always already feared. Only the congenitally weak-kneed need tremble.

Strauss derived this talk of philosophy and theology in part from Rosenzweig, who had invoked their relation in his discussion of the miracle. But Strauss departed from Rosenzweig's position in important respects, and in ways that attest to the twofold nature of his intervention. What Strauss described as two incommensurable systems, Rosenzweig cast as newly complementary languages. Strauss had set out to separate what Rosenzweig had hoped to join in symbiosis. Where Strauss spoke of mutual exclusivity, Rosenzweig spoke of "reciprocal need." Rosenzweig was frank about the dangers precipitated by this rapprochement. Philosophy might be reduced to theology's handmaiden. On the other hand, it might also make theology superfluous. How, then, to relieve the mutual distrust and ensure a workable marriage? "Hardly otherwise," he answered, "than by demonstrating that both sides need something which in each case only the other party can supply." This was, he added, "after all really the case," and Rosenzweig welcomed the prospect. "The theologian whom philosophy requires for the sake of its scientific status is himself a theologian who requires philosophy—for the sake of his integrity. What was for philosophy a demand in the interests of objectivity, will turn out to be a demand in the interests of subjectivity for theology. They are dependent on each other and so generate jointly a new type, be it philosopher or theologian, situated between theology and philosophy."[31]

Rosenzweig went further. He located in their interdependence what Strauss secured in their separation: the possibility of experiencing miracles.[32] For Strauss, by contrast, all hope for agreement on the miracle foundered on the rocks of incommensurability: reason versus revelation, Athens against Jerusalem. The opposition arises not only with respect to theology's little worm; it is the singular theme of *Spinoza's Critique*. Their differences derive in part from the historical status of their investigations, or from the status of the historical within them. Like Strauss, Rosenzweig took aim at an Enlightenment position that compromised the status of the miracle as a sign of providence and as creation's redeemed promise.

Rosenzweig could envision in his time—indeed, expected—circumstances that would restore to the miracle its due. By contrast, Strauss usually left the historical foundations of his analysis behind. What began as a historical observation of Enlightenment failures lost its historicity, and devolved instead into ahistorical—and for that reason immensely powerful—pronouncements on the relation between reason and faith. For example: "Before philosophizing can even be begun, belief in revelation, which calls trust in human reason into question, must itself first be questioned. In this sense the critique of revealed religion is not the achievement, but the very basis of free science." Or: "For reason, no proof can be adduced that a miracle has occurred." Or again: "Theology, which has its basis in the Scriptures, and philosophy are in their bases and in their aims entirely different, so different that there is no transition and bridge from one to the other."[33] Strauss insisted on an absolutism of difference that Rosenzweig did not. But why?

He did so to nip in the bud the challenge exemplified by the pantheist language of heresy. Consider for a moment its threat. To insist as Strauss did on the nonrelational difference of philosophy and theology made the fact of heresy incoherent. Here is Strauss: "From the attitude of obedience, rebellion can never arise. Every rebellion presupposes readiness and capacity for rebellion, liberty to reject Scripture, 'as we reject the Koran and the Talmud [as Spinoza put it],' hence rebellion itself. There is no gradual transition in this. Apostasy as such is not to be justified. Therefore it is of no account which particular grounds Spinoza adduces for his own apostasy."[34] The orthodox and the heterodox lack common ground by which to make sense of their difference. To commit apostasy is to have always rebelled.

But it then becomes difficult to account for heresy's historical fact. It becomes difficult to account for the move from piety to sacrilege, from disciple to renegade, let alone for the persistent renewal of this itinerary in the heretic's own recollection. Precisely this problem produced Strauss's most emphatic—and problematic—pronouncements on Spinoza's Judaism. Strauss did not deny the fact of Spinoza's Jewish origins. He did not dispute it here, in his book of 1930, nor did he do so in his essay of 1932, on Spinoza's last will and testament. He admitted the fact of the philosopher's Jewish origins, but promptly moved to discount it:

Spinoza was born and brought up as a Jew. However matters may stand with the cogency of the critique by means of which he justifies his apostasy from Judaism, the result, at the least the result, is the radical and continuing distance from Judaism. The actual distance from Judaism creates an entirely new situation for the critique. It is no longer needful for Spinoza to justify his apostasy from Judaism before the tribunal of Judaism. On the contrary, he requires of Judaism that it should justify itself before the tribunal of reason, of humanity. . . . What is demanded is the positive justification of Judaism on grounds that are external to Judaism, and before a judge who, perhaps devoid of hatred, certainly devoid of love, tests with inexorable severity the arguments advanced—with "a free mind."

The philosopher stands beyond it all. His heresy is by far the most radical, for his is a heresy *beyond* heresy. It transcends itself and so leaves its lowly origins behind.[35]

Strauss had in effect followed Barth's language of division, but in a way Barth had neither envisioned nor desired. Barth threw in his lot with revelation, and with it reduced theology to a protracted statement on human ignorance of the divine. Strauss intuited that the move with which Barth and Gogarten had secured revelation and divine transcendence could secure the possibility of philosophy as well.[36] As he put it in a letter to Gerhard Krüger, "My [Spinoza] book [was] a single *answer* [from the perspective of] unbelief to the belief of the Barth-Gogarten tradition, *at least in its intent*."[37] The remark is important: it alerts us to what Strauss himself thought at stake. With God absented from the world, man might go about his philosophical business unperturbed by the threat of divine intervention. Jonas had argued in a similar vein: natural science in the tradition of Francis Bacon owed its victory to God's absence. Strauss also embraced God's absence—not on behalf of natural science and the ethos of human self-assertion underwriting it, but on behalf of philosophy and the *limits* on human self-assertion his understanding of it implied. In other words, Strauss's philosophical project had its origins in precisely those theological debates that provoked Jonas to a philosophy of life. But the Straussian revival came in the form of a search for a natural standard—not divine, and not (or not first) human—by which to measure the rightfulness of human action.

MENDELSSOHN

If theological in origin, however, Strauss's project was flatly heathen in intent. The authority of nature ought not, on Strauss's view, derive in any way from God. This was the predicament bequeathed to the modern world by Spinoza and Hobbes. To pave the way for the revival of natural right, Strauss therefore had first to put an end to the fiction of a theological-philosophical rapprochement. He did so first with a qualified embrace of Jacobi, second with an attack on the Jewish Spinozists of his age. He did so finally by considering the arguments of Moses

Mendelssohn, the last of the personalities at issue in the pantheism controversy of old, in an essay on Mendelssohn's contributions to the debate.[38]

The essay has received little attention.[39] That is a shame, since it reveals much about the way Strauss's commitments had developed over the most formative years of his career. The piece concludes a span in which Strauss encountered the pantheism controversy, resurrected it, internalized and applied its lessons. All the themes of *Spinoza's Critique*—an updated epicureanism, the autonomy of the philosopher, the (non)relation of reason and faith—surface in this essay also, but with one crucial difference: Strauss could here assume vindicated the positions he had earlier to justify. The piece also says much about Strauss's approach to modern Judaism, not to mention the theological-political problem of interwar Europe. Strauss rejected in the end the Jew who did most to balance the claims of reason and revelation. He did so even as he embraced Jacobi, the Christian whose insistence on their irreconcilable difference Strauss had come to share.

The pantheism controversy was to be won or lost on the plausibility of a "purified" or "refined" Spinozism. Mendelssohn had ascribed this position to his friend Lessing. The move was a defense, designed to protect his deceased friend from the taint of Spinozism in the wake of Jacobi's revelations. But what did it mean to Mendelssohn to be a Spinozist in the first place? In the context of the controversy, it meant either to reject or to affirm a world outside and independent of God. It therefore invoked the question of pantheism—whether it was not in fact acosmism—in its most acute and basic form.

Mendelssohn had taken up this question nearly thirty years before Jacobi's attack. In one of his earliest works, his *Philosophische Gespräche* (1755), he had come to the defense of the philosopher Gottfried Wilhelm Leibniz, who affirmed such a world, against Spinoza, who, it seemed, did not. Mendelssohn argued in the tradition of the "theological Wolffians," followers of a man who had mobilized Leibnizian philosophy in the service of a supra-confessional theology at once rational and natural, and with the intent to ground rather than contest revealed religion.[40] Mendelssohn therefore belittled Spinoza's system as absurd and declared his principles distasteful.

But he had also undertaken a partial rehabilitation of Spinoza. Leibniz had argued for a kind of twofold creation: the world was at first only one of many possible ones within God's mind, and was only then preferred and made real because best. On Mendelssohn's reading, Spinoza affirmed the first of these (if only in part). But Spinoza could not follow through to its Leibnizian completion, since he refused to acknowledge a world outside and independent of God. The upshot of all this was a Spinoza understood as a necessary precursor to a theism developed fully by Leibniz. This true bequest of his to Western thought had gone unrecognized, and Mendelssohn considered it his sacred honor, in 1755, to rectify the matter. Spinoza's was a "sacrifice for the sake of the human mind; a sacrifice, however, that deserves to be adorned with flowers." Mendelssohn therefore bemoaned Spinoza's ill fortune, suffered at the hands of hostile interpreters: "How unjust is the implacable hatred of the learned towards such a hapless one!"[41]

Mendelssohn came to rue those words. But he did not disavow the reasoning that led him to pen them. It reappeared almost verbatim in his conflict with Jacobi, but ascribed by him to *Lessing*, not Spinoza. Lessing, Mendelssohn wrote, affirmed the "intra-deical world" which the theist also was compelled to admit; he failed only to recognize that world as independent of God.[42] Lessing's refined Spinozism, what Mendelssohn had earlier identified as Spinozism plain and simple, was marginally compatible with a theism that posited a breach between a transcendent god and a worldly world. To distinguish Lessing's position from Spinoza's, then, required less the invention of a purified pantheism than it did the invention of a new and radicalized Spinoza.

So proceeded Mendelssohn's defense of Lessing from Jacobi's putative slander. But Mendelssohn himself could not endorse the position, which had its ground in the absence of a criterion by which to distinguish a thing from its godly intellection. Whether or not—and how—to guarantee the independence and autonomy of the world from God, the sovereign "thinginess" of things, thus arose as one of the fundamental points of dispute. From Jacobi's perspective, the need was superfluous, grounded as it was on the assumption that pantheism superseded Spinoza's thought, was hence autonomous and open to "purification." Spinozism contained pantheism, but the converse did not necessarily hold. Spinozism was both "the exhaustion of a possibility and a blind alley." Jacobi's polemic against Mendelssohn meant to demonstrate precisely this irretrievable obsolescence of the Spinozist position.[43] If correct, Spinozism was beyond repair, a purified version of it not only implausible but also impossible.

As in so many other aspects of the controversy, Jacobi's remonstrations elicited the opposite of their intended effect. To ascribe to Lessing pantheist inclinations did less to delegitimize him than to make them palatable to the leading lights of German letters, and to declare Spinoza a dead end only inspired those same luminaries to prove Jacobi wrong. This they did, whether in Schelling's *Naturphilosophie*, Herder's theory of the organism, Goethe's so-called *herrlich-leuchtende Natur* (roughly, "brilliantly illuminating nature"), or Hegel's philosophical system. Still, in all this Mendelssohn shared much with Jacobi, his erstwhile adversary.

Both, after all, hoped to save divine transcendence along with worldly immanence, the both of them threatened by the pantheist equation *deus sive natura*. But they differed, for one, on the question of means. Jacobi favored a leap of faith, Mendelssohn the form of reason associated with common sense, a *gesunder Menschenverstand*. They differed also on the possibility of the sort of intermediate position ascribed by Mendelssohn to Lessing. This was not only because Jacobi understood Spinoza as the be-all and end-all of reason, as an incarnation of the nihilism that follows necessarily from unchecked rational inquiry, but also, if not primarily, because he understood faith and reason as a necessary opposition—"reason is proud, and faith is humble"—while Mendelssohn believed them, at worst, only contingently opposed, and at best, fundamentally in accord. This last made Jacobi's position, for all its inconsistencies and occasional incoherence, more palatable to Strauss, given his conclusions in *Spinoza's Critique*, than the arguments of his own coreligionist. Strauss in effect ushered out the era of German-Jewish history inaugurated by Mendelssohn, and he did so by resurrecting those arguments that Mendelssohn had done so much to defeat, and which in the end had sent him, exhausted, to his grave.

The way in which Strauss adjudicated their claims reveals much. Mendelssohn came out the worse for it in nearly every respect, the brunt of criticism both for those moods he shared with Spinoza and for those he did not. To begin, Strauss located in Mendelssohn's interventions an epicurean motive much like the one he had earlier identified in Spinoza. Like Spinoza, Mendelssohn had hoped systematically to defeat the terror of the hidden god. Like Spinoza, he had thrown in his lot with modern, as opposed to ancient, metaphysics not least on account of its revaluation of worldliness in the face of a threat from beyond. As Mendelssohn understood and appropriated it, modern metaphysics "fulfilled itself insofar as it eliminated for man the fear of divine wrath and of death." But Mendelssohn's position had to appear suspect to one who broached such questions in a lexicon derived above all from Barth. True to form, Strauss abruptly dismissed it, without explanation, as blind to the "inner questionableness" of what Mendelssohn himself had admitted to be, in a letter to a friend, his own "rather epicurean theism."[44]

Mendelssohn shared with Spinoza not only the epicurean motive, but also, for a time, its means: the conceit of philosophical demonstration. Mendelssohn had, of course, deployed the tools of his trade to shore up belief in a transcendent God, rather than to undermine it. He hoped to ensure the tranquility of the soul, threatened as it was by the "fright of superstition" on one side, the "despair of unbelief" on the other, by carving out a middle ground that would preserve God's transcendence and, as a corollary, the autonomy and independence of man from the divine. He had first hoped to do all this by dint of reason. His invocation of "common sense" thus signaled a partial defeat, for it counted as a retreat from the stricter rationality of his original stance. For Strauss, Mendelssohn's tacit recognition that the attempt to ground faith "by means of faithless speculation" had foundered only confirmed the conclusions he had reached already in *Spinoza's Critique*. The language of incommensurability had ensured Spinoza's failure, to compel unbelief by means of philosophy. So too, Strauss thought, did it ensure the failure of Mendelssohn's attempted reversal, to defend revealed religion, or revealed legislation, out of the sources of reason.[45]

Mendelssohn's position Strauss characterized as beyond repair. But not Jacobi's. Strauss sided squarely with Jacobi on the question of Lessing's "purified" Spinozism. He in fact concluded ninety pages of analysis with precisely that point: "If Lessing had indeed undertaken a transformation of Spinozism, his intent was certainly not to 'purify' or 'refine' it, or, to adopt an expression which Lessing himself had used in a related context, to satisfy oneself 'with a pleasant aspect,' by means of which one could deflect 'all suspicion of freethinking.' If Jacobi was at all moved by Lessing's spirit, so it was surely in his critique of the conception of a 'purified' Spinozism. The lines which he devotes to this concept . . . would have, perhaps, not put to shame even Lessing himself." Strauss dismissed the possibility, or at least the fact, of a purified Spinozism, which from his point of view, like Jacobi's, was less a purification than an adulteration of a completed system. Mendelssohn's imputation to Lessing of a purified pantheism Strauss wrote off as chicanery, impelled not by a burning need for truth, but by shame.[46]

Strauss ripped Mendelssohn in two, the productive tension of his scheme resolved toward its poles. In the end Strauss found more compelling *both* of the competing heretical alternatives to Mendelssohnian moderation than Mendelssohn himself: both gnosticism and Spinozism. He had adapted from the language of interwar gnosticism much of his intellectual arsenal. And Spinoza, whatever his deficiencies, had at least sought in no way to reconcile revelation with reason, religion with philosophy. If predicated on God's absence, however, Strauss's option for philosophy did not preclude a reenchantment of the world. It meant only that the reenchantment would have to proceed by different means. It would have to do without the divine and derive from the philosophical tradition itself. He had already attempted to do precisely that, in his Spinoza book, as he noted to Gerhard Krüger. But Strauss failed in his first effort, hindered as he later put it by a deficient prose style. In the early 1930s he decided to try again.

CHAPTER SEVEN

From God to Nature

THE PANTHEISM controversy of the late eighteenth century resolved itself in several ways. One was in renewed appreciation for the category of the organism, and with it, the notion of teleology applied to the natural world. This was the achievement of Johann Gottfried Herder. Herder's creative misreading of Spinoza's *Ethics* was one of the first to give the lie to Jacobi's dictum that Spinozism represented the dead end of unchecked, reasoned human inquiry. Herder did not throw in his lot with the apparent mechanism of Spinoza's scheme. Nor did he share in its atheism and fatalism, estimations at any rate adopted preeminently by Spinoza's critics. For Herder, Spinoza had erected not a materialist or mechanist universe, but a vitalist one. Neither matter nor machine, the cosmos was instead a self-animating version of both: the cosmos as organism. As with Jonas, the category of organism dovetailed with the notion that an immanent purpose, or set of them, suffuses the natural world. In Herder's case, this affinity followed from the holism implicit in Spinoza's notion of substance, understood as nature's active, creative force and endowed with an intrinsic or immanent infinity.[1] The pantheism controversy of the early twentieth century also had its denouement, or one of them, in the recovery of a teleological notion of nature. It went by an ancient name, physis, and found its champion in Leo Strauss.[2]

Such language brings Hans Jonas to mind. Jonas, after all, rehabilitated this notion of nature to contest the revival of gnostic and Pauline theology in the interwar period. It was Strauss who first pointed out to Jonas, in 1958, the hidden implications that made a single project of his diverse investigations—early studies of Paul and the gnostics, followed by a philosophical biology, an environmental ethics, and writings in post-Holocaust theology. Gnosticism had presented the most radical challenge in Western history to the Greek notion of physis, Strauss argued, and he claimed to discover in Jonas a concerted attempt to save it. This diagnosis was something of a habit for Strauss. Two years later he identified similar motives, if unarticulated, in the work of Gershom Scholem, whose meditations on religious nihilism he thought a covert and inverted restoration of the category. It was in his letter to Jonas, however, that Strauss pointed to the task at hand: "Our problem now is to recover physis."[3]

The plural possessive was no slip of the tongue. Strauss could recognize the hidden implications of Jonas's work because he had embarked upon, and by 1958 largely completed, his own revival of the idea for the needs of the twentieth century. His recovery came to fruition in his masterpiece, *Natural Right and History*, published in 1953. There he expressed his desire to revive a classic doctrine of natural right "connected with a teleological view of the universe." There Strauss affirmed—if with some modifications—its basic conviction, that "all natural beings have a natural end, a natural destiny, which determines what kind of operation is good for them." But the Straussian renewal proceeded by different means and had a decidedly dissimilar end. For Jonas, the revival of physis took the form of a philosophical biology in a spirit at once indebted and opposed to Heidegger, and its aftereffects came in the form of the German Greens. For Strauss, it came in the avowedly political guise of natural right—the belief in a natural realm of justice prior to law, or beyond it. It also helped inspire a sort of politics—American neoconservatism—rather different from the one that found retrospective sanction in the thought of Jonas. Behind and beyond their apparent diversity there nonetheless remains the fact of their shared theological parentage. Both were born of an interwar encounter with the gnostic challenge writ large.

This challenge explains both the fact and fashion of a determined shift in Strauss's thought as he left the pantheism controversy behind. Strauss's early work was animated by the opposition of orthodoxy and Enlightenment. He encountered it first in Jacobi, then in Spinoza, and finally brought his conclusions to bear on Mendelssohn. But by the 1950s, the distinction between reason and revelation had given way to another: between nomos and physis, or as Strauss put it in *Natural Right*, between convention, human convention above all, and nature. The question of nature had displaced the question of God, and it is an account of this transition or transformation that just might cure Strauss of the schizophrenia—Jew or Greek, Greek or Jew—to which warring interpretations have consigned him.

Hobbes: Nature, Art, and Liberalism

The moment of the shift is easy to specify. It commenced in the early 1930s, a time that found Strauss stationed alternatively in Berlin, Paris, and London. His work from the period asked above all after two giants in the history of philosophy, Moses Maimonides and Thomas Hobbes. Both investigations, however, concerned at heart a single question: the source of authority for the right way of life when neither God nor nature can provide.

Hobbes first. Strauss published a book about Hobbes in 1936, the fruit of several years of archival inquiry, a series of essays (among them one on Carl Schmitt), and an unpublished German manuscript.[4] Ostensibly, Strauss sought to decouple the moral foundations of Hobbesian thought from the natural-scientific accretions of its method. This in itself is noteworthy: Strauss hoped to "save" Hobbes from a natural-scientific tradition he had embraced, but which Strauss, centuries later, would identify as complicit with a form of human self-assertion run amok. But Strauss in fact spoke to a more fundamental—and acutely modern—crisis. Strauss put it this way in his book: "Since there is no superhuman order which binds man from the beginning, since man has no set place in the universe, but has to make one for himself, he can extend the limits of his power at will."[5] Hobbes had in fact done much to create this predicament. His critique of revelation made God unavailable as a source for political authority. His critique of traditional concepts of natural right did the same for the ancient Greek notion of the cosmos and of man's position within it. In their place Hobbes substituted the authority of man alone. Only human artifice, he thought, could provide a measure of certainty in a world that had little to none.

Strauss's interpretation has much to recommend it. *Leviathan*, after all, commences with a sharp attack on man's capacity to know the world in which he lives. It opens by describing an epistemological crisis, and arrives at questions of politics—its putative subject—only after it has demonstrated the futility of an appeal to knowledge authorized either by God (through revelation) or by nature (positively construed). Hobbes did so for a reason: the civil strife that rocked seventeenth-century England was unleashed by partisans for whom these views were paramount. Puritans hostile to official creed invoked divine "inspiration" and a claim to grace to justify their violent opposition to the crown. Others fomented disobedience on the strength of a classical republican argument that revived ancient Greek ideas about the relation of nature and politics. The republican city-state was natural, this reasoning went, and man ought so to live in freedom. Hobbes proposed this understanding of the theological-political predicament of his time the better to set the stage for his solution: the Leviathan, an absolute state understood at once as "artificial creature" and "mortall God." Man, in other words, would have to arrogate to himself the power that once flowed either from divine revelation or from a cosmology that specified the natural and right way for man to live. As Strauss put it in an unpublished manuscript, in a passage he underlined for emphasis: "Hobbes begins not with the question of the [natural] order or the [divine] law, because he denies the very existence of an order or a law that precedes human will."[6]

The priority Hobbes granted to human will had a consequence: Hobbes unleashed human artifice from the constraints that had bound it. In particular, Hobbes struck a death blow to a notion of nature understood as a model commanding human imitation, and so nature lost its character as archetype. Artifice changed, too. No longer a mimetic reproduction or cultivation of an order prior to man, it was instead understood as "sovereign invention."[7] The knowledge of the artificer was once understood in altogether different terms, and it was this sort of knowledge Strauss aimed to save: "For the originators of the tradition, for Socrates-Plato, the knowledge that comprises the standard for the artist involves a looking-beyond-at-something, namely to a form, an *order* that the artist wishes to produce. And the knowledge of the artist is on this view excellent, because real knowledge is the recognition of the form or the order through which and on whose behalf every thing is what it is."[8] For Hobbes, every possible human orientation in the world had its foundation in human artifice, since what man made was all he might conclusively know. But for Strauss and the tradition he aimed to revive, true knowledge took as its object not nomos or human convention, but physis, its natural model and precursor.

Strauss discovered in Hobbes much of what Jonas and Blumenberg had discovered in Bacon. Both Hobbes and Bacon lionized a spirit of human self-assertion, and notwithstanding important differences, both did so in part by privileging a natural-scientific approach to nature that emphasized technical control and exploitation over reverence, wonder, and awe. Jonas had drawn attention to the way in which the gnostic spirit of interwar Europe had abetted a natural-scientific ethos—Bacon's bequest—that devalued nature and called for its overcoming. Strauss argued likewise, but in reference to Hobbes. He stipulated that the Hobbesian recasting of the relation between art and nature was prepared first and foremost by his critique of revelation.[9] The effect of that critique had not been to deny God, but as the latter-day gnostics had done, to distance him irretrievably from those who would claim to hear his call. What the pious heard was not God, Hobbes insisted, but man. God may not have been silenced. But Hobbes made it plain that man did not have the ears to hear him. In other words, Hobbes offered for Strauss something of what Bacon had for Jonas: a means by which to grapple with both the neo-gnostic spirit of the day as well as the crisis of human self-assertion with which it was complicit.

But Hobbes offered something more. Not only had he unbound human artifice. He did so in the service of a political program—as Strauss saw it, in the service of what became modern, liberal civilization. To contest his recasting of the relation between art and nature meant also to contest his political and civilizational bequest. It was *the* philosophical means by which to do so. It was also a matter of pressing concern. The interwar origins of this stance are made plain in Strauss's comments on Carl Schmitt, who had done much to revive Hobbes for the needs of the twentieth century. In 1927 (and again in 1932), Schmitt published *The Concept of the Political*. The book aimed to recover the existential stakes of political life obscured by the liberal project, which Schmitt described as an "extraordinarily intricate coalition of economy, freedom, technology, ethics, and parliamentarianism."[10] All this had conspired to rid the world of that which had made life worth living in the first place—the sense of vitality that came with the need for totalities of men to decide upon their enemies and defend themselves against them. The prospect of a thoroughly managed and pacified world frightened Schmitt, and led him to wonder of its proponents: "For what would they be free?"[11]

Strauss penned an important response to Schmitt's essay, in which he largely concurred in Schmitt's assessment of modern life. But he also thought deficient Schmitt's attempts to overcome its spirit. He paraphrased Schmitt's position this way: "We may say in summary that liberalism, sheltered by and engrossed in a world of culture, forgets the foundation of culture, the state of nature, that is, human nature in its dangerousness and endangeredness." The forgetting was twofold. Liberal civilization had lost a sense for the Hobbesian war of all against all to which it had first appeared as a response. Still more, it had lost a sense for the natural ground of human activity altogether, preferring instead to cast human artifice as "sovereign creation," as the " 'pure product' of the human spirit." It embraced a "spirit of technicity" instead, and in this it lived out its Hobbesian bequest. Strauss could therefore anoint Hobbes as the one who completed the foundation of liberalism, notwithstanding the emphatically illiberal character of the state Hobbes preferred.[12]

But Strauss felt compelled to remind his readers, Schmitt among them, that "culture is always the *culture of nature*. This expression means, primarily, that culture develops the natural predisposition; it is careful nurture of nature—whether of the soil or of the human spirit makes no difference; it thus *obeys* the orders that nature itself gives." To escape the horizon of liberalism meant to disavow altogether its impoverished notion of man in the state of nature—for Hobbes and the liberal tradition a danger to be neutralized, but for Schmitt embraced. Schmitt failed for Strauss insofar as his critique of liberal civilization remained indebted to its foundational premise—debased nature. "The affirmation of the political as such," Strauss concluded, "proves to be a liberalism with the opposite polarity."[13]

Against a spirit that disavowed altogether a decision on the enemy, Schmitt had held up the imperative to decide, irrespective of content. It was on its face an *empty* decisionism. It only exacerbated the crisis of human self-assertion Strauss hoped to resolve, for it made an imperative out of the purest assertion of will. Strauss therefore undertook to save Schmitt from himself. Had Schmitt hewn to his deepest aim (or the one Strauss imputed to him), he would have abandoned the "polemic against liberalism" in favor of liberalism's "opposite in spirit and faith, which, as it seems, still has no name." If anonymous, this spirit nonetheless had a program: it sought after "the order of the human things" by means of a "pure and whole knowledge" independent of any historical epoch in particular. Such knowledge, Strauss concluded, was to be discovered only by means of a "return to the origin," or to what Schmitt had described as "undamaged, noncorrupt nature."[14] In other words, Strauss did to Schmitt precisely what he had done to Hobbes. He "reoriented" and redirected them to a natural right tradition each had inadvertently lost. Hobbes's error had inaugurated the liberal epoch; Schmitt's error threatened to sustain it, notwithstanding his own most emphatic wishes to see it die. If Strauss on Hobbes appears at first glance an antiquarian matter, Strauss on Schmitt makes it clear that it was no such thing. The Hobbesian predicament—what to do when nature is mute and God, interrupted—Strauss described as his own. Strauss simply came to different, and as *he* understood it, more illiberal conclusions.

This is a contested point, and deserves explanation. Strauss is sometimes described as a friend to liberal democracy. This claim comes in two forms: that Strauss's philosophical teaching lends itself to liberalism, and that Strauss supported liberal democratic regimes (at least out of pragmatism if not always out of conviction). The first claim is difficult to sustain, given Strauss's appreciative remarks about Schmitt. If there is a liberalism in his teaching, it will have to be discovered elsewhere.[15] As for the second claim: it may be true with respect to his later years, but not his early ones. Not even the Nazi takeover of Germany—not at first, anyway—convinced Strauss to repudiate the authoritarian right. Here, for example, is a letter Strauss wrote to Karl Löwith in May of 1933, shortly after his remarks on Schmitt:

Just because Germany has turned to the Right and has expelled us it simply does not follow that the principles of the Right are therefore to be rejected. On the contrary: only on the basis of principles of the Right—on the basis of fascist, authoritarian, *imperial* principles—is it possible in a dignified manner, without the ridiculous and pitiful appeal to the "inalienable rights of man," to protest against the nasty abomination [i.e., Nazism]. I read Caesar's commentaries with deeper understanding, and I think about Virgil's [exhortation]: *Tu regere imperio . . . parcere subjectis et debellare superbos.* [Roman! let this be your care, this your art; to rule over the nations and impose the ways of peace, to spare the underdog, and pull down the proud (Aeneid VI. 851).] There is no reason to prostrate oneself before crosses, including the cross of liberalism, so long as somewhere in the world a spark of the *roman* idea still glimmers.[16]

What is one to make of such a statement? What kind of empire could Strauss have had in mind in May of 1933? What kind of fascism? It is difficult to say. Perhaps all this was born with disgust for the weakness of the liberal Weimar regime, with its incapacity to protect its Jews, let alone itself. The implication: the liberal position was not invalidated but defeated by the contingencies of circumstance. Liberalism ought not be rejected but reestablished on new foundations. On the other hand, Strauss rejected a liberal "crusade," the notion of liberal empire as it were, and in the name of authoritarian principles. Muscular liberalism, it seems, was not enough for Strauss in 1933. The question is why.[17]

FROM GOD TO NATURE

In part, the answer has to do with the source and scope of Strauss's animus. The illiberal bent of his thought in this period was not limited to its politics. It was deeper, more wide-ranging. It was civilizational, and a second project, this one in the person of Maimonides, made plain his illiberalism's theological origins and ends.

The series of essays collected in Strauss's work of 1935, *Philosophie und Gesetz* (Philosophy and Law), putatively took as its object the status of revelation in the thought of Maimonides and his predecessors. It entered the world on March 30, 1935, as one of five monographs on the "great eagle" published in time for the celebrations of his eight hundredth birthday. But the origins and intent of the text belie the rationale imputed to it in retrospect. It is at its core a commentary on the perils of human self-assertion, and still more than the work on Hobbes throws in relief the process by which the question of nature evolved for Strauss out of the question of God, how the pantheism controversy of interwar Europe had (like its predecessor) its conclusion in the recovery of physis.

Strauss once spoke of his introduction to *Philosophy and Law* as "the best which I have written." That he considered it his best did little, however, to ensure its univocal reception. Julius Guttmann claimed to find in Strauss a champion of psychological and philosophical existentialism, and not without justice. His friend Karl Löwith conjectured that he had thrown in his lot with the orthodox, an assessment that Strauss irritably dismissed: "By the way," he retorted, "I am *not* an orthodox Jew." Strauss's lifelong friend and confidante, Jacob Klein, nonetheless arrived at a like-minded appraisal: "One could, *following* your account, come to the conclusion: why not orthodoxy?!" But this fragile consensus on Strauss the crypto-Jew shattered under the hammer blows of an incredulous Gershom Scholem. Scholem wrote to his friend Walter Benjamin of his dismay as he ventured into the text's first pages, only to find there a thinly disguised brief for unbelief. Scholem complained that the book "begins with an unfeigned and copiously argued (if completely ludicrous) affirmation of atheism as the most important Jewish watchword." Scholem reacted with incomprehension to the "admirable boldness" with which Strauss had professed his atheism (even as he had designs on a chair in Jewish studies, and in Jerusalem no less). Scholem thought it unmatched in impunity. "It even outdoes the first forty pages of your postdoctoral dissertation!" he wrote to his friend—words that Benjamin and all those who have labored over him could not fail to appreciate. "I admire this ethical stance," Scholem concluded, "and regret the—obviously conscious and deliberately provoked—suicide of such a capable mind."[18]

That Strauss's book could elicit this welter of response, so heated and from such capable observers, says at once a great deal and very little. It reflects much of the text's oracular light, as if it were a revelation without content, open to the most wide-ranging and incompatible of readings. *What* Strauss had in mind was simply not apparent, or at least not readily so. Even the man Strauss considered his philosophical fellow traveler— even Jacob Klein did not quite know what to make of it. Following the publication of *Philosophy and Law*, Klein posed to Strauss the simple question: "Wozu?" To what end? To answer Klein's query, we would do best to shield our eyes for the moment from the bright radiance of the book's philosophical sun, and content ourselves with a more modest view—the one illuminated by the dim bulb of its intellectual-historical context.

The book documents Strauss's struggle with the gnostic challenge and the legacy of the crisis theologians in particular. This legacy loomed large, above all in the criticisms Strauss directed toward Julius Guttmann, a doyen in the field of Jewish thought and author of the classic historical account of Jewish philosophy.[19] Strauss's objections were numerous and complicated, but boiled down to two.

First, Guttmann had put man before God, if more by accident than design. Guttmann had hoped to describe the "specifically religious world and its truth." This meant to distinguish religion from other dimensions of human consciousness and culture (such as morality). The problem, for Strauss, was that consciousness and culture (as Guttmann understood it) proceed from man. They smack of human artifice, of the "sovereign invention" Strauss had recognized—and rejected—as Hobbes's bequest to the modern age. "Religion in its *proper sense* does not have this character," he observed. In this, at least, Strauss thought orthodoxy akin to the physis-tradition of ancient Greek philosophy. Both stressed human obedience; both denied the prerogative to reduce the world to an object for the exercise of human will. "The claim to universality on the part of 'culture,' which in its own view rests on spontaneous production [by man]," Strauss explained, "seems to be opposed by the claim to universality on the part of religion, which in its own view is not produced by man but *given* to him."[20] Guttmann had set out to grant religion its autonomy. But he had succeeded only in reducing it to one of several modes of human consciousness, and had so denied the claims of religion to supra-human origins and universal truth.[21]

This objection was hardly a novel one for Strauss. By 1935, he had levied it for at least a decade. But he followed it with a second that helps us understand the great shift in his thought: from the problem of God to the problem of nature, from the question of reason and revelation to the problems of nomos and physis. Guttmann, it turns out, had not only put man before God. He had put man before nature. "No longer," Strauss observed, "or less and less does modern philosophy [of religion] understand man as a member of the cosmos, as one (though exceptional) natural being among others; on the contrary, it understands nature from man, or, more precisely, from consciousness as man's defining property." Strauss explained the trouble with this view from the standpoint of religion: it precluded the discovery of God as creator of the world. It understood God as "produced" by human consciousness, and so the raw fact of God's reality had become "essentially unintelligible." But the formulation speaks first to Strauss's disaffection with an ethos of human self-assertion that posits man over and against the *world*. He refers here, not first to the eclipse of God, but to the eclipse of nature. And so we come to the crux of the matter: the *same arguments* Strauss used to secure the primacy of God to man—arguments derived from crisis theology—could be used to secure the primacy of nature also. This helps account for the ease with which Strauss spoke his new tongue. The languages of revelation and physis, of God and nature, were not autonomous languages at all. They were dialects.

We also find here signs of Strauss's disaffection with a theology whose arguments he had often embraced. Strauss once mobilized the theologians of crisis to secure the priority of God to all human knowing. But he now found them guilty of a version of the sin they had helped him discern in others. "If it comes down to the fundamental distinction man/nature and if, accordingly, it is asserted that the existence of God is not intelligible from nature," as the latter-day gnostics (and even Bultmann) had argued, "then one loses the sole guarantee that the existence of God will not get completely 'internalized' and thereby evaporated." If not intelligible from nature, God would have to be made intelligible from man—and so, Strauss feared, reduced to him.[22]

He found corroboration of his fears in the fact that existential theology could account only with the greatest difficulty for a doctrine of creation "as the creation also of *non*-human nature." This symptom Strauss detected most conspicuously in the work of Friedrich Gogarten, for a time a close associate of Barth. "We believe we are doing Gogarten no injustice if we say that for him . . . creation has meaning only as the creation of man." Strauss here replicated the critique levied by Alexander Altmann against the representatives of dialectical theology: they had saved God, but at creation's expense.[23] They lost at the same time a view of nature that long served as an alternative: a Greek cosmology that imputed an immanent purposefulness to the natural world. "It is on the basis of this development," Strauss declared, on the basis of the displacement of "consciousness" (Schleiermacher, Guttmann) by "existence" (Barth), that the "fundamental cosmological distinction eternal/corruptible . . . finally becomes completely obsolete."[24] In other words, the rise of existential theology brought to its completion a predicament whose origins Strauss discerned in Hobbes—it had rid the world of any source of authority save man. Neither God (exiled from the world) nor nature (understood as transient) could provide an enduring standard by which to know whether what man chooses to do is right.

To defeat the theologians of crisis meant, then, to save a notion of nature that did not oppose man, but sustained him, a nature that did not diminish man so much as ground him in something greater. It therefore meant also to contest the view of nature developed by Hobbes: a state of war, a realm of anxiety, a natural world without *summum bonum*, and so a human life oriented in fear toward the *summum malum* of death. It meant to contest the elevation of art and denigration of nature that followed in the form of modern natural science, not to mention modern, liberal civilization itself, which Strauss thought inaugurated and intellectually "completed" by Hobbes's critique. To defeat the theologians of crisis meant in the end to save the cosmos, or the possibility of cosmology in its original Greek sense. As Strauss later put it, "all philosophy is cosmology ultimately," and so it meant to secure the possibility of philosophy as well.[25]

All this recalls Jonas. Jonas had argued that natural-scientific thought in the tradition of Bacon had acquiesced to divine transcendence, but only the better to banish the divine from the world. Transcendence was *all* that was left over to God, as his power to intervene in and upon the world had been usurped by man. The result: man devolved into a creature for whom the natural world presented at most an occasion for the exercise of his will. Once thought a solution, natural science had instead come to reproduce the gnostic problem. In *Philosophy and Law*, Strauss concurred in the assessment, and also in the premonition of the solution's failure. "Doubts about the success of civilization soon became doubts about the possibility of civilization. Finally the belief is perishing that man can, by pushing back the 'limits of Nature' further and further, advance to ever greater 'freedom,' that he can 'subjugate' nature, 'prescribe his own laws' for her," and at its most egregious, " 'generate' her by dint of pure thought."[26]

A glance at Strauss's correspondence confirms the importance of this point. In June of 1935, Strauss penned a letter to Jonas, then in Palestine. *Philosophy and Law* had appeared two months before, and Strauss wished to remit to him a copy. "Above all," however, Strauss wanted "finally to say something" to Jonas about *Gnosis und spätantiker Geist*, which had appeared a year earlier, and which Strauss had in the meantime largely read to completion. It is in this letter that Strauss redescribed his project in the terms set out by Jonas. It is there that he revealed their affinity: above all a diagnosis of modernity riven by the recrudescence of gnosticism. It is there, also, that he hinted at their shared response.

Strauss spoke with evident appreciation. As a professed *am-ha'arez gamur* in things gnostic, as a total novice, he could not address the text's details. "But insofar as your thesis is concerned, it is both at first glance and after some consideration so convincing, that even one (such as myself) who knows the texts not at all, feels justified in saying: only so *can* it be; only so does [the phenomenon] have meaning." Strauss echoed the diagnosis of modernity as beset by a neo-gnostic spirit. He wrote with praise for "the historical understanding of the modern" he discovered in the book, "upon whose 'gnostic' character you correctly and repeatedly point out." Jonas had stressed a notion of the world understood as an "adversarial power." He had described the "opposition of the self to the world," the " 'common loneliness (of the isolated self) in a world become alien' " and the "despair of natural theology" prompted by the gnostic spirit. Above all, he had underscored the notion of the "just life as antinatural" and the "anthropological orientation of [what passed for gnostic] 'cosmology.'" "In all of these points," Strauss wrote, "I agree completely." He concurred also in the links Jonas forged between gnostic theology and Heideggerian thought. "The victory of the gnostic in modern philosophy," Strauss affirmed, "especially in its most recent form, in Heidegger, enables the recognition of the singularly gnostic roots of our world."[27]

At the conclusion of his list of affinities came a directive. Offered on its face to Jonas, it applied to himself just as much. "I believe that here," only after the diagnosis, "does the actual problem—both the interpretive and the philosophical one—first *begin*." Indeed, Strauss had already mobilized to address it. His work on Hobbes and Maimonides heralded the recovery of physis—his own overcoming of the neo-gnostic spirit—that achieved its full form in *Natural Right and History*. But what, exactly, did it mean for Strauss to overcome gnosticism? For Jonas, it meant to contest *das Fremde*, the spirit of alienation he found in the theologians of crisis, but more ominously in natural science, their erstwhile partner. For Strauss, too, it meant to defeat the fetish for human self-assertion. It meant also to defeat the condition of its possibility, a notion of nature rid of immanent purpose. Ten days after he had written to Jonas, Strauss wrote to his friend Karl Löwith. There he spoke of the need to contest "the rebellion against the indifference of the universe, against its aimlessness," which lay at the root of modern civilization. Strauss meant to contest not the rebellion per se, but the false assumptions upon which it was founded. "We must recall our natural being in order to remove, by means of thought, the unnatural conditions" under which he believed modern man to live.[28]

To recall man's natural ends, his physis, meant also to stake a claim with respect to nomos. Jonas and Strauss count as antinomians of sorts. They contested nomos in order to defeat an ethos of unbridled human self-assertion. But they did so in different ways. Jonas underscored the cellular foundations man shares with his earthly cousins, from lowly amoeba to mountain sloth, and so to dispute the sort of freedom to make of the earth what man wills. He had important things to say about man's kinship with redwoods and ventworms, with the beluga whale and the common cold. But he had relatively little to say about his *political* relations with fellow men and women. Rarely did he comment on the politics of physis. Rarely did he speak of its political embodiment. And when he did, it was clear that he believed the fate of the natural world to trump all other concerns. For example, he could speak well—albeit in a thought experiment and with serious qualifications—of the totalitarian regimes of cold war Europe. They were best suited to enforce the compulsory limits to human behavior required by an Earth under siege. Strauss would not have entertained such thoughts for an instant.

Strauss directed his energies not to organic nature, but to the nature of man. In *Philosophy and Law*, he bemoaned the victory of natural science as the basic threat to the version of nature he hoped to recover. Its triumph, as he explained again in *Natural Right*, inhered in the demise of the Aristotelian cosmology. "The fundamental dilemma, in whose grip we are, is caused by the victory of modern natural science" over the Greek cosmos. "An adequate solution to the problem of natural right cannot be found before this basic problem has been solved." Jonas expended much effort in the attempt to revive Aristotelianism, if not its full cosmology then at least the particulars most suited to a philosophy of the organism. He disputed Bacon's triumph, denied it had ever been argued. But Strauss eschewed this tack. Though he did refer to Bacon on occasion, and as an exponent of the view he wished to contest, he did so rarely. He devoted less attention to Bacon's than to Hobbes's recasting of the relation between art and nature, with the corollary stress on the political such a choice would imply. So too did he discount the details of Aristotelian cosmology and physics. "I am not an Aristotelian," he explained, a short time after *Natural Right* appeared in German translation. "I am not an Aristotelian since I am not satisfied that the visible universe is eternal, to say nothing of other perhaps more important reasons." Not the Aristotelian cosmology, but Aristotelian, and especially Platonic politics had earned his allegiance. "I can only say that what Aristotle and Plato say about man and the affairs of men makes infinitely more sense to me than what the moderns have said or say." And it was this tradition, on some accounts invented by Strauss as much as discovered by him, that he associated with physis and natural right.[29] He made nature the subject of philosophy in general, political philosophy in particular.

But what did this tradition hold? For Jonas, physis referred to the unconscious willing and striving embedded in all organic activity. For Strauss, physis referred to a realm of justice prior to law and so independent of human convention. Strictly understood, Platonic natural right meant "that which is right by itself and not in particular through man's making it right." It is the "same as the 'idea of justice.' " The fact that the idea of justice required institutional embodiment did not make such institutions, for Strauss, by definition illegitimate or antinatural. Neither Strauss nor Jonas opposed human convention as such. Strauss made this argument in his essay on Schmitt, and again in a 1941 lecture at the New School for Social Research. Strauss devoted the talk to the problem of German nihilism, and cast the then-present war as a contest of German and Anglo-Saxon principles. Strauss favored English prudence over German radicalism, with the curious result that "it are the English, and not the Germans, who deserve to have, and to remain, an imperial nation." But he also stressed the compatibility of nature with political institutions, with willful human action in and upon the world. "Civilization is the conscious culture of reason," he asserted. "This means that civilization is not identical with human life or human existence." On the one hand, this implied that "there were, and there are, many human beings who do not partake of civilization." On the other, it meant that "civilization has a natural basis which it *finds*, which it does not create, on which it is dependent, and on which it has only a very limited influence. Conquest of nature, if not taken as a highly poetic overstatement, is a nonsensical expression." With this, he departed decisively from the tack Jonas had adopted of late in Palestine. He departed still further with his "proof," that the natural basis of civilization was to be discerned in the fact that "all civilized communities as well as uncivilized ones are in need of armed force which they must use against their enemies from without and against the criminals within." Strauss found in the human capacity for controlled and social violence what Jonas had found in digestion.[30]

The politics of physis surfaced also in his correspondence with his friend Karl Löwith. His allegiances had evidently left Löwith incredulous, and Strauss felt compelled to reaffirm a basic conviction. "I *really* believe, although to you this apparently appears fantastic, that the perfect political order, as Plato and Aristotle have sketched it, *is* the perfect political order." Strauss was quick to admit the impossibility of the city-state's reconstitution. "I know very well that *today* it cannot be restored." But it did at least serve as an ideal, one more attuned to the natural and the right than its modern deviation. "I know very well that *today* it cannot be restored, but the famous atomic bombs—not to mention at all cities with a million inhabitants, gadgets, funeral homes, 'ideologies'— show that the contemporary solution, that is, the completely modern solution, is *contra naturam*. Whoever concedes that Horace did not speak nonsense when he said *Naturam furca expelles, tamen usque recurret* [expel nature with a hayfork, but it always returns] concedes thereby precisely the legitimacy *in principle* of Platonic-Aristotelian politics." "Details," Strauss concluded, "can be disputed, although I myself might actually agree with everything that Plato and Aristotle demand (but this I tell only you)."[31]

His disbelief quelled, Löwith asked for specification instead. "Where do you draw the line between natural and unnatural?" he asked. "For the Greeks it was—I commend them for this—completely natural to consort with women, youths and animals. The bourgeois marriage is just as unnatural as pederasty, and Japanese geishas are just as natural for the man as [Oscar] Wilde's friend was for him. The creation of a perfect political order—be it social and political or in private morals—is," Löwith concluded, "always afflicted with the unnatural—simply qua order." Strauss did not leave Löwith's challenge unanswered. Only the moderns, Strauss insisted, are so "crazy" as to "believe that the 'creation' of a 'work of art' is more worthy of wonder and more mysterious than the reproduction of a dog." Whether bovine or canine, feline or ursine, procreation superseded convention because it was natural; it is "higher in rank than everything men have made." On this view, nature trumps art. "When you say that the *polis* is *contra naturam* like all human institutions," he wrote to Löwith, "you only repeat a Greek political thesis," albeit not the one Strauss favored. Strauss contested not the thesis, however, but its presupposition: "The fact that [the polis] is institutional is still no proof that it is *contra naturam*." On the contrary, Strauss believed that "some institutions *assist* natural tendencies," and had already argued precisely that, to his students in New York, five years before.[32]

The question thus becomes: what *institutions* manage to get the natural right? The problem is a difficult one. It is made no easier by the heated polemic prompted by the rise to prominence of Strauss's students and disciples. It is easy, for example, to see how Strauss has been put to use in America's culture wars. Allan Bloom voiced a typical Straussian griev-ance in his 1987 best-seller, *The Closing of the American Mind.* "Everything has become culture," he complained. Civilization under-stood as the careful cultivation of nature had fallen by the wayside, as "culture" had come to refer to "drug culture, the rock culture, the street-gang culture, and so on endlessly and without discrimination. The failure of culture is now culture." The premise: human action in and upon the world had lost sight of its natural—hence, moral—foundations. Others influenced by Strauss have made similar arguments, if in a different register. Among them must be counted Leon Kass (former chief of President Bush's council on bioethics), who has invoked a "more ancient and teleological understanding of nature" to inveigh on behalf of the institution of "exogamous, monogamous marriage" as best suited to rearing "decent and upright children, that is, children who are truly human." Still others have applied the Straussian criterion in questions of politics, with mixed results.[33]

Whether their answers at the turn of the twenty-first century mirror in aspect those of Strauss in the middle of the twentieth is up for debate. I think it unlikely. But whatever answers Strauss may have broached, they are secondary, secondary to the fact of the question itself. The question was born of a need for an authority to pronounce on the rightfulness of human action. The authority once vested in God had been lost. The authority usurped by man in God's absence had led the world awry. Strauss revived an ancient approach to the relation of nature and politics in order to reverse the excesses of human self-assertion, and to do so without resort to divine command. It was a call to human excellence, but also—and first—to humility. It is worth asking, however, whether the call has drowned in the cacophony of its unintended consequences.

It effectively changes the civilizational calculus. Strauss's call can preempt the question "How will an institution help us live?" with the question "Is an institution natural, and therefore right?" Intended to rein in human excess, it has the means to unleash it all the more. It potentially (though not necessarily) grants to man the authority vested in an absolute God or in a timeless natural order, all the while denying precisely that fact. After all, *who* in the end is to say? Strauss once chided his friend Scholem for privileging a divine "who" over a natural "what" as the measure for that which is right. Hobbes would have responded to them both: neither God nor nature can speak its intent without a human mouthpiece through which it might be voiced. As Hobbes demonstrated, to speak on behalf of the divine is a dangerous business. To speak on behalf of nature is, too.

CHAPTER EIGHT

Natural Right and Judaism

Natural Right and History speaks little of heresy and not at all of Judaism. The book opens with accounts of the twin threat to natural right doctrine, embodied on the one hand by a historicism that denies the validity of enduring standards of right, and on the other by Max Weber's distinction between fact and value, which helped banish questions of right—even its lexicon—from the modern study of politics. It then turns to the primeval origins of natural right, which Strauss declared coeval with the discovery of nature and philosophy. From there it proceeds to discussions of its classic incarnations in Aristotle and Plato, to its modern revisions in Hobbes and Locke, and finally to its modern crises in Burke and Rousseau. Maimonides comes in for a single citation. He is relegated to a lonely footnote, lost in the book's impersonal expanse. For these reasons, some of Strauss's Jewish champions have largely ignored *Natural Right*; it seems to bear not at all on his Jewish commitments, or his more obviously Jewish writings. Some even find him congenial to Jewish orthodoxy, given his insistence on the enduring validity of the orthodox argument. His philosophical champions have at their most egregious dismissed his "exoteric" forays into Jewish scholarship as but a smoke screen, calculated to deflect attention from his commitment to the philosopher's dangerous truths. At their best, they have acknowledged the authenticity of these researches, but have relegated them to a philosophical ghetto, as inessential to the core teachings of the master.[1]

Both, I believe, are mistaken. This is because *Natural Right* floats in a galaxy starred just as much by heresy and Judaism as by Greek political theory. If not evident on its face, it becomes so when we consider the term's semantic pairs or counter-concepts. To begin, Strauss opposed the natural to the conventional, and so reproduced the distinction between physis and nomos. We have just seen how Strauss privileged the natural over human creation. But he privileged it over the positings of all persons, whether human or divine. In the preface to *Natural Right*'s seventh impression, composed seventeen years after the book's arrival, Strauss felt obliged to dispel its misreadings. "Nothing that I have learned [in the interim]," he frankly announced, "has shaken my inclination to prefer 'natural right,' especially in its classic form, to the reigning relativism, positivist or historicist." To avoid a common misunderstanding, however, he thought it prudent to add the remark "that the appeal to a higher law, if that law is understood in terms of 'our' tradition as distinguished from 'nature,' is historicist in character, if not in intention." It too succumbed to the ravages of the relativist plague. "The case is obviously different," Strauss allowed, "if appeal is made to the divine law." Still, he insisted, "the divine law is not the natural law, let alone natural right."[2] Divine law is not natural law because it is posited, in history, by God. It is not always already given. Nor is it by definition accessible to reason, or open to knowledge. It is the product of a voluntarist, personal (and possibly capricious) lawgiver. Nomos applied for Strauss to the laws of both man and God.[3] And so he came to privilege the natural over the divine. Or as he put it in a letter to his friend Scholem, "What gives the certainty that a Who, as distinguished from a What, is 'the last word of all theory?'"[4]

Strauss also privileged right over law: right, which Strauss understood as justice, has no necessary relation with law, understood in terms of procedure. It is crucial to grasp that natural right and natural law are for Strauss not terms of identity but distinction. The German term, *Naturrecht*, allows of both translations. This gave rise to some confusion, evaded not even by the author of the foreword to Strauss's book. But over time, Strauss left little doubt as to the one he intended and preferred.[5] In a 1946 lecture, he spoke explicitly of natural right as a system of "trans-legal standards." In *Natural Right and History*, he emphasized the autonomy of right from law: "If justice is to remain good, we must conceive of it as essentially independent of law. We shall then define justice as the habit of giving to everyone what is due to him according to nature."[6] Later, he quashed the minority position, first in a letter to a student on Montesquieu—"the crucial point in the arguments is that these relations of justice are not yet *laws*"—and in a letter to Helmut Kuhn, who reviewed *Natural Right*'s German edition: "I spoke in the very title of my book of natural right and not of natural law."[7] Samuel Moyn has pointed out one of the implications of all this. Strauss was not an antinomian so much as an ante-nomian; he did not contest law so much as he discovered in nature a realm of justice prior to and independent of law.

To sum up, Strauss contrasted the natural with the divine, and right he distinguished from law. If Judaism is understood as a religion of divinely revealed law (and Strauss understood it that way), then natural right must count as the most potent of its heretical alternatives. On this view, to enshrine natural right meant at once to abandon the Mendelssohnian tradition and dialectically to preserve it. To enshrine it meant to speak a last word on the pantheism controversy of old. To enshrine it was, above all, to offer a philosophical substitute for God. In their silence on *Natural Right*, Strauss's Jewish champions were perhaps more prescient than they knew. Strauss was no adherent of orthodoxy. But he *could* be recuperated in precisely the way he had denied it to Spinoza, as an identifiably Jewish heretic.

That he could not throw in his lot with religion Strauss made quite clear in a letter to Gershom Scholem. Scholem had just completed his book, *On the Kabbalah and its Symbolism*. Strauss praised it in unusually loving detail:

> Never before have I been so deeply impressed by your thought. You even succeeded in warming and softening my cold and hard heart—especially by [the end] where you bring "home" to me your message by revealing the sources of such things as smirot of erev shabbat which I used to sing as a child in utter ignorance of their "background." I understood perhaps for the first time the infinite attraction exercised by this deep, and rich world, your home, which enigmatically and indissolubly unites the universal and the particular, the human and the Jewish—which transcends all moralism and punitiveness without disintegrating into aestheticism or the like. You are a blessed man because you have achieved a harmony of mind and heart on such a high level, and you are a blessing to every Jew now living. As a consequence, you have the right and the duty to speak up. Unfortunately, I am constitutionally unable to follow you—or if you wish, I too have sworn to a flag, the oath to the flag being (in the beautiful Arabic Latin created by some of our ancestors, which to Cicero would appear to be *in ultimate turpitudinis*) [at the ultimate end of the shameful]: *moriatur anima mea mortem* [sic] *philosophorum*.[8]

"Let my soul die the death of the philosophers," Strauss wished for himself, a death that the biblical verse upon which his own was based had reserved not for the philosopher but the just.

Though sworn to philosophy, Strauss refused to declare reason the victor in its battle with revelation. Revelation could bear this uncertainty, Strauss thought. But philosophy could not. "Philosophy must admit the possibility of revelation." It was not self-evidently the "right way of life." But in this case, Strauss surmised, "the choice of philosophy is based on faith."[9] Religion may look to God, philosophy may look to nature, the one to revealed law, the other to a natural realm of justice prior and superior to law. But to decide for either is fiat in the end. In place of fideism, Strauss developed a species of physiodicy.

The term is Joseph Cropsey's.[10] He declined to specify its meaning, but it should be apparent what its use means here. It resonates with a more common expression, theodicy, and in its resonance echoes also its intent. Physis here usurps God's place. Theodicy implies faith, a faith that God in his mystery will defeat in the end what appears to man as autonomous and unvanquished evil. Physiodicy, too, implies faith, faith by the philosopher in the natural ground of his own activity. It implies, as Strauss admitted, that "the quest for evident knowledge rests itself on an unevident premise."[11] Or to borrow a phrase from Franz Rosenzweig, philosophy was "atheistic theology."[12] Strauss would no doubt have objected. To discover natural right was for him an exercise in human reason. But it would have been difficult for him to dispute the fact that natural right performed for him the same sort of work performed for the man of religion by God. It promised a standard by which to measure all others, free of human whim and caprice. "Natural right is right that is independent of human arbitrariness," he wrote in a lecture. "The problem of natural right is as serious as our need for standards, accessible to the knowledge of man as man. . . . If there are no such standards, all human action is blind: because it does not know whether its ultimate aims are *right*. If there are no such standards, *everything* is permitted or," he penciled in, "legitimate."[13] Right may be independent of law, but the reverse, if the good is to be served, does not hold.

But all this begs a simple question: can natural right—even its question—be discovered merely on the strength of its need? David Baumgardt, for one, did not think so. Like Strauss, Baumgardt set up philosophical shop in America after emigration from Germany. He, too, was ambivalent about nomos, and turned to nature for aid in dispelling it. Though he did not achieve fame on the Straussian scale, he did go on to inspire a number of younger scholars, in part on the strength of an elaborate ethics of hedonism in the Benthamite tradition.[14] Baumgardt was not the fairest of Strauss's readers. But he did well to point out how Strauss had sought in natural right a philosophical surrogate for God. "In the theory of natural right," he wrote in criticism, "the burning thirst for a clear and simple criterion of right and wrong has led us to maintain falsely that the mere thirst proves the existence of water or even wine. . . . If we still try to rely on the possession of simple absolute knowledge in morals, we only deceive ourselves with the vain boast of being 'like God' in absolute ethical judgment." Baumgardt thought this discovery of natural right better described as an invention in disguise. To "discover" natural right therefore smacked of idolatry, for it meant to put man in God's place. In the words of Genesis, "you will be like God knowing good and evil."[15] Something of a displaced need for God lay at the root of this unending quest for natural right. This, perhaps, was the bequest of the Jew Strauss was to the philosopher he wished to become.

There was something of Spinoza in Strauss as well. The option for natural right, after all, reveals a deep Epicurean current in Straussian thought. Spinoza's Epicureanism, as Strauss saw it at least, had inhered in his hope to defeat divine revelation with a system in which it had no room. He erected a seamless and knowable world by philosophical means; he hoped to make revelation supererogatory. Strauss seems to have done Spinoza one better. Not the *Ethics*, but natural right would take the place of revelation. Not the *Ethics*, but natural right would make it superfluous. All this made Strauss an antinomian in more than a merely philosophical sense, as one who contested nomos with a version of physis. He had rebelled against God, but found he could not do without him, and so set out to discover, or erect, a new idol in God's place.

To point to the Spinoza in Strauss is also, I think, to hint at the partial failure of his project. Strauss was prompted to save both philosophy and religion from the threat posed by the synthesis of the Jewish Spinozists, and adapted Barth's talk of God's radical transcendence for the job. He hoped to compartmentalize them, to set each on opposite sides of an abyss, and then to destroy the bridge. That bridge was the problem of heresy. Heresy undoes Strauss's scheme because its mark excludes and includes at once; the mark sets the transgressor apart from the community, but in the act of marking implicitly includes him as well, all the more if it holds out, as it did with Spinoza, the promise of return. Heresy defies talk of incommensurability. It does not allow for a relation defined by its total and utter lack, the sort of otherness that lent Barth's thought its force, and on which Strauss had also relied.

It is therefore no surprise that the problem of heresy would elicit the most categorical, paradoxical, and, I think, incoherent language in Strauss's writings. He found himself compelled to extirpate that which in fact did most to define him. Philosophy as Strauss understood it *was* heresy, prompted as it was by disaffection with God's law.[16] Gerhard Krüger once called him an "unbeliever"—not as a term of abuse, but to distinguish him from someone merely indifferent to the claims of revelation. "You orient yourself—even if in negative fashion—toward revealed religion," Krüger wrote.[17] Whatever its direction, the fact of this orientation belied Strauss's claims about the indifference—the neutrality as he once put it in reference to Spinoza—of philosophy to religion. Philosophy unfolded for Strauss within the horizon of revealed religion. As his friend Jonas put it, Strauss suffered from the "spiritual necessity" of "becoming an atheist in order to be a philosopher."[18] Not *being* an atheist, but *becoming* one: it is under the sign of this becoming, persistently renewed and always incomplete, that we ought to understand Strauss's life and career. On this view, the moment of his matchless philosophical triumph—*Natural Right and History*—was also the moment of his most ardent heresy; and so the moment in which he sided most vigorously with philosophy was also that moment in which he was most deeply, if dialectically, a Jew.

Or at least a certain kind of Jew: Strauss seemed to think of his age as one in which a heretical Judaism had become normative rather than deviant. That he expended great effort in the hope of dismantling it only testifies to its currency. So does the fact that he did so with arguments adapted from one dialect of heresy, the gnostic, deployed against its pantheist cousin. But by the end of his life, Strauss seems to have made his peace with the heretical world he inhabited, and with the heretical Jews among whom he lived. That, at any rate, seems to me the only way to account for a last and cryptic letter to his friend Scholem. There Strauss spoke of the Sabbatian phenomenon, that labyrinth of law and transgression, of redemption through sin, as akin to the shared life story of his, and Scholem's, intellectual world. By the fall of 1973, Scholem had completed the English translation and expansion of his masterpiece, his biography of Sabbatai Sevi, and had remitted to Strauss a copy. Strauss wrote in a feeble hand, in little more than chicken scratch. But his physical frailty only set in stark relief the force of his thanks and his praise. "Dear Scholem!"

> You see again from my handwriting that my fingers refuse their services. Therefore only this much. I have read your book on the deified *meshumad* [apostate] in the capacity of a docile pupil and learned something of greater or lesser importance from practically every line. You wrote a true biography—the *bios* not only of Sabbatai but *pos* [in a manner] of our whole *ethnos*.[19]

"For you and all Israel I wish everything good," Strauss wrote to his friend. "*Shalom u-Bracha*." May peace and blessings be upon you. And so he brought to an end a letter and with it a career that had commenced with a blessing—or a Benedictus—of a rather different sort.

So too did he bring with it an end to a life. Two days later, and by the time Scholem read these lines, he had died.

PART THREE

Redemption through Sin

IN THE BEGINNING, God did not create the heavens and God did not create the earth. The earth was not unformed. It was not void, and darkness did not rest upon the face of the deep. God's spirit did not hover above the waters. God did not let there be light, God did not see that it was good, God did not divide it from the darkness. There was not evening. There was not morning. There was not one day. "In the beginning," rather, "there was a cigar." Adjacent to the cigar was a candelabra. Its candles burned every Sabbath eve in the window of a Jewish apartment in Berlin, but on each of these evenings there occurred also something monstrous. Following the Sabbath meal, a liberal, Jewish citizen of the German Empire kindled his cigar from the holy candle and recited over it—the cigar, not the candle—a curious benediction: *baure pri tobakko*. Blessed art Thou who has created the fruit of tobacco.[1]

So proceeds Gershom Scholem's version of the Genesis story. Altered slightly from the prevailing sentiment of the last three thousand years, it nonetheless did better to align with the spirit of his age. Only several years later did Scholem, a child at the time, recognize his father's act for the transgression it was. He apparently knew nothing of the injunction against the kindling of fire on the Sabbath, a remarkable fact that attests to the depths of Jewish ignorance that reigned in the bourgeois, assimilated circle of German Jews out of which Scholem's revolt would emerge.

The story is of course a farce. But it is also, in a way, a foundation. For it narrates in the space of a few lines the array of themes to which Scholem devoted thousands of pages over the course of a career and a life: the crisis of liberal Judaism in Germany, Jewish heresy as the ground for modern Jewish identity, the freedom to create tradition as much as to live it, the unexpected persistence of discourses of the divine among those for whom God had long been dead or missing. It also invokes in ironic fashion the core of Scholem's most celebrated researches: the notion of a divine command fulfilled through transgression, or in its more radical and systematic guise, a program of redemption through sin.

This program Scholem did more than anyone else to resurrect in his time, personified for him by the Sabbatian controversies of the seventeenth and eighteenth centuries. But he was by no means alone. The interwar period witnessed an explosion of interest in heresy as a historical phenomenon and a conceptual problem. Mostly Protestant "gnostics" competed for supremacy with a pantheist sensibility associated with the interconfessional (and interdisciplinary) revival of Spinoza. Jews—and Scholem's circle in particular—engaged in these debates as well, and with important consequences. Scholem intervened in a special capacity. In Scholem we find an attempt—largely unconscious of itself as such but no less true for the fact—to speak Jewish revisions of these languages and so to transform them both. The great span of his work on the history of

Jewish mysticism is best understood, as I hope to show, in just these terms: as a contest between competing Jewish revisions of the gnostic and pantheist options. More than most, Scholem lays bare the deep complicity of these rival tongues, and he does so by speaking them together, at the same time.

How and why are difficult questions to answer, and they are two of the burdens taken up in the following chapters. They are also best approached by a story, or a series of them, that proceeds with an eye to Scholem the person, an eye to Scholem the scholar, and with both eyes to what joins person to thought. The first follows Scholem from a stormy adolescence in Berlin to adulthood in Jerusalem. It tracks his self-emancipation from an adolescent refusal of the world to its measured, if sometimes reluctant embrace. It also traces the evolution of his Zionism, which in this period was less political than existential: from a self-overcoming of the Diasporic Jew, modeled on the example of Friedrich Nietzsche's *Zarathustra*, to a more ambivalent form of Jewish identity inspired by the heretics he studied. The second, parallel story encompasses the expanse of his scholarship, and redescribes it in the terms bequeathed to Scholem by the languages of heresy between the wars.

The third strand of the story can be encapsulated in a phrase: from nihilism to nothingness. Scholem discovered the nihilist refusal of the world in some of those he studied, and also in himself. In both instances, it was born of a keen sense for God's absence, and for the dereliction of the world God had left behind. But this gnostic sensibility proved unsatisfying in the end, too easy and too dangerous, and so Scholem set out to find an antidote. He unearthed it in a strange idea: that God manifests himself in the world—in the process of life itself—as a peculiar form of nothingness. God was absent, but also present. Stated a bit differently: the idea accepts the neo-gnostic premise, or a form of it, but reverses the conclusions. To think of the world as suffused with God's nothingness is to affirm the world against those who demean it or pay it no heed. Scholem discovered the idea in his researches in the kabbalah, but a version of it also informed his efforts to recast Jewish identity in a heretical mold. In other words, the idea of not-being would prove crucial to his understandings of both his world and himself.

This may sound both abstract and idiosyncratic. The first is probably true. It is safe to say, after all, that most of us do not amble through life with a keen, conscious sense for the nothingness and not-being that suffuse our world. If we notice it at all, it manifests itself as a pervasive but unlocalizable sense of unease. But Scholem was not most of us, and neither were his intellectual contemporaries. If abstract, the idea was anything but idiosyncratic—Scholem's talk of nothingness and not-being situates him squarely in the philosophical milieu of the interwar years.

His affirmation of the idea, for example, makes him sound a lot like Martin Heidegger (in certain of his moods), and certainly more like Heidegger than Nietzsche. It also pulls him into the intellectual orbit of Jonas and Strauss. Both had revived the ancient Greek distinction between physis and nomos for the needs of the twentieth century, and both came down on the side of the first. They discovered in the autonomy of nature a check against the autonomy of man; they discovered in human worldliness a check against human aspirations to godliness. They were antinomians who appealed to nature to cast aspersions on the rule of human convention. Scholem was also an antinomian of sorts. It was expressed historically in his work on Sabbatai Sevi. It was expressed politically in his occasional brief for anarchism. And when he spoke of not-being and nothingness, he expressed it in philosophical terms also. Or as Strauss put it in a letter to Scholem: "What you call *nihil* the *falasifa* call *physis*."[2]

Something about Scholem's approach to nothingness (nihil), Strauss thought, made him akin to the *falasifa*, a group of medieval Islamic Aristotelians. This sounds strange. But if Strauss was right, and I think he was, it meant that Scholem undertook in his way what Strauss and Jonas had identified as the task of philosophy in a technological age: the recovery of physis. Scholem's recovery would proceed a bit differently. Still, he aimed (like Jonas) to save the world from its gnostic denigration and (like Strauss) from its pantheist annihilation, and he did both by appropriating these languages of heresy for what he thought were Jewish ends. Scholem aimed to save the world as a scene for Jewish endeavor, as a scene for Jewish self-assertion, as a scene for what he considered authentic Jewish life. Scholem had to save the world—not negate it, as he once had done—in order to save the Jews. And the problem of heresy gave him the conceptual vocabulary with which to do it.[3]

CHAPTER NINE

Redemption through Sin

By the 1950s, Hans Jonas managed finally to secure what had eluded him since 1933 and what remains to this day the grail of academic life—a permanent job. After two decades of wandering, learning, and soldiering most of all, Jonas arrived at the New School for Social Research in New York. There ensued a period of intense creativity. It led him from the phenomenon of life to the imperative of responsibility, from a philosophical biology to an environmental ethics and to work in post-Holocaust thought. But Jonas had not left his gnostic friends behind. They followed him from Berlin to Jerusalem, to Canada and New York, a pack of feral dogs half tamed by his attentions, and in 1958 he thanked them for their loyalty. In that year Jonas issued an English edition of his gnosis book. It commenced with a few lines of prose that surely rank among the finest he would ever pen. "Out of the mist of the beginning of our era," he wrote,

> there looms a pageant of mythical figures whose vast, superhuman contours might people the walls and ceiling of another Sistine Chapel. Their countenances and gestures, the roles in which they are cast, the drama which they enact, would yield images different from the biblical ones on which the imagination of the beholder was reared, yet strangely familiar to him and disturbingly moving. . . . The tale has found no Michelangelo to retell it, no Dante and no Milton. The sterner discipline of biblical creed weathered the storm of those days, and both Old and New Testament were left to inform the mind and imagination of Western man. Those teachings, which in the feverish hour of transition challenged, tempted, tried to twist the new faith are forgotten, their written record buried in the tomes of their refuters or in the sands of ancient lands.

"Our art and literature and much else would be different," Jonas concluded, "had the gnostic message prevailed."[1]

The same might be said, in Jewish history at least, of another foundational set of heresies. By 1936, in the 280 years since their inception, and in the 100 or so since their demise, the Sabbatian controversies had found no Jonas to retell them, no Gebhardt, and no Strauss. To be sure, they had not gone unnoticed. From their inception they elicited heated debate among Jews; among Muslims, concern; and among Christians, a good deal of derision.[2] But their written record had long since vanished. Their tomes had been left to languish in dark corners of libraries across the continent and beyond. So too had the Sabbatian impulse evaporated. In part, the sterner discipline of rabbinic creed had weathered the Sabbatian storm, and had done much to quash the memory of the Sabbatians' anarchic will to freedom from law. In the East, the advent of Hasidism had sublimated—and neutralized—the more ardent of their messianic energies. In the West, in Germany especially, the Sabbatians suffered a less ambiguous fate. To the exponents of Jewish enlightenment and emancipation, their Sabbatian forebears were potentially the source of considerable embarrassment. Sabbatian "irrationalism," "particularism," and "enthusiasm" set the movement squarely in opposition to the Enlightenment program, predicated as it was on a system of reasonable, measured, and universalized belief. To these champions of light, the Sabbatian mystics appeared as daughters of darkness. They were best left shackled and gagged, consigned to the dank cellar of Jewish historical consciousness, even if they had paved the way for Enlightenment indifference to the law with a program of its willful transgression. This, at least, is how Gershom Scholem was to speak of their fate in 1936, in his essay "Redemption through Sin."[3] To hear Scholem tell it, the Sabbatians had fallen on hard times indeed. But to hear Scholem tell it is to hear it told wrong.

To understand why, it helps to consider the business of Jewish memorialization, which flourished in the interwar period. In 1927 Jews honored their own arch-heretic, Baruch Spinoza. In 1932 they marked his tercentenary. In 1935 they celebrated the eight hundredth birthday of Moses Maimonides. By comparison, 1925 came and went without much ado. To be sure, a short piece published in *Davar*, the mouthpiece of the Socialist Zionist movement in Palestine, did seek to fill this uncharacteristic void in the hit parade of Jewish memory. Its author, Zalman Rubashov (or Shazar, 1899–1973), would become the third president of Israel, and his article aimed to build the state, if in unorthodox fashion. He could not have picked a less propitious date for its publication. It appeared on the eve of the ninth day of the month of Av, traditionally marked as the day on which ancient Jewish sovereignty had twice been destroyed. But tradition has it also that lamentation will give way to joy. On some accounts, the messiah is to be born on that day, and for this reason would-be redeemers have sometimes claimed it as their own. Sabbatai Sevi, exceptional as he was, was no exception in this regard, and after three hundred years, Rubashov thought it high time to memorialize him.

His own "rebellious generation," he thought, had failed to grant this predecessor his due. Rubashov chalked up the defect to a signal lack of historical imagination. Had his contemporaries grasped the "paternity and pedigree" that yoked them to the Sabbatians, they would have accorded to the day the splendor it deserved. The Sabbatians, after all, had vanquished medieval Judaism and "forced open the gates of modern Hebrew history." They had managed to ignite "new fires" from the "eternal rocks of religion." They had prefigured the Zionist movement of his day by mobilizing a "popular movement of a breadth such that the exile had never known," even if they had erected an "idol to the nation" and devolved into a "monster and disgrace" in the process. "Many layers of culture and history separate us from that epoch," he admitted. "Distant is the man, distant is the generation and foreign are the paths. But the eternal flame will not snuff out."[4]

Rubashov's lament expressed what was in fact a common complaint: that successive generations of Jews had repressed the memory of their Sabbatian forebears. As a result, contemporaries no longer knew to appraise them with the sympathy they deserved, if they knew to appraise them at all. To an extent he was surely justified. No group of admirers or self-professed Sabbatians rallied in The Hague to celebrate the apostate messiah, as they would do for Spinoza several years later. No one thought to found a Sabbatai Sevi Society, a Nathan of Gaza Foundation, an Abraham Cardozo Institute, or a Jacob Frank House (Sevi's prophet, apologist, and self-styled incarnation, respectively). No profusion of literature on the scale enjoyed by Spinoza arose in celebration of his contemporary: no Sabbatian equivalent of the *Chronicon Spinozanum*, nothing for Sevi like the sort of "Spinoza for beginners" guide that appeared in interwar Europe.[5] Astronomers, jurists, occultists, teachers, even the German dental association could put in a few good words for Spinoza. But they had nothing to say, good or bad, about Sabbatai Sevi.

Nonetheless, Rubashov's recovery of Sabbatai Sevi belied the complaint even as he made it: his recovery was neither unique among the Jews of his age nor unprecedented among those before it. The Sabbatians had not merely vanished in the age of Enlightenment, and by 1925 had in any event made a remarkable comeback in historical memory, Jewish and otherwise. Scholars had published a slew of monographs, essays, and documents, while leading German-Jewish writers such as Jakob Wassermann, Lion Feuchtwanger, Felix Theilhaber, Josef Kastein and Esriel Carlebach made them a mainstay of the popular imagination.[6]

But why would heretics like Sabbatai Sevi and Spinoza prove so attractive in the first place? It is easy to see how German Jews whose relation to Judaism was defined above all by estrangement could find in the heretics of Jewish history a set of useful ancestors. For many, the fact of their heresy was all that remained of their Jewishness save the name. But heretics served a more specific purpose. They could be mobilized in the service of a Jewish peoplehood understood as prior to religious creed or practice. They were conduits for debate about a more recent development in the course of Jewish history: the advent of modern Jewish nationalism.[7] The upshot of Jewish peoplehood was a revision of religious forms of identity grounded either in Jewish law (orthodoxy) or in a secularized and universal version of a Jewish prophetic mission (liberal, reform). The test of its strength, then, inhered in its capacity to repatriate Judaism's heretics: the more offensive the heretic and odious his crime, the deeper the national bond required to include him.[8] The move routed two foes in a single stroke. It of course ruined the lawful piety of the orthodox. But it also reversed the nineteenth-century, liberal embrace of a figure like Spinoza, who for the liberal had made it incumbent upon the Jew-in-particular to become a man-in-general. To repair Spinoza to the fold, rather than trail after him beyond it, meant to yoke him into the service of a Jewish nationhood against which the orthodox and reform, though erstwhile enemies, could nonetheless join in opposition.

Arguments about Jewish self-assertion and self-creation were pursued through the Sabbatians in particular. Zalman Rubashov recalled as formative a childhood incident in Russia, in which a neighbor inveighed against the Zionist sin of "hastening the end" of exile (d'chikat ha-ketz) by working for the Jewish return to Palestine. In this, they reproduced the crime of the Sabbatians. They had arrogated to man what was best left to God.[9] Meanwhile, in the West, Theodor Herzl imagined in his novel *Altneuland* a future Jewish state in which *Sabbatai Sevi*, the opera, would play to wide acclaim. But to imagine it did not necessarily mean to approve of it, and elsewhere, Herzl felt obliged to defend Zionism against the charge that it, too, would destroy the Jewish people as it met its inevitable and ignominious end. Sabbatianism had failed, he argued, insofar as it refused to loose itself from Oriental enthusiasm. Zionism, on the other hand, would succeed "because we have machines," because it harnessed for the Jewish people a Western will to human self-assertion in a hostile and unforgiving world.[10]

Whatever Herzl's ambivalence, other Zionist intellectuals were quick to discover in the Sabbatian movement an important prefiguration of their own. For the most part, they belonged to what David Biale has described as the revolutionary and counterhistorical revision of the *Wissenschaft des Judentums* (Science of Judaism).[11] In its origins, the *Wissenschaft des Judentums* thought of itself in terms akin to Minerva's owl. It flew at dusk, which meant that it appeared in the twilight years of the object it described. Jewish history might be written, but only because it was over. Leopold Zunz had argued this point in his programmatic essay, *Etwas über die rabbinische Literatur* (1818), often understood as the foundational document of the movement.[12] But the advent of Jewish nationalism toward the end of the nineteenth century changed all that.

What had presented as a corpse to the coroners of the *Wissenschaft des Judentums* appeared as a living, breathing organism to the practitioners of the new scholarship. The metaphor says much: Zionists for the most part adapted organological metaphors for collective Jewish identity. They privileged the Jewish people over the Jewish religion and held up the willfulness, striving, and self-assertion of the Jewish organism as the measure of its "life." The Sabbatian revolt against the law, the scope of the mass movement and the activism of its program, the revival of a Jewish nation: all this appealed to a group of Zionists who hoped for something of the same. Here is Scholem, for example, after a memorable conversation with Walter Benjamin in 1927 about Abraham Miguel Cardozo, one of the premier theologians of the Sabbatian movement: "Was Judaism still alive," he wondered, "or did it exist only as an object of cognition?"[13] The same question underwrote Scholem's investigations in "Redemption through Sin." There he would speak of a Zionism that enabled like-minded scholars to "detect in Sabbatianism's throes those gropings toward a healthier national existence which must have seemed like an undiluted nightmare to the peaceable Jewish bourgeois of the nineteenth century."[14] The program is clear: heresy in the service of Jewish self-assertion.

How heretical? Totally, and the example of Jacob Frank (1726–1791) best demonstrates it. By nearly all accounts, Frank and his followers represented the total devolution of the Sabbatian impulse. A professed "reincarnation" of Sabbatai Sevi, Frank was something of a malefactor magnet. He attracted a group of former Sabbatians in Poland, led them in a series of savage transgressions, and enjoined them to follow him into the bosom of the Catholic Church. They promptly beset their former coreligionists in public disputations with charges of a blood libel, even as they continued to practice in secret the Sabbatian principle of the holiness of sin. The group ultimately splintered and died: some dissolved into the fabric of Polish life, others fomented revolution in France (where references to their leader Jacob raised suspicions about their supposed Jacobin loyalties), and still others became proponents of Jewish enlightenment and assimilation, in Austria especially.[15] Heinrich Graetz, the leading Jewish historian of the nineteenth century, had dismissed them as a gang of "common liars and adventurers."[16] Scholem would denounce Frank as "one of the most frightening phenomena in the whole of Jewish history," a "strongman-messiah" who debased even the doctrine of redemption through sin.[17] "It is one thing to worship God," Frank is reported to have said, "and quite another to follow the path that I have taken."[18]

But Rubashov had a soft spot for this early-modern Manson. The year 1912 found him at work on the Frankists in the bucolic German town of Freiburg.[19] And in 1923 he published in book form his essay *Al Tile Beit*

Frank (On the Ruins of the House of Frank). "The gods they worshiped I do not know, their paths of worship are strange to me and foreign, and the price they paid on their behalf—it is loathsome," Rubashov began. "But nonetheless. . ." But nonetheless he undertook to grasp the Frankists as his siblings. He imagined that he shared their distaste for the dim and dirty claptrap rooms that passed for eastern European Hebrew schools. And he concluded that his Jewish present had flourished in a garden nourished by the Frankist past.[20] In "Redemption through Sin," Scholem professed similar ambivalence: disgust at Frank's debauchery and excess, but admiration for the genuine "creed of life" at work in his grotesqueries. With Rubashov he shared a neo-romantic sensibility for which creation proceeds out of negation, a world on the heels of its ruin.[21]

Scholem's brief for the heretics, it should now be clear, was by no means his alone. By the time he wrote "Redemption through Sin," one could complain of a Sabbatian absence in Jewish historical memory only out of ignorance or blindness or a will to either one. Nor could one argue in 1935 that the Sabbatians had vanished from the scholarly radar, Jewish or otherwise. What, then, was the innovation and significance of Scholem's essay? It did not inhere in his recuperation of the Sabbatians for Jewish historical memory. Others had done that, too. It did not inhere in original archival scholarship. The sources assembled by Scholem in the piece had in large part been collected by others, and pale in comparison with those he would later discover as he plumbed the libraries of New York and Oxford, Paris and Italy, Germany and Poland throughout the 1930s, '40s, and '50s.[22] Nor did the essay represent a summation of Scholem's research. It was in fact one of the first he devoted to the theme, followed by nearly forty more, a two-volume Hebrew biography, and a thousand-page English revision.[23] It was more of a program than a summation. In retrospect, the essay is a promissory note. But what exactly did it promise?

It is difficult to say. The essay had many possible futures.[24] Scholem might have developed any number of themes whose implications spoke as much to his present as to an imagined Jewish past. Most obviously, "Redemption through Sin" functioned as a salvo in debates about Jewish self-creation and national difference by describing heresy as a mode of Jewish self-assertion. It wrecked orthodoxy by recovering for the Jewish people even those Sabbatian radicals who thought it their task, not only that of their apostate messiah, to advance the cause of redemption through the doctrine of the holiness of sin.[25] It destroyed a reform, liberal scheme that could tolerate heresy more easily than its orthodox cousin, but which could tolerate Jewish nationhood even less. It also proposed a crucial distinction between the sort of Jew and his relation to the world espoused by the Sabbatians on one hand, the Frankists on the other: or, *between heresy as a mode of Jewish self-assertion and a ruinous Jewish nihilism*.[26]

All these themes would surface in the essay's most important iteration. Scholem would return to "Redemption through Sin" almost forty years later. He would reproduce pages of it verbatim (if in German), but would resituate the essay and so rewrite it. In 1974 he delivered a talk to the scholars of comparative religion assembled at Eranos called "Der Nihilismus als Religiöses Phänomen" (Nihilism as a Religious Phenomenon). The essay situates Sabbatian and Frankist nihilism in the context of a two-thousand-year history of competing languages of heresy, which Scholem had by 1974 come to understand also as two complementary languages of nihilism: the gnostic and the pantheist. By 1974, that is, Scholem had adapted the interwar discourse of heresy. By 1974, he had made that tongue his own, and the great expanse of his corpus is best understood as a record of how he did it. In other words, Scholem wrote a history of Jewish mysticism as a history of Jewish revisions (or as he would put it, sublimations) of the gnostic and pantheist impulses. This was no mere historiographic exercise. The guiding force behind these revisions was to save the relative autonomy of the world as a scene for Jewish self-assertion, or as a scene for what Scholem considered authentic Jewish life.

CHAPTER TEN

Jewish Gnosticism

Have we completely separated from You
Oh God? In darkness
Shall we no longer be overtaken by any whiff
Of Your peace, of Your message?
—Gershom Scholem, *With a Copy of Kafka's* The Trial

In 1958, Hans Jonas wondered out loud what might have become of Western civilization had the gnostic message prevailed. The formulation is symptomatic. Jonas hoped to defeat the gnostic threat but could do so only by first resurrecting it. He did well to contest the gnostic denigration of worldliness with a philosophy of the organism and an environmental ethics. He did less well to contain the proliferation of the name, and in fact contributed to the expansion of its currency. Before Jonas, gnosticism could be specified as an adaptation of Greek, Jewish, Christian, or Persian thought. After him, and against his wishes, it became shorthand for the modern condition. Asked in 1975 whether religious patterns of thought endured among the moderns, Jonas answered in the affirmative, and he sustained his claim with an example: "I receive letters from people . . . who tell me that by reading *The Gnostic Religion* they felt helped in their self-knowledge." More often than not, the letters arrived from California, and all this, Jonas added, "sometimes makes me feel uncomfortable."[1]

Jonas had thought of his book as a casket for his gnostic friends. It proved to be a chrysalis instead. For the gnostic message prevailed, and not only among Golden State spiritualists who looked to Jonas for guidance in their quest for self-discovery. They and others participated in a wholesale revival of the term, and as they understood it, of the gnostic ethos also. Jonas had abetted them in this endeavor. But so had the work of his friend Gershom Scholem, whose researches in the history of Jewish mysticism did much, perhaps more than Jonas himself, to revive the gnostic spirit for the needs of the twentieth century.

Jonas did not begrudge the acclaim paid his friend. But he did in the end begrudge its source, a diffuse but widespread sense that the gnostic era is also our own. With two exceptions—Heidegger and Barth—Jonas had always resisted the urge to find in the world around him an irruption of the ancient heresy. A distinguished series of critics, however, has gravitated to Scholem on precisely this count. "As much as the stories and parables of Kafka," the critic Harold Bloom has claimed, "Scholem's work helped inaugurate [an age of] Jewish gnosticism." Bloom described Scholem as the quintessentially Miltonic figure of modern scholarship. Like Milton and all those who make themselves appear "early" and their interpretive rivals "late"—like those, that is, whose interpretations overwhelm every alternative—Scholem was a "sect of one."[2]

Bloom had one thing absolutely right: Scholem's vast corpus ought to be understood as an attempt to write the history of Jewish mysticism as a contest between gnostic and Neoplatonic principles, or in the terms more appropriate to Scholem's age, between gnostic and pantheist languages of heresy. Judaism could abide neither the gnostic divorce of God from world nor their pantheist conflation. But it could—and kabbalah on Scholem's account did—internalize gnosticism by positing a dualism immanent to the Godhead itself, and it could countenance a Neoplatonic or panentheist scheme for which creation is understood as the self-emanation of the divine. Kabbalah, in other words, offered Scholem a means to speak Jewish dialects of the gnostic and pantheist languages of heresy current in interwar Europe—and to speak these otherwise competing languages together.

Bloom was right about another thing, too: though gnosticism does not vanquish its pantheist opponent in Scholem's corpus, it does prevail. The gnostic motif simply dominates Scholem's work, from his earliest diaries, reviews, and dissertation to his essays, books, seminars, and broadcasts. He claimed to discover the gnostic spirit at work among Jews in the Near East of late antiquity, in thirteenth-century Spain, in sixteenth-century Palestine, in seventeenth-century Amsterdam, in eighteenth-century Poland, and in twentieth-century Prague. He found it in Moses de Leon (ca. 1240-1305) and the brothers Cohen of Castile, in Isaac Luria (1534-1572) and in Sabbatai Sevi (1626-1676), in Nathan of Gaza (1643-1680), Jacob Frank (1726-1791), and Franz Kafka (1883-1924). He found it in the *Shiur Komah* and the *Sefer Ha-Bahir*, in the *Zohar* and the *Treatise on the Emanations of the Left*, in the *Book of the Words of the Lord* and *The Trial*. Gnosticism could refer in his work to a hidden God and to an androgynous God, to metaphysical dualism and to the ascent of the soul, to sexual libertinism and to the scattering of the holy sparks, and most importantly, to something called "myth." (In his more programmatic statements, Scholem took care to distance himself from the exponents of kabbalistic "pantheism," from those kabbalists most indebted to a Neoplatonic theory of creation as the self-emanation of God.) Scholem's gnoseophilia did know bounds. But they were loose ones.

What, then, does it mean that Scholem was so intent on introducing into kabbalah and the course of Jewish history the gnostic principle, however he may have defined it? Why would Scholem have opted for Jewish gnosticism even—or especially—in those cases where the option came at the expense of the historical record, a record to which he—a professed historian—otherwise pledged fidelity? To reduce his option to a matter of "taste" or to a rebellious hankering for the nasty and taboo will not suffice.[3] Neither will it do to chalk it up to the influence of his friend Jonas, or to the scholarship of the *religionsgeschichtliche Schule*, or to that of the *Wissenschaft des Judentums*. To be sure, each supplied Scholem with elements of a scholarly vocabulary. But the advent of Scholem's "gnostic" sensibility—his sense for God's absence and a pervasive unease about the world—predated his encounters with them all. As Jonas wrote of the gnostic spirit of late antiquity, so we might say of Scholem: the gnostic spirit was in his case more of a *Daseinshaltung* than a syncretistic hodgepodge of influence and origins. Nor will it do merely to highlight the willfulness of Scholem's choice.[4] It is a necessary step, but only a first one, since it immediately begs the question: why?

I would like to offer an account guided by the premise that "Jewish gnosticism" originates as much in interwar Europe as in any of the epochs in which Scholem thought it to operate. This is hardly a controversial claim, or should not be. Jewish gnosticism arose out of a series of hermeneutic fusions between past and present unique to the 1920s and '30s. It arose as a Jewish revision of the gnostic language of heresy. Scholem's stance on the scholarship of his time helps to explain the phenomenon. But so does the relation of his Jewish gnosticism to his other intellectual and political commitments. What, in particular, does this most willful of his choices for the Jewish past have to do with his Zionism, the most obvious and willful of his choices for the Jewish present?

WRITING A *ZARATHUSTRA* FOR THE JEWS

"Who among us young Jews has not seen himself as Jesus and the Messiah of the oppressed?"[5] This remarkable apology precedes the most highly charged passage in Scholem's early journals. He fancied himself the "chosen one," the "expected one," and in a play on his Hebrew surname, called himself "Scholem, the perfected one."[6] In his own defense, he cast his messianic fantasy as the "unconscious product of an irrepressible poetic force," and he attributed it to a yearning: "[my] yearning for the new, [for the] unwrought that should come to us, that I wish to and cannot announce, my yearning for objective and subjective redemption."[7]

The preface was intended as a prophylactic. Scholem wanted to deflect the criticisms his imaginary readers might voice against his "megaloma-nia." Evidently, he was unconcerned that the preface also cast his kingship in Christian terms. Not all young Jews aspired to become Jesus, after all, an occupational fantasy that Scholem, dejected, would months later recant.[8] Whatever future it augured, however, this adolescent fantasy does reveal one thing at least: Scholem pined for sweeping transformation—both for himself and for the world in which he lived. This was no call for liberal reform. It was a call for existential revolution, a thoroughgoing reorientation of the self. The invention of self writ small in this fragment and writ large in the diaries was meant to erase every trace of exile and to emerge—cleansed, pure and whole—as something prophesied by a Jewish version of Nietzsche's *Zarathustra*. "This book," Scholem wrote, "is in fact a new Bible. Oh yes, to write something like this, that is an ideal for me. That is it. To write a *Judenzarathustra* . . . whoever could do such a thing." The *Judenzarathustra* called not only for a new Jew (Scholem) but also for wholesale overcoming: of a liberal bourgeoisie, all forms of German-Jewish symbiosis, and not least a European culture of which both were symptom and symbol. "Zion" was the alternative Scholem proclaimed. It was the "measure of all things," the "solution to all imperfections."[9]

But why take these journals seriously at all? We do not encounter a mature scholar. We find instead a talented and troubled young man. His diaries are by turns outlandish, venomous, brilliant, and not a little disturbed (and for all these reasons immensely fun to read). Here, for example, is what Scholem wrote of Martin Buber (a Zionist inspired by Nietzsche and a popularizer of Hasidic folktales) following a talk by Buber at a Berlin community center:

> What one would dare nowhere else: to speak before an assembly without a study of the sources, one does with Hasidism. And those congregated there stood in *aesthetic ecstasy* and whispered so to speak: ah, ah, religiosity—Religiosity. It is unheard of shamelessness. . . . These people who have absolutely no conception of Jewry, that they pass the time with Jewish "religiosity" (what does that mean in Hebrew?) and aestheticize with it in front of *goyim* and young girls, *I do not recognize them as Zionists.*

They had "prostituted reverence as such." They were "liars" who "in the mornings defiled the youth entrusted to them and in the evenings defiled themselves."[10]

Harsh words, but hardly untypical. Here is Scholem on the youth movements of his time, charged with the task of spiritual renewal, but stymied by their older leaders:

Youth should be ideal, so I hear it everywhere from the pig-dogs, the filthy, squealing, that means, youth should be dumb and allow the Knights of Schmutz to stuff crap in the mouth, that youth should strike itself dead for these people, but we do not want, we do not want, we do not want, you—people! Youth should be ideal, yes, we say it here without your filthy undertone, ideal, that means oriented *against you*, against all that is lowly and impure.[11]

And here he is on Theodor Herzl, foremost representative of the Zionist movement:

It is good that he has died, otherwise we would have been compelled to try him for high treason against the Jewish people, we, his own students. . . . His only thought was: the Jewish *State*. And that we reject. For we preach anarchism. We do not want a state, but a free society. . . . We do not go to Palestine to found a state—oh, you little Philistines—and to ensnare ourselves in new chains [forged] out of the old, we go to Palestine out of thirst for freedom and yearning for the future, for the future belongs to the Orient."[12]

Again, why take an adolescent narcissist seriously? Scholem's early writings have a thematic logic, but not an expository one. They are the product of a febrile mind playing games of association, the traces of a wild and woolly "metaphysicizing." Read with caution and care, however, these notebooks tell us much. They provide wonderful material to consider (radical, Jewish) selfhood as lived out, so to speak, on the page. Above all, they document the advent of problems later refined and explored in his scholarship. They help us grapple with an enduring conundrum: the relation between his life and work, his person and thought. They also make plain why Scholem found so attractive the gospel of the alien god.

Scholem's story is a Jewish story. It is also a European one. This sounds banal, but it also runs against Scholem's self-estimation—his earliest understanding of Zionism was so radical that it could not admit of European origins and ends. But Scholem articulated a Jewish version of a European crisis, and his response, if in the language of Zion, was indebted to the Europe he hoped to leave behind. It was, after all, embedded in the very name of his endeavor—to write a *Zarathustra* for the Jews. For this reason, Scholem's early Zionism proved a chimera. Jerusalem was not to be his fate and destiny—not Jerusalem alone, but Berlin as well. Zion as Scholem first imagined it was an illusion, and his later acknowledgment of the fact, formative.

As for Scholem's imagination, it was born of a world gone bad. It is impossible to overstate the importance of this sensibility. Crisis was paramount, and was embodied for him in one figure above all: the "Angel of Uncertainty." This angel was no corpulent cherub—he had no divine master and brought no glad tidings. He sneered at Scholem, lashed him with his whip. Scholem could not imagine life without the Angel's sadistic prodding, for the Angel of Uncertainty had become his "fate and destiny," his "taskmaster and instigator." The pain, however, was welcome. The Angel may have "thrown [Scholem] out into the world," but in this had created the precondition for greatness. It all came down to gathering oneself up in the face of adversity, and responding with what Scholem called a *selbstherrliche Gesetzgebung*, a lawgiving at once autocratic, *selbstherrlich*, but more literally self-ruling, *selbst-herrlich*. This response, he believed, was both "magnificent and necessary" (it was also copied from Nietzsche's playbook).[13]

All this spoke to Scholem's solution—Zion—but first and foremost to the "logic" of crisis thought in general. "Decision" and "deed" were its watchwords, undertaken both to stare down the "gaping chasms" and "frightening paradoxes" of interwar life and to transcend the world as it was. It is easy to discern the affinity of this language for the anti-liberalism and world-alienation associated with the theologians of crisis, not to mention so many of Scholem's modernist contemporaries. Many of them repudiated "culture"—understood as incurably bourgeois—whether in the form of the German-Jewish obsession with *Bildung* (self-cultivation), or in the form of the "cultural Protestantism" that had made of God a mere experience of man. Scholem was no different. Here, for example, is Scholem speaking to "his people":

> You are Orientals and not Europeans, you are Jews and humans, not Germans and decadents, your God is called Haschem, and not the belly. You have gone [morally] bankrupt, or you make, and this is worse still, compromises. Because, so you say, one must not attempt to run through the wall with [one's] head, [for] the head will split apart! . . . We, however, the coming generation, we believe this. . . . We believe that we must run into the wall with our heads and that the *wall* will split in two, not our heads.

These were wall runners and enthusiasts, the *Mauerrenner und Schwärmer* who would "leave culture in its disreputable form in Europe" and "create over there, where our hearts are, a true people without all these lies and deceptions. It is our task: to bring about the deed, the redeeming deed. . . . To run against the wall with our heads and not only to believe, no, to know that it will smash in—that is laid upon us."[14]

Scholem's animus toward liberal civilization, not to mention the reigning forms of (post-liberal) Zionism, is obvious. But his radicalism also created insuperable difficulties. The point of smashing into walls is, presumably, to break through to the other side. For Scholem, this meant Zion. But Zion was for him so pure, so unadulterated, that even the memory of that which came before—*Galut*, exile—threatened to pollute it. It was Eden, but before the Fall, not after its restitution. For this reason, Scholem imagined that those who will "live Zion" will fail to understand those who have enabled it. "When Zion is spoken of, so their lips [will] smile and know no longer of the crisis of those who went." They are "entirely free," severed from Diaspora altogether.[15] They live in a house of language in which "exile" has not been exiled so much as made unintelligible. Zion does not mean for them what it did for Scholem. It is no alternative. It is all they know.

Scholem was obsessed with this existential plenitude, and it loomed large as he considered the programs tendered by the Zionist youth groups of Berlin. According to these groups, he reasoned, "Zionism is the demand of a great life in the Land of Israel. If the great life allows its realization only in the primal forms of human society," forms unavailable to those born of exile, then the Zionist act would entail the "sacrifice of the self, so that our children [might] find a free path toward a free earth. The Zionist act, then, would be suicide." Scholem distinguished two fates, equally wanting: "the going over as one who defiles, as one who has not yet become Jewish, and suicide."[16]

Scholem struggled to discover an alternative. As opposed to the defilers, Scholem celebrated modes of becoming that promised an instantaneous transformation of state. With the advocates of suicide, however, and with Nietzsche too, Scholem grappled with the problem of memory. He emphasized modes of becoming that suppressed traces of origins, that denied the fact and the signs of their becoming. After all, to bash one's head against the wall seems calculated to induce amnesia. But whereas the advocates of suicide countenanced only death, Scholem's *Judenzarathustra* held out the promise for a form of rebirth. Whereas the advocates of suicide could produce only a proleptic writing of their own demise, Scholem imagined in the *Judenzarathustra* a form of writing that would displace his death as German Jew on to the figure of an other. It would open a space for the writing of his life as Scholem, while erasing the traces of the death that enabled it.

Scholem returned to this line of thought when he mulled over his name. He had a predilection for onomancy—to divine fate from the letters of a name—and the impulse that once led him to proclaim his kingship as Scholem, "the perfected one," he sustained unabated several years later: "All that I now wish for I could summarize in epigrammatic [fashion], that one might be able to inscribe in my gravestone without lying: He was his name or: *schmo haja hu*, that means: He was Scholem, that is whole, he was so as his name demanded it from him, he lived his name, to be whole and undivided."[17]

Scholem rarely considered his first name, though he would have done well to do so. Gershom, after all, recalls the Diasporic origins Scholem elsewhere aimed to suppress. The name combines two words: the *ger* of Gershom refers to the biblical figure of the "stranger" or "resident alien," while its *sham* locates the Israelites "there" in Egypt. Moses conjured the name for his eldest son as a reminder: "he called his name Gershom, for he said, 'I have been a stranger in an alien land.' " Like the Exodus tale itself, this story of naming stresses a sense of always coming from somewhere else.[18]

In other words, Scholem named himself in a way that preserved memories of his enslavement to the *chukkat gojim*, to the rule of non-Jews, whose shackles he desperately sought to shed. There is an irony here, an irony with a set of historical and philosophical correlates. German and Jew are joined most deeply, that is, at just those points where Scholem fulminated against modern, hybrid, German-Jewish identities. That he proclaimed his kingship in Christian terms; that he wrote of Zion as a Jewish version of *Heimat* (a German term for "homeland"); that he rejected the state as a European idolatry even as he embraced an anarchism of European origin; that his rhetoric of crisis and deed, his animus for ideologies of progress, his metaphors of the abyss, the chasm, and the paradox echoed the themes developed by so many of his European contemporaries: these examples and others attest to a thoroughly European imagination. They also reveal the terms in which Scholem rejected hybrid, German-Jewish identity as infused and enabled by it. But perhaps this should come as no surprise. Scholem's case recalls once more Nietzsche's youthful vanguard destined to fashion a "more beautiful and blessed humanity." This vanguard suffers from both a malady (the burden of history) and its homeopathic antidotes (what Nietzsche called the un-historical and super-historical sensibilities) within which the traces of the sickness they aim to heal are inscribed.[19]

It will not do, however, to leave the matter at that. Scholem ought not be made a victim of a familiar conceit: that the orthodox thrives upon the heterodox, dogma upon its alternatives. We need to acknowledge a second impulse, subordinate to Scholem's Nietzschean moods and infrequent at this point in his life, but present nonetheless. Scholem's act of naming, after all, was purposeful. He considered it "no scandal" to have set himself "upon the correct path out of a manifestly un-Jewish milieu."[20] From this perspective, his naming was a renunciation of the Jewish self-overcoming he derived from Nietzsche, or at least an intuitive recognition of its futility. In these moods, he recognized that he was destined also to be among those he would forty years later call "men from afar." In these moods, Scholem recognized that it was not the Scholem heralded by the *Judenzarathustra* that was to be his fate and destiny, but also the *ger*; not Jerusalem alone, but Berlin as well. That which distinguishes them doubles as the mark that divides those willing to make their peace with the partial heteronomy of a hybrid condition from those who resist it at all costs. It divides those who want to make do with their lot from those intent on plenitude, those for whom Diaspora need not be erased from those for whom nothing but Zion will suffice.

BERNE, 1918

Fast-forward several years. In the summer of 1917, at twenty years of age, Scholem was called to war. He had spent two years assiduous in his efforts to avoid the draft, but could do so no longer. He feigned mental illness instead. Army doctors watched over him for six weeks and eventually ruled him, in January of 1918, mentally unfit for military service. But they had evidently declared him acceptable for the academy: armed not with a gun but a discharge, Scholem went first to the university at Jena and then in May left Germany altogether for Switzerland, where his friend Walter Benjamin had made a home in exile with his wife near Berne. Scholem admired Benjamin. In the months before his departure, he could hardly contain himself as he recalled his first encounters with Benjamin as the "greatest experience of my life." He reckoned Benjamin "the miracle that in every generation comes only once." Benjamin stood as a foundation at the "center of [his] life, he and no other." Words to describe the gratitude he felt for "this prophet of God" eluded him. Scholem "yearned indescribably" for him.[21]

Things did not turn out as planned. Scholem seems to have fallen for Dora, Walter's wife, as a strange sort of mother figure, and his estimations of Benjamin fluctuated wildly. Scholem arrived on May 4, a Saturday. Benjamin met him at the station in Berne. "Our togetherness," Scholem wrote that evening, "has already astonished me." The next day brought similar appraisals of Benjamin's wife, "the most beautiful on this earth." "She knows how very much I love her." But the following days ushered in dolor and despair. "My life converges upon suicide," Scholem wrote.

> That is the naked truth, which has for four weeks been tumbling around in my head like a mill-wheel. Never before have I thought of death with such intensity and proximity, of self-murder, as in these weeks. Day for day, night for night. And Walter and Dora, instead of

helping, only make it worse. They hound me literally to my death. There are moments—God and them both, forgive me!—when I consider them wholly ignoble people.

And still further: "I can not live with Walter and Dora. *I can not, God*. Walter may be what he always is, there is a limit which he does not transgress. That I must experience daily. Metaphysics makes him crazy. His perception is no longer human, but that which is entrusted by God to the insane." Insane or not, within two weeks Scholem had set Goethe and Plato in comparison, to their detriment, with his friend. "*If* one will at one time begin to understand him," a coming-to-pass that Scholem doubted Benjamin would live to see—if it should come to pass at all, "one will understand his life as the miracle" that defies all commentary save silence. One week Scholem thought Benjamin a miracle. The next, when Scholem returned a borrowed book in less than timely fashion, he thought him a hysterical despot instead.[22]

And so on. Still, the time was a heady one. Together, Scholem and Benjamin founded a farcical university, called Muri. With Dora they discussed poetry, wrote and devoted poems to one another. Benjamin embarked on some of his most celebrated texts. Scholem decided upon a course of study in kabbalah. He also arrived at some of his most enduring insights. In particular, Scholem committed to paper some thoughts on the problem of nature in general, and the landscape in particular. They tell us much about how a maturing Scholem imagined himself as a being in the world, and convey a sense for why Scholem found so appealing the gospel of the alien god.

Scholem's reflections came prompted by the view from his "watchtower," his rooftop perch on the edge of town. "The cornfield under my window shows me anew," he wrote on a glorious day in late June, "what a fullness and greatness can lie in such a simple speck of nature. I know now, how deep and beautiful is the comparison of the sea with the cornfield through which the wind blows. The waves overtake one another . . . and there is a rush and a movement within it all that gives rise to moments in which I am," he concluded, "wholly deceived." So Scholem wrote in a first indication of his unease. Something about the reverie and its promise gnawed at him. "Before me are alone the fields, the forest and the mountains beyond. There the world ends." But the proximity of the world only made manifest Scholem's more primary sense of alienation. "It hurts."[23]

Scholem thought he was destined never to feel at one with nature. "I live off [the fact] that the landscape is *outside* of me," he insisted. The prospect of union with the natural world Scholem dismissed as a false promise, as the "great swindle of pantheism." Quite the contrary proved true: "Im

Abstande erst erzeugt sich ja mein Leben," Scholem wrote. "My life arises first out of *distance* [from nature]." To be as one with the landscape, that, Scholem added, is "the great and horrible magic act of the modern." But not even the most accomplished of epochal prestidigitators—the modern age—could make disappear a single, obstinate fact. "I am," Scholem wrote. "'I am': that is always a lament."[24]

Scholem's word for lament, *Klage*, allows of another translation. It means also complaint or accusation, and there can be little doubt Scholem had this in mind. Already for several years he had mulled over the peculiarities of a language used to levy a complaint against God. How is God to be accused? And if guilty, how is he to be punished?

Scholem's stylized musings do not always make sense. But whatever their literary merit and logical coherence, they do communicate a few basic postulates. First, lamentation is not one language among others. It is the language of counter-revelation itself—revelation's "deep antipode." On the one hand, this meant that the lament shared with revelation its formal characteristics—both were languages of "form without content" or "validity without meaning."[25] But if revelation manifests itself as a voice that enters the world from afar, lamentation is the voice of the world shouted into the void. (As Hans Jonas might have put it, it is the outcry of mute things themselves, for Jonas the new revelation man must heed.) "The order of creation itself," Scholem hypothesized, "protects the lament from destruction." He spoke of the lament of natural things, likening their cry to the scream of a birth.[26] To be in this world—for Scholem to lament "I am"—is therefore to be natural, but also deficient. Scholem's is a world that screams in protest. It is a world that defies God's claims upon it with a language of lamentation all its own. It is a world that announces its relative autonomy, but also its want. It is not a gnostic world of autonomous evil. But it is a world—a creation—characterized by a deficit or unredeemable promise.

It should come, then, as little surprise that Scholem would also refer to the world as a "Welt-Golus," a world-exile, or that he would affirm the kabbalistic notion of the *shvirat ha-kelim*, the breaking of the vessels, as a "gruesome truth," or that he would state as his aim "the total negation of this time." It should come as little surprise that he would declare the landscape a death shroud, *Landschaft* as *Leichentuch*, or that he would note with appreciation the resonance of the Hebrew *tzalmon*, landscape, with *tzel* and *tzalmavet*, a shadowy darkness and a world of death. Neither should it surprise that he would entertain as "outstanding" the idea that the world was not created by God, but by the devil, nor that he would cite God's absence as the fundament of the modern condition. Scholem's sense of alienation was wildly overdetermined: from God, who had absconded from the scene of his creation; from the world, insofar as he refused the seductions of natural beauty as pantheist deceit; but also, and most insidiously, in the world. To be is to be in the world, but without a home, in exile, foreign. It is to lament.[27]

Some of these—the *deus absconditus*, creation as a scene of exile and alienation, being-in-the-world as lament—made Scholem receptive to the gospel of the alien god. They read like a gnostic catechism, at least as described by Jonas, his early guide to the world of archons and aeons. But even these most intense of Scholem's gnostic moods could not quash an alternative already there at the outset. Even the most acidulous despair of the world could not induce him to abandon it altogether. It remained, after all, God's creation, and despite his absence he had once pronounced it to be good. However much Scholem's God had absented himself, he nonetheless remained a Jewish, not a gnostic, God. As Hans Jonas wrote of the gnostic divine, "Some positive attributes and metaphors do apply to him: Light, Life, Spirit, Father, the Good." But others—"Creator, Ruler, Judge"—did not.[28] By contrast, Scholem sanctified just those features in his appreciation for *Gericht*, which in the German incorporates complaint and lament, witness, judgment, and execution. In November of 1918, at least, Scholem fixed on the category as that which "orders my life today."[29]

To reject the comeliness of the world as deceit, then, did not necessarily mean to reject the world itself. It meant to reject one way of relating to it, a malaise Scholem associated with modern Judaism and the modern world in general (the one "collapsed" into the other). Both, he thought, privileged a false experience of the world, "Natur*genuss*," or "*enjoyment* of nature." Both reduced the natural world to a means to the end of human gratification. And so both modernity and modern Judaism might be overcome, as he wrote to his friend Heller, by establishing "a relation to the things of this world" characterized by "true freedom, purity, and rigor."[30] What that meant went unspecified. But his aim shared much with that he would later ascribe to the Jewish mystic, who in paradoxical fashion "lives and acts in perpetual rebellion against a world with which he strives with all his zeal to be at peace." The contradictions—indeed, the near incoherence of this position— Scholem considered not debilitating but fruitful, the product of a gnostic return in the heart of Judaism.[31]

Scholem did not elaborate on the point, at least not in 1918, in his diaries. He did not yet have at his disposal a means to express this sensibility, had he even recognized it for what it was. To Heller he confided his despair, for example, about the pseudo-metaphysical posturing into which he lapsed in pursuit of these thoughts. Neither had Scholem yet discovered a suitable subject through which to develop these concerns. He would find it shortly, in the kabbalah, and he would discover in historical discourse a language formally suited to the task.

KABBALAH AND MYTH

"The task is certainly not to find refutations of myth or of pantheism, but to annihilate them." These words are not Scholem's, at least not originally, though anyone would be forgiven for thinking they were. A similar formulation appeared in a letter Scholem wrote in 1937 to the publisher Zalman Schocken, and has since become hallmark Scholemiana. Scholem promised a candid word on his decision to study kabbalah, and spoke in part of how he hoped to discover there a sublimation—literally a negation, suspension, and raising up—of both myth and pantheism. In Scholemspeak, myth and gnosticism were interchangeable, and so his remark of 1937 meant in effect: I set out to write a history of the kabbalah as a history of Jewish attempts to speak both gnostic and pantheist languages of heresy at once; I set out also to show that the kabbalists did so not only while remaining Jews, but by making these heretical languages, or their adaptations, constitutive of Judaism itself. "The comment, first made to me by a pious Jew, that there was nonetheless something to [pantheism and myth] struck me as far more important," Scholem averred, than the order to defeat them. To demonstrate the patent falsehood of the gnostic and pantheist stance posed no challenge at all. The gnostic divorce of God from world made it the equally vacuous reversal of their pantheist conflation. Scholem rejected both as incompatible with a Jewish view for which creature and creator are autonomous yet allied, in which God and world are far, yet near.

The remark was not Scholem's, not in its origins anyway. Neither was it the remark of a pious Jew as he claimed. It was, rather, a directive from his friend Benjamin, as Scholem dutifully recorded in his diaries of 1918. What Benjamin meant by the phrase remains unclear. What Scholem understood it to mean does not. To Benjamin's remark he added the following diagnosis: "This," the attempt to construct antitheses to pantheism and to myth, had been "the principally false stance of Jewish religious philosophy from Rambam to [Hermann] Cohen." Eight hundred years of a Jewish philosophical tradition had gone about the task altogether wrong. The stance neither annihilates nor sublimates. It does not preserve or sustain those aspects of the gnostic and pantheist positions amenable to Jewish thought. "It 'refutes' " instead.[32] Scholem's decision to contest this tradition with an alternative in which myth had a central role to play, his decision, as it were, to remythologize a Jewish past by discovering a form of gnosticism at its core—all this ought to be appreciated for the decisive choice that it was.

That he chose there can be no doubt. Scholem arrived at his conclusions about Jewish gnosticism the way some are encouraged to vote—early and often.[33] Scholem took the directive to heart, but also, it seems, too far.

The votes for Jewish gnosticism suffer from ruinous flaws, and so Scholem's option has roused over the years a number of calls for a recount.[34] Whatever the plausibility of his claims, however, they are historically intelligible as one instance of a wider phenomenon: the gnostic language of heresy spoken by his contemporaries, Jewish and non-Jewish, between the world wars. His sense for creation as a scene of exile and alienation, of being-in-the-world as lament, of God's absence— all these reveal him as a Jewish practitioner of the gnostic discourse that his Protestant contemporaries had developed. His myth was for the Jewish people, but it was a version of a myth embraced by other modern malcontents. That he chose there can be no doubt, but the real questions are why and how.

Why: because the problem raised by the kabbalists was, he thought, his own. "If, finally, you ask me what kind of value I attach to Jewish mysticism," he wrote in his masterly synthetic account of 1941, *Major Trends in Jewish Mysticism*, "I would say this":

> Authoritative Jewish theology, both mediaeval and modern, in repre-sentatives like Saadia, Maimonides and Hermann Cohen, has taken upon itself the task of formulating an antithesis to pantheism and mystical theology, i.e.: to prove them wrong. In this endeavour it has shown itself tireless. What is really required, however, is an under-standing of these phenomena which yet does not lead away from monotheism; and once their significance is grasped, that elusive something in them which may be of value must be clearly defined. To have posed this problem is the historic achievement of Kabbalism. The varying answers it supplied to the question may be as inadequate as you like; I shall certainly be the last to deny that its representatives often lost their way and went over the edge of the precipice.

"But the fact remains," Scholem concluded, "that they faced a problem which others were more concerned to ignore." Almost as a footnote, but with a crucial switch in tense, he specified the problem of Jewish gnosticism and pantheism still further. Pivotal to the kabbalists, it was also one "which is of the greatest importance for Jewish theology [today]."[35] Little wonder, then, that Scholem should have dedicated the book to the memory of his friend Benjamin, who took his own life in 1940 at Port Bou, Spain, as he fled from the Nazi terror—little wonder that Scholem should have written the book in his name, because in some strange and small way, his friend had shown him how to write it.

How: in part by making these interpretive choices the foundation of his generalized theory of religion. Take the problem of God's absence. In his diaries at the beginning of his adult life and in a lecture delivered toward its end, Scholem described the modern condition as a world rid of God.[36]

In his scholarship, he went further, and described it as the religious condition *tout court*. Religion, he held, arises there where an abyss or chasm opens up in the relation between man and God. It is a second course of sorts, for it follows upon the great primordial soup of the spirit, a mythical stage in which reigns an "essential unity which precedes duality and in fact knows nothing of it." Gods inhabit the earth; man encounters them at every step, and so nature functions as the scene of man's encounter with the divine. All this changes with religion. It dissolves the "dream-harmony" of man, world, and God. It creates a vast abyss, conceived as absolute, between God, the infinite and transcendental Being, and Man, the finite creature." Dualism rules the day, once man recognizes this gulf that admits of no span save the voice, of God's revelation in one direction, of human supplication in the other. Monotheism is born in crisis, is crisis. Or in language akin to Barth's, monotheism lives in consciousness of an "abyss which can never be bridged," of a divine conceived as infinite, transcendent, and radically, if not wholly other.[37]

But Scholem spoke the gnostic language of heresy in a Jewish idiom, and the act of translation required alterations to the original. As an example, take gnostic dualism. For the most part, the kabbalists revised the gnostic scheme by locating this split within a single Godhead, rather than divide these principles among two powers in heaven. "All the energy of 'orthodox' Kabbalistic speculation is bent to the task of escaping from dualistic consequences," Scholem argued. "Otherwise they would not have been able to maintain themselves within the Jewish community."[38]

The Judaism in the gnosticism is important. The gnostics of late antiquity had divorced God from the world the better to escape it. The neo-gnostics of Scholem's time, Barth especially, had hoped to save God from worldly corruption, and so threatened to exile God from his creation. Scholem also spoke of an abyss between God and world. But he did so in a different register, not (or not only) in order to save God from the dereliction of the world, but as Strauss and Jonas had done, to save the relative autonomy of the world (a version of it) from God, and thereby to affirm it. Dualism—not so much; dialectic—yes. As we will see in a moment, he pursued the same strategy when he set out to "raise pantheism" also.

CHAPTER ELEVEN

Raising Pantheism

THE QUESTION of Spinoza's pantheism has been shot through from the very beginning by the question of its kabbalistic origins. Or at least since 1699—in that year appeared a three-hundred-page book by Johann Georg Wachter (1663-1757): *Der Spinozismus im Jüdenthumb / oder / die von dem heutigen Jüdenthumb / und dessen Geheimen Kabbala vergötterte Welt / an Mose Germano sonsten Johann Peter Speeth von Augsburg / gebürtig befunden und widerleget* (Spinozism in Judaism, or the World as Divinized by Contemporary Judaism and its Secret Kabbala). Wachter based his book on a lengthier collection of writings, a three-thousand-page behemoth called *Kabbala Denudata* (Kabbala Unveiled) compiled by the scholar Christian Knorr von Rosenroth (1677-1684). With Knorr's help, Wachter likened the teaching of Spinoza's *Ethics* to that of Spinoza's kabbalist forebears. Both, Wachter claimed, equated God with nature, and both, he argued further, were for that reason atheist.

Whatever the rightness of his first argument, his second was specious on its face, and Wachter retracted the charge of atheism some years later. It was born of a curious dispute. For some years, Wachter had engaged with a fellow German named Johann Peter Speeth, a disciple of the mystic Jakob Böhme. Peter Speeth had grown progressively disenchanted with Christian theosophy and eventually moved to Amsterdam. There he converted to Judaism and undertook to defend his new faith in a series of writings that aroused Wachter's ire, and eventually, his book. He also changed his name. Johann Peter Speeth became—Moses the German, and so the stage was set for a minor, if delightful chapter in the history of ideas.

The chapter, on the kabbalistic origins of Spinozist pantheism, proved a protracted one. Wachter's book prompted an attack on his work by the Jena theologian Johann Franciscus Buddeus (1667-1729).[1] Buddeus distinguished between the kabbalah of the Zohar, which he wrongly dated to the second century, and the newfangled corruptions of more recent kabbalistic texts, such as those of Isaac Luria and Abraham Cohen Herrera. The antagonists faced off on Herrera's work in particular, since it was largely Herrera's position in which Wachter had discovered a precursor to Spinoza. Born Alonso Nuñes, Herrera became Herrera when his family—Marranos—left Cordoba for Italy to return to the Jewish fold. There he studied philosophy with Italian Neoplatonists, learned Hebrew, and composed a philosophical defense of kabbalah in Spanish called *Puerta del Cielo* (The Gates of Heaven). The original went unpublished until 1987, but shortly after Herrera's death there appeared in 1655 a Hebrew abbreviation and translation of his book in Amsterdam (thanks to Isaac Aboab, a scholar in the Amsterdam community).[2] It appeared, in other words, a year before Spinoza left that same community, and Wachter thought this no coincidence. He discovered in the book (or in an abridged Latin form of the abbreviated Hebrew translation of the Spanish original) enough parallels with Spinoza's *Ethics* to declare them kin, and undesirable ones at that.

Wachter's attack on Spinoza the kabbalist set the terms for several centuries of interpretation, despite his best efforts to reverse it from the start. His retraction of 1706 stipulated that neither Spinoza nor the kabbalists in fact espoused atheism, that neither had divinized the world, that the Spinozist distinction between *natura naturans* and *natura naturata* implicitly signaled an enduring theism, and that Herrera, too, had not taught the identity of God and world. But the retraction—written in Latin rather than German—had little effect, and so the argument of *Spinozismus im Jüdenthumb* endured. In 1717 the theologian Jacob Reimmann advanced the thesis, following Wachter, that Herrera had set out to make visible the invisible essence of the divine, and so had openly promoted atheism. Leibniz, too, accepted the argument of Spinoza's kabbalistic inheritance. He thought it accounted for the doctrine of the unity of infinite substance, at least to judge by his remarks in the margins of Wachter's book. Wachter's thesis surfaced also in the work of the first general history of the Jews, written by the French Huguenot Jacques Basnage.[3] By the end of the eighteenth century, the force of Wachter's thesis had attenuated not a bit, as both of the major protagonists of the pantheism controversy—Moses Mendelssohn and Friedrich Heinrich Jacobi—accepted his arguments at face value. Mendelssohn had read *Spinozismus im Jüdenthumb*, and was only too happy to follow Wachter in consigning Spinozistic thought to the dung-heap of kabbalistic *Schwärmerei*. Jacobi, by contrast, had familiarized himself with Wachter's retraction, his *Elucidarius cabalisticus*, which insisted as much as its predecessor on the affinities Spinoza shared with kabbalah, and deviated only in the implications to be drawn from the fact.[4]

Wachter's fortunes lapsed through most of the nineteenth century, though the links he had forged between Spinoza and the kabbalah endured.[5] He enjoyed a comeback, however, in the first decades of the twentieth, thanks largely to the efforts of the Polish Jesuit and Spinoza scholar Stanislaus von Dunin-Borkowski. Following Wachter,

Dunin-Borkowski thought it certain that Spinoza had read Herrera, and had in fact derived much of the first book of the *Ethics* from the *Gates of Heaven*. "Only blind prejudice," he thought, could lead one to overlook the line of influence. Both developed doctrines of the unity, the necessity, the perfection and infinity of the first cause, understood as identical with God.[6] Others at the time also picked up where Wachter had left off. Sigmund Gelbhaus, Carl Gebhardt, Fritz Mauthner, and others flatly declared Spinozism a form of mysticism, though they generally declined to reveal Spinoza as a kabbalist in disguise.[7] Whatever the plausibility of their claims, one thing is certain: the question of Spinoza's pantheism has in large part hinged on the question of its kabbalistic origins. The pantheism controversies of the late eighteenth and early twentieth centuries have taken the problem of Jewish mysticism as one of their crucial subtexts.

This helps make intelligible one of the oddities of Gershom Scholem's career. For all his interest in the heretical and heterodox, for all his delight in transgression, Scholem paid little attention to Spinoza. To be sure, he procured for himself a copy of the *Theological-Political Treatise* at the age of sixteen, and paged through Spinoza's letters several years later. But the treatise he left on the shelf unread, while the letters interested him but little. "There are very important things that I do not know and for the foreseeable future will not know," he admitted in 1918. Among them he included Spinoza and Goethe, the arch-heretic's greatest German champion. Goethe's call, for one, emptied out into the void. Scholem could not hear it, and the same, it seems, held for Spinoza. "I do not read them, I do not speak of them."[8]

Scholem's silence was not total. In 1928, for example, he appealed to Carl Gebhardt's thesis, that Spinoza must be understood as an outcome of the Marrano sensibility at the heart of seventeenth-century Judaism. But he adduced Gebhardt only to set in relief the alternative Marrano option for Sabbatai Sevi.[9] Scholem would address Spinoza at length only in the last decade of his life, and then still indirectly via Wachter and Herrera.[10] He declined to say why. Perhaps he preferred the Sabbatians to Spinoza because they had never thought themselves to depart from the fold; for all their ambivalence about the law of Moses, they threw in their lot, like Scholem, with the Jews.[11] Or perhaps Scholem recognized the role Spinoza had played in the advent of the German-Jewish synthesis he hoped to undo. That Scholem failed to heed Goethe's call he imagined of great importance, proof that the "Jewish genius in me has forsaken the German world." Perhaps Spinoza's call failed for the same reason as had Goethe's: "I have grown up so wholly and totally outside all truly German cultural contexts," Scholem wrote, a German totality to which Spinoza, after several centuries of interpretation, also belonged. "I often feel," he continued, "as if I were a new land."[12]

Whatever its roots, Scholem's indifference to Spinoza by no means betokened indifference to the problem of pantheism. Nor did it mean that Scholem failed to intervene in the pantheism controversy Strauss had done most to revive. On the contrary, Scholem engaged with the problem often, so much so that his peculiar devaluation of the pantheist option became one of the hallmarks of his scholarship and his thought, the flip side of his enthusiasm for Jewish gnosticism. In his diaries, he explicitly resisted the "pantheist swindle" implicit in the deceit of natural beauty. In his scholarship, he addressed the question throughout his life.[13] It is fair (and important) to say that Scholem described all the most crucial episodes in the history of Jewish mysticism—or at least those episodes he did not think gnostic in character—as Jewish flirtations with pantheism.[14] In other words, Scholem did not need Spinoza to address the question of pantheism. He had at his disposal the history of kabbalah instead.[15] Kabbalah had appeared as a subtext to discussions about Spinoza for Wachter and for those who wrote in his wake. Scholem reversed the terms of those arguments. To Scholem, kabbalah appeared as their condition of possibility, and he treated it as such.

Scholem never allied himself with pantheism, "that most convenient and lazy of theories."[16] For all his distrust of the pantheist position and his enthusiasm for the gnostic, however, the lessons Scholem drew from both proved complementary. His "Jewish gnosticism" was less concerned with establishing God's radical transcendence than with the autonomy of the world as a scene for human endeavor. Jewish pantheism, to countenance a term that Scholem did not, achieved something similar. The Judaism in the pantheism ensured a gap, some gap, however amorphous or ill-defined, between creature and creator; it saved worldliness from the obliteration it otherwise would meet in the greater totality that is God (acosmism), and it saved a weak form of human autonomy for the same reason. The pantheism in the Judaism, on the other hand, ensured a divine presence in the world that Jewish gnosticism, in the more extreme of its incarnations, threatened to expunge. It inoculated Judaism from the contagion spread by the modern Marcionites: cosmic despair. It defeated a sense of "absolute homelessness" and its corollary, "absolute Godlessness."[17] Jewish pantheism offered a vital corrective, also, to a Jewish gnosticism for which cosmic despair meant complicity with a Jew run amok. It ensured, in other words, that Scholem would give up on unbridled Jewish self-assertion. It ensured he would give up on his *Zarathustra* for the Jews.

GOD AND WORLD

Pantheism arose as a problem for the kabbalists, and hence for Scholem, in two basic forms: in Jewish adaptations of Neoplatonist theories of creation, and in Jewish descriptions of the mystical encounter with the divine. The former asked after the relation between God and world, the latter between God and man. Wachter had stressed the former, and it is instructive to return for a moment to his question. Did he, perhaps, get it right in *Spinozismus im Jüdenthumb*? Does kabbalah teach of a *Welt-werdung Gottes*, a "worldification" of God, or of a *vergötterte Welt*, a divinized world? It is difficult to say. The question, as Scholem acknowledged, remains open.[18] The majority of kabbalists held to personalist and theistic ideas about the Godhead. But a sizable minority advanced positions akin, if not quite identical, to pantheism. Of these, Moses Cordovero (1522-1570) was most important. Cordovero lived for the most part in Safed, where he moved in the circle of kabbalists that included Isaac Luria, and was in fact for a time his teacher. He produced his first major work, the *Pardes Rimonim* (Garden of Pomegranates), at age twenty-seven, followed by a second systematic book ten years later, and finally an extensive commentary on the Zohar. In his literary fecundity, Scholem likened him to Aquinas.[19]

Scholem's initial treatment of Cordovero came in the form of a series of arguments from the mid-1920s to the early 1930s. In fits of rage, he skewered those hapless souls whose sin was to think differently than he. To take one example: a scholar by the name of S. A. Horodezky had called Cordovero a pantheist, "for the first time" in Jewish history, "before Spinoza." Horodezky advanced the claim on the basis of these of Cordovero's words: "God is all that exists, but not all that exists is God. All has come from him; there is no thing free of the divine."[20] This left Scholem incredulous. Horodezky had failed to make a basic distinction. Pantheism ought not be equated with panentheism; a scheme that posits the identity of God and world ought not be confused with one that understands the world as an emanation of the divine.[21]

The extra syllable speaks volumes, and Scholem's insistence on pronouncing it says much about his intellectual commitments. Panentheism preserves some sort of autonomy for the world. That is its basic point. Pantheism, as Scholem imagined it, does not. Indeed, panentheism as a term was coined in the nineteenth century by scholars eager to distinguish it from a pantheism in which the world was reduced to God. Scholem dismissed pantheism as incoherent on its face, and favored the term acosmism in its stead.[22] For most, the former pleases and reassures, as it speaks of a divine that is present, here, in and around us; the latter disquiets and alarms, as it evokes an image of a world destroyed, obliterated.

But not for Scholem: he conflated the two, pantheism and acosmism, and belittled them both in favor of the panentheist alternative. The panentheist view, as he put it, "offered a clear compromise between pure theism and pure pantheism and left room for a personalistic depiction of the Godhead."[23] It offered, in other words, a way to be both Jewish and pantheist, yet neither, and all at the same time. But panentheism carries with it a different, if still related, set of problems. To ensure the autonomy of both God and world, it must essay an answer to the question: where does God end and world begin?

Cordovero labored on precisely this problem. He specified it as a question of the transition from the *ein-sof*, literally "that without end" or "that which is infinite," to the first of the divine emanations or *sefirot*, called *keter* or crown. Scholem held him in great esteem on this count. For an appreciation of the complexity involved, of the sheer dialectical will exerted in Cordovero's effort to resist the pantheist swindle, it is worth quoting Scholem at some length. But be warned. Scholem's Cordovero gives the likes of Hegel and Adorno, the most masterful of modern dialecticians, a real run for their money:

> Cordovero understood full well that the salient point of the whole theory of emanation was the transition from *Ein-Sof* to the Sefirah *keter* and he devoted great effort to its solution. The *Sefirot*, he argues, owe the source of their existence to *Ein-Sof*, but this existence is "hidden" in the same sense that the spark of fire is hidden in the rock until it is struck with metal. Moreover, this aspect of their existence is incomparably more rarified than their existence once they have been emanated to their respective places, for in their emanated existence they assume a totally new guise. Even in their ultimate, "hidden" mode of existence, however, when they are comprehended in the substance of *Ein-Sof* and united with it perfectly, they are nevertheless not truly identical with this substance, which apprehends them while remaining unapprehended by them. This being the case, should it be said that the first change in their ontological status takes place in their hidden existence or not until their manifest one? Cordovero avoided giving an unequivocal answer to this question, while at the same time developing the theory that even the highest aspects of the *Keter* which he called "the *Keter* of the *Keter*," "the *Keter* of the *Keter* of the *Keter*," and so forth, approach the substance of *Ein-Sof* asymptotically until the human intellect can no longer distinguish them. Nevertheless they retain an identity distinct from it, so that there is a kind of leap between *Ein-Sof* and their hidden existence within it that continually approaches to infinity. The existence of these inward stages is considered by

Cordovero to represent an entirely new departure within the Godhead and the coming into being of this hidden existence, or "Will of Wills" as he calls it, is what constitutes the act of creation from nothingness in its literal sense.[24]

So said Scholem of Cordovero, the greatest of the kabbalah's theoreticians. He had similar things to say about Isaac Luria, the greatest of its post-expulsion visionaries. He pursued the same strategy with Luria as he had with his colleague in the circle of kabbalists at Safed. On the face of it, Luria's innovations erected an added defense against the pantheist drift of Cordovero's scheme. Luria's doctrine of *tzimtzum*, God's originary self-contraction or effacement, meant that the world was created literally of nothing, as a ray of light streamed out from the space of God's retreat to the void left in his wake, to unfold as "God the Creator [i.e., in one of his manifestations], in the primordial space of His own creation." Scholem appreciated this move as a "counterpoise" to the pantheist tendencies in the theory of emanation.[25] Luria wrote not of a progressive series of emanations from the Godhead, but of an endless, dialectical process of retraction and disclosure, of concealment and revelation. Every act of creation follows on the heels of a self-evacuation of the divine. As with Cordovero, it came down for Scholem to specifying a break in the process by which God becomes world; there must come a point at which creation is no longer substantially one with God. Luria's great achievement was to do just that, but in a way that preserved God, or at least something of him, in the world. Or as Scholem put it: "Not only is there a residue of divine manifestation in every being, but under the aspect of *Tsimtsum* it also acquires a reality of its own which guards it against the danger of dissolution into the non-individual being of the divine 'all in all.'"[26]

The sensibility at work in Scholem's scholarly choices propelled his programmatic statements also. In 1958, he published a series of "unhistorical theses" on kabbalah. Leo Strauss, for one, thought them magnificent. "You seem to think, and I believe rightly, that the time has now come for letting the cat—or rather her 10 invisible kittens—out of your old sorcerer's bag." Strauss confessed his pleasure at their unexpected company, but seemed also at a loss as to what to do with them. "I like the auras and the inaudible purrings of those of them of whom I have become aware, but they do not feel at home with me because I do not know with what to feed them, and even if I did, I am almost sure that I could not get the proper food for them. I myself am entirely comfortable with them because the dogs and hares which are my teachers had already taught me the exciting things with which your kittens are trying to tease me. Where would people like myself have to begin," Strauss asked in conclusion, "in order to understand?"[27] The same might be asked of Strauss. What he meant by all this is unclear. What Scholem wrote to prompt it is also obscure, but less so, and revealing.

The theses range widely in tone and in theme: from philology to the public status of secrets, from the epistemology of Torah to the materialism of symbols, from the transparency of law to illuminated mirrors. They address the problem of pantheism also, and in ways that disclose what Scholem thought at stake in his scholarship. Consider this passage, from thesis seven:

> One might consider the doctrine of emanation as the true misfortune of kabbala. . . . Cordovero would have been more at home as a phenomenologist than as a disciple of Plotinus. The attempt to build up (and to think to the end) the thought of the kabbalists without the use of the doctrine of emanation would be the payment of the debt which a true student of Cordovero would have to take upon himself, if ever there should be one.[28]

Scholem pointed here to an unredeemed promise in Cordovero's thought. Trapped by the language of a Neoplatonic scheme unsuited to it in the end—it lacked the dialectical defense against pantheism and posited a nonpersonalist God to boot—the truth toward which Cordovero strove remained inaccessible. Scholem felt it necessary to save kabbalah from emanation, or to divorce Cordovero from his Neoplatonic inheritance.

Though antiquarian or idiosyncratic on its face, the move in fact spoke to the vital theological questions of the era. It came down in the end to rescuing a form of divine transcendence. Scholem had no need for the radical transcendence of Barth's deity. But he did need enough of it to save creation from the pantheist threat. As he put it in his thesis number five, "Without transcendence the Nothing extends here down into the Something. One could say that those early kabbalists who wished to accord only a difference of name, not essence, to the Ein-Sof and 'ajin [God's nothingness] in fact crossed out the first act of the cosmic drama which contained the dialectical exposition of the whole. . . . The mystic who approaches his experiences undialectically inevitably arrives at pantheism."[29] Scholem's recovery of divine transcendence shared more with Strauss than with Barth. Strauss adapted the gnostic discourse of divine transcendence not, as Barth had done, to save God, but to save the world. Strauss did so to secure the possibility of philosophy, which he understood as the pursuit of authentic human life. Scholem did so to secure the autonomy of the world as the scene for authentic Jewish life.

GOD AND MAN

Scholem made similar arguments about the relation of God to man. This version of the problem surfaced in kabbalistic discussions of *devekut*, a term that refers to the manner by which man "cleaves" or "adheres" to God (*devek*, for example, means glue). The Bible commands it of the Jew. "Thou shalt fear the Lord thy God; Him shalt thou serve; and to Him shalt thou cleave, and by His name shalt thou swear": so proceeds the Deuteronomic imperative. But what this ought to mean in practice has been up for debate from the beginning. For some in late antiquity, it meant to enjoin pious deeds, and in one example from the school of R. Ishmael, this could include marrying off a daughter to a promising young scholar. Followers of R. Akiva tended toward a more literal interpretation: cleaving meant cleaving, some sort of attachment, real contact with the divine. Mystical variations arose in medieval Jewish texts usually as one (or a combination) of three ideal types: Aristotelian, Neoplatonic, and hermetic. The first involved the union of knower with known; to know God amounted to mystical union. The second involved the union of the human soul with its root, either the universal soul, or in rarer cases, God; here, imagery of ascent predominated. The third evolved out of magical rites designed to draw the divine spirit down into the world, and took the form of a mysticism of descent.[30]

For Scholem, however, none of this mattered so much as one overriding point: whatever its form, *devekut* had to be distinguished from the union of man and God characteristic, he thought, of non-Jewish forms of mysticism. *Devekut* aspired to communion, to a being-with and not to a being-as. Even the most rapturous of mystical moments were thought to preserve a "proper sense of distance." This was the case for the thirteenth-century kabbalist Abraham Abulafia, whose frankly ecstatic kabbalism nonetheless did not countenance, according to Scholem, a wholesale erasure of personality.[31] The same held for Hasidism, the movement with which *devekut* is most commonly associated. Scholem thought the content of Hasidic doctrine hardly new. Others had long spoken of the immanence of the divine in all things. Their novelty inhered in the centrality they accorded to the command to cleave—it superseded even Torah study—and also in their ardor, in "the primitive enthusiasm with which it was expounded and the truly pantheistic exhilaration evoked by the belief that God 'surrounds everything and pervades everything.'" Their zeal aroused the ire of the orthodox establishment and also of their most implacable enemy, the Vilna *Gaon* (a leading kabbalist himself, notwithstanding his status as the animator of a *mitnaged* movement renowned more for its sober commitment to study than to mystical contemplation). Hasidim, in turn, accused the Gaon of an overly literal notion of the abyss implicit in the Lurianic *tzimtzum*, and so of a misplaced, reified sense of God's radical transcendence. In other words, Scholem described the upheavals of the Hasidic advent and the *mitnagdic* response in terms oddly redolent of his own time: as a battle between pantheists exulting in the immanence of the divine, and a theist who stressed its absolute transcendence.

The "radicalism" of this pantheist position, Scholem tells us, waned only when the movement detached itself from its crude and "primitive" origins in Podolia and was joined by more "learned and sophisticated minds."[32] Over time, and after a series of tumultuous battles with the orthodox establishment, Hasidism's leading exponents eschewed talk of unity with God. This held in even the most extreme of cases, for Scholem that of Dov Baer (known also as the Maggid of Mezeritsch). Though Dov Baer referred not only to *devekut* but also to *ahdut* (union or oneness), and though his disciples described *ahdut* as a prelude to annihilation, Scholem insisted on difference within unity. "This union is, in fact, not at all the pantheistic obliteration of the self within the divine mind which [Baer] likes to call the Naught, but pierces through this state on to the rediscovery of man's spiritual identity. He finds himself because he finds God." Scholem insisted, in other words, on a God and a man understood as separate and distinct personalities. "Man is still man," Scholem wrote, "nay, he has, in truth, only then started to be man, and it is only logical that only then will he be called upon to fulfill his destiny in the society of men."[33]

Scholem had discovered in kabbalist Neoplatonism an opportunity to ask after the relation between God and world. In *devekut*, he found a suitable object through which to ask after the relation between God and man. In both instances, he insisted on a basic autonomy for all the parties involved, guided by a need to preserve the integrity of world and man from an unwittingly rapacious God. As he put it in Berne, with Benjamin, "Im *Abstande* erst erzeugt sich ja mein Leben." The line captures perfectly the sentiment at work in his writings on pantheism. Only out of some irreducible distance from God can meaningful life emerge. Or as Jonas wrote toward the end of his life, God deserves praise not for his providence, but first for his absence, as it is the condition for human mortality, for an emphatically human life. Scholem penned those words as he gazed out upon the Swiss countryside, upon the waves rippling through the grass; he referred there not to his alienation from *God*, but to the alienation, or the transcendence, of man from the *world*. The same sentiment, in other words, underwrote his Jewish revisions of both the gnostic and pantheist languages of heresy.

But the questions Scholem posed in his encounters with pantheism and gnosticism do not yet exhaust the more basic problem at stake. They imply, but do not yet ask, two more. Can man have a relation to the world independent of his relation with God? Can man have a relation to God independent of his relation with the world? The difficulty of these questions inheres in the fact that man is both creature and creator, in some small way both world and God. Jonas and Strauss asked these questions, each in his way. However disparate their points of ingress, they also arrived at similar answers. Both ruled decisively in favor of a man understood as creature first, creator second. Both discovered in physis an antidote to nomos, in the autonomy of the world an arrest on the unchecked autonomy of man.

Scholem posed these questions also. If not always in such stark and unadorned form, they are nonetheless implicated from the first of his writings to the last. He has also left answers. Rarely did he deign to announce them as such. But they *are* there, at least for those who care to look. Among those who cared most must be counted Leo Strauss.

CHAPTER TWELVE

From Nihilism to Nothingness

> Only thus shall Your face be revealed, Oh God,
> To a generation that has thrown You off.
> Your nothingness is all that is left
> For him to experience of You.
> —Gershom Scholem, *With a Copy of Kafka's* The Trial

IN 1957, Gershom Scholem entered the second half of a life that aspired, in the tradition of Jewish lives, to 120 years. The occasion, and also the appearance of his essay "Schöpfung aus Nichts und Selbstverschränkung Gottes" (Creation from Nothing and God's Self-Contraction), prompted a note of congratulations from his friend Leo Strauss. "Of all your publications which I know," Strauss wrote from Chicago, "this one impressed me most."[1]

It is curious that Strauss would say so. Scholem's compact account of creation out of nothing in the history of monotheistic religions—and in Jewish mysticism above all—reads as does so much of his work: his vital interest in the subject matter is plain but vague, and the inquiry as a whole is presented in patient and philological style. Its avowed theme would also seem far removed from the questions Strauss took as his own. The motley crew of mystics and enthusiasts that inhabit the dim recesses of Scholem's text differs considerably from the stable of thoroughbred philosophers—Spinoza, Hobbes, Aristotle, Plato—to which Strauss preferred to attend. But Strauss nonetheless heard in Scholem's essay the muted call of shared conviction. Something about the links Scholem forged between the categories of creation and (divine) nothingness struck Strauss as far more pressing than their delimited thematic scope would suggest. The atheist intent on discovering in nature a set of enduring standards by which to judge the rightness of human action thought he detected a comparable, if not identical impulse in the work of his friend. In his letter, Strauss spoke in praise of a critique levied not "chiefly or merely as an historian," but as one brought with Scholem's "full vigor and at the peak of [his] power." The attack appeared bent on extirpating the "Root of Orthodoxy" itself.[2] Scholem's links, as Strauss seemed to have it, were in fact a set of shackles, and Scholem's remarkably unremarkable rhetoric served only to mask his intent: to bind the rabbis, to free Judaism from its captors and the hegemony of their law.

Scholem replied as do many made nervous by the questionable uses to which their intellectual labor is put: with polite equivocation.[3] His unease was apt. Scholem's guiding impulse—to blur the distinction between heresy and Jewish normativity—opposed in no uncertain terms a Straussian scheme that made heresy unintelligible on its face. Scholem had devoted his life to the mystics, Strauss to the philosophers. Scholem developed an anarchic and historicist notion of Judaism; Strauss hoped to make an end run around historicism altogether, and discovered authentic Judaism in the enduring demands of biblical religion. But for all that, Strauss remained appreciative of his friend. As he put it three years later, in 1960, he reckoned Scholem "the only antiphilosophic contemporary—for you are consistent enough to be antiphilosophic—from whom I learn something with pleasure."[4] Scholem repaid the sentiment in kind. Already in 1933 Scholem had professed admiration for the most "excellent head" set atop his friend's comparably dwarfish frame. Several years later he bemoaned his failure to lure Strauss to Jerusalem on a permanent basis.[5] Theirs was more than personal friendship; each thought of the other as intellectual kin.

But on what grounds? Their estimations on this count were various, mutable—and also at odds. In 1935 Scholem seemed to think that Strauss shared his desire "wholly to rewrite" the "inner history" of Judaism and the Jewish people, notwithstanding their substantially different points of departure. "We would have had much to do together," he believed, had Strauss come in the end to Palestine.[6] Scholem parroted here a line of talk that Strauss himself first vocalized in 1933. Nearly three decades later, Strauss spoke specifically of an "important sphere of agreement" that united their otherwise far-flung projects: first, their shared diagnosis of Martin Buber as a master of empty posturing, and of his soul, a "morass." But Strauss thought it more important that he and Scholem agreed on something else: "that modern rationalism or enlightenment with all the doctrines peculiar to it and in all its forms (German idealism, positivism, romanticism) is finished."[7] Strauss allowed that Scholem may not have emancipated himself entirely from romanticism, and Strauss was right to do so. Scholem found intellectual inspiration in the German romantics, and was himself a nominal exponent of a neo-romanticism in vogue among both Jews and gentiles of his time. Strauss was certainly incorrect about Scholem's relation to a positivist tradition in the philological sciences; Scholem did not do away with that tradition so much as sublimate and transform it. And as we will shortly see, Scholem's encounter with German idealism traced a similar arc.

However each hoped to enlist the other, their deepest and most important affinity inhered in another project altogether. They generally did not recognize it as such, but of the two, Strauss at least came close. He did so in a remarkable letter composed on the occasion of Scholem's book, *On the Kabbalah and Its Symbolism*. He began by pointing, appreciably, to their differences. But in a turn of epistolary disposition, Strauss went on to suggest a hidden point of agreement:

> Your justification in your letter to me includes the sentence that the "philosophic and nihilistic implications" of your second chapter were not likely to escape me. As you see . . . indeed they did not. I was very much impressed by them and confirmed in what a simple man would describe as *apiquorsut* [heresy]. Still, you confirm my diagnosis of you by using "philosophic" and "nihilistic" synonymously: what you call *nihil*, the *falasifa* call *physis*. Period.[8]

Evidently, Strauss thought Scholem's discussion of divine nothingness had much in common with the appreciation of the falasifa—the medieval, Islamic Aristotelians—for the purposiveness embedded in the natural world. The declaration is resolute. It is obscure. It is paradoxical. But it is also of great consequence, and the task of the pages that follow is in part to make good on its promise.

Redeemed, the promise would reveal the hidden core of Scholem's thought as a version of others we have already encountered. Like Jonas and Strauss, Scholem embarked on a Jewish recovery of nature as a substitute, supplement, or ground for law. He, too, hoped to disclose value in a world apparently made worthless by God's absence. He, too, would come to contest the spirit of the day for which God's evacuation from his creation had left the world as nothing. All this marked a sharp departure from his early attempts to write a *Zarathustra* for the Jews, to negate his fallen German-Jewish world and to create a new one out of nothing but himself. The ethos of nothingness no longer granted license to unfettered Jewish self-creation. God's absence no longer meant, as both Jonas and Strauss had diagnosed, complicity with a man run amok. Rather, the answer Scholem discovered in the kabbalah defeated the ethos of nothingness at its core, even as it affirmed that ethos at the very same time. For the kabbalists occasionally described creation as shot through with the nothingness of an otherwise absent divine. Scholem was no kabbalist. Their era was not his. But for both, to affirm the nothingness in the world meant also to discover there traces of the divine. It could therefore mean, as Jonas had argued, to acknowledge the claims of that world on man as the claims of the divine as well.

NIHILISM AS A JEWISH PHENOMENON

Nihilism, Nietzsche's most unhomely of guests, had by the early 1970s made himself quite at home in European culture, when Scholem devoted a lecture to the topic at Eranos. Friedrich Heinrich Jacobi was first to name him, or so many have thought, nearly a century before Nietzsche announced his presence at the door. Jacobi thought him to appear wherever rational inquiry went unchecked by faith, and for Jacobi this meant Spinoza and Johann Gottlieb Fichte before all others. Over the next few generations, nihilism featured regularly in the work of the German romantics. He also wandered east, where he was warmly received among the political and intellectual malcontents of nineteenth-century Russia. Ivan Turgenev did most perhaps to secure his lasting fame by casting him for a starring role in the novel *Fathers and Sons* (1862). In the person of Bazarov, the nihilist announced himself the enemy of all authority grounded in faith, and as a fervent champion of a godless natural science. Among Russian anarchists like Kropotkin, he avowed his hostility to repressive institutions and his allegiance to an anarchic ideal of community built upon the ruins of law. In the person of Bakunin, he announced in the will to destroy an even deeper will to create. By the time he returned to Germany in the person of Nietzsche, his reputation as a force of the profane well preceded him.

In the century that followed, nihilism became the common currency of a series of European generations that witnessed carnage and senseless destruction on an unprecedented scale. Here is how Leo Strauss parodied the sentiment in 1941, in a lecture to his students at the New School for Social Research:

> "Nihilism," they [the nihilists] would say, is a slogan used by those who do not understand the new, who see merely the rejection of *their* cherished ideals, the destruction of *their* spiritual property, who judge the new by its first words and deeds, which are, of necessity, a caricature rather than an adequate expression. How can a reasonable man expect an adequate expression of the ideal of a new epoch at its beginning, considering that the owl of Minerva starts its flight when the sun is setting? the Nazis? Hitler? The less is said about him, the better. He will soon be forgotten. He is merely the rather contemptible *tool* of "History": the midwife who assists at the birth of the new epoch, of a new spirit, and a midwife usually understands nothing of the genius at whose birth she assists; she is not even supposed to be a competent gynaecologist. A new reality is in the making; it is transforming the whole world; in the meantime there is: nothing, but—a fertile nothing. The Nazis are as unsubstantial as clouds; the sky is hidden at present by

many clouds which announce a devastating storm, but at the same time the long needed rain which will bring new life to the dried up soil; and (here I am almost quoting) do not lose hope; what appears to you the end of the world, is merely the end of an epoch, of the epoch which began in 1517 or so.[9]

Strauss confessed his inability to comprehend such unbounded faith in the future. It smacked of a liberal brief for progress definitively quashed by the time he came of age, intellectually speaking, in interwar Europe. He professed his desire instead for an enduring, known, and stable standard, an antidote to the nihilist toxins inside the veins of modern thought.[10] His solution, a partial recovery of Greek notions about the link between nature and politics, was not without its problems. But he at least did well to point to nihilism's remarkable capacity to present itself as novel, all the more so given that Nietzsche's erstwhile guest had by Strauss's time made himself a well-worn fixture on the European scene.[11]

The same impulse—to "denovel" what announced itself as new—underwrote Scholem's lecture also, which he called "Nihilism as a Religious Phenomenon." Scholem launched the lecture with a historical précis of nihilism over the preceding 150 years as a preeminently secular phenomenon. He then moved to overturn that tradition of interpretation as blind to nihilism's deeper and more archaic religious origins. In its profane forms, as Karl Jaspers had diagnosed in 1919, nihilism expressed several competing tendencies. On the one hand, it could refer to the prerogative of a man understood in existential terms to transcend, negate, or deny his creaturely worldhood, as one whose freedom was born of world-despair and attained in self-creation, one for whom nature proved a burden to be shed or an obstacle to be overcome, as opposed to a template for right living. This, Jaspers had argued, was a nihilism of the deed, which Scholem thought best incarnated in *Caligula*, the drama by Albert Camus. On the other hand, nihilism could adopt quietistic forms, in which negation of the world proceeded not in action but in metaphysical contemplation. Nihilism's more recent history obscured its wellsprings, Scholem thought, and so he set out to discover the early religious tributaries that converged in the great waterway of its later profanations. These he described, significantly, as gnostic and pantheist forms of nihilism.[12]

Indeed, Scholem described nearly two millennia of religious nihilism as a contest—and as a deeper complicity—of the languages of heresy made available to him by a whole gamut of thinkers in interwar Europe. Gnostic nihilism had its heyday in late antiquity and entailed a "negation of the values of the world and of creation itself." To depart from the world meant also to overcome it. Over and against gnostic nihilism, however, Scholem held up a form of nihilism characteristic, he thought, of medieval Christian heresies, for which "the affirmation of the divine character of the world" was the product of an "excessive pantheism." For the first, "*super*worldly being" was at once "*anti*worldly being," conceived in explicit rejoinder to both the Greek cosmos and the Jewish story of creation. This ethos had best been defined by his friend Hans Jonas in the first of his volumes on gnosis and the spirit of late antiquity, and Scholem could do no better than to quote him: "The sublime unity of God and cosmos is rent asunder, a monstrous chasm ensues; God and world are made foreign to one another, set in opposition. . . . God is the world-alien, the world-alienating, the anti-worldly. The gnostic concept of God is first and foremost a nihilistic one. God—*das Nichts der Welt.*"[13]

The gnostic nihilist is therefore made free "through the transcendence from the world and its law." By contrast, the pantheist nihilist finds freedom "through divinization of the world." If the gnostic nihilist had called to rebellion against the law of the cosmos in the name of an otherworldly morality, the pantheist nihilist had urged, in the name of the cosmos, the subversion of an unnatural and so ungodly law. In the end, Scholem thought their freedom had more to unite than distinguish them, since both discovered license in a conflation of man with God, whether this transpired upon the scene of the world or beyond it.[14]

The lecture deserves attention for other reasons. Its remainder restates the argument—the very words—Scholem committed to paper in "Redemption through Sin" forty years before. But the earlier essay he had written in Hebrew, with the effect that his best friend Benjamin (and Strauss, too) could not read his most important piece of scholarship at the time of publication. Scholem's choice of language was no accident. As we have seen, the essay was intended as a salvo in debates about the consolidations of Jewish nationalism in Palestine, as a commentary on Jewish self-creation at a time when Jewish self-determination had become the most importunate of problems. But Scholem composed and delivered "Nihilism as a Religious Phenomenon" in German, in Switzerland, and to an audience with an avowed interest in the comparative dimensions of the religious experience. The essay restated the argument of its predecessor, but also resituated and so rewrote it. Not the Zionist project but the human prospect itself was now at stake. The essay reveals to us how he imagined his most important work to speak beyond its original disciplinary, confessional, and political-existential boundaries.

The "architecture" of the piece, its argumentative conceit, does most to make plain its interwar origins. The distinction between gnostic and pantheist forms of nihilism, that is, derives directly from the interwar scene, where mostly Protestant "gnostics" and a whole assortment of Spinozist pantheists competed for supremacy. As Scholem invoked the distinction, however, so too did he ruin it: first, by pointing to their formal coherence; and second, by holding up in the persons of Jacob Frank and his followers an example that combined them both. To be sure, gnostic nihilism predominated in Frank's case over its pantheist cousin. Neither Frank nor his disciples were aware of the fact, but they revived, according to Scholem, an "age-old tradition" of gnostic myth not only in the general drift of their activities and thought, but also in the specifics of their symbols. Both were born of the most savage of revolts against the Judaism of the Bible. Both transformed the snake of Eden into a symbol of gnosis, thought to instruct the adept to despise the laws and institutions of the world. Both spoke of a hidden light of salvation visible only to the lucky few. Both spoke less of world than of "world-ruin."[15] In sum, both taught the destruction of all worldly values, positive laws, and religions as a means toward something called "life." Both taught descent first, ascent later (if in Frank's case at all). Both taught a gospel of redemption through sin.[16]

The irruptions of the gnostic language of heresy recur in this essay with a frequency impossible to ignore. For the gnostic, Scholem tells us, the self is "wholly alien" or other to the world. The self is *das ganz Fremde*. It is a lost spark of a transcendent God, alien to the world, but for the moment captive to the guardians of a miserable cosmic prison. Scholem spoke here in a lexicon more readily identified in others of his time: the Protestant theologians Rudolf Otto and Karl Barth in particular. "How other?" Barth famously asked in reference to his God. "Totally other!" Citing Jonas once again, Scholem described this stance as the "anarchy of the break," as the "nihilism of the 'Between the Times' which fills the space of lawlessness with the self-ruling arbitrariness of the liberated self." The citation is important because it yokes Scholem to the discourse of gnosticism associated with Barth and his associates. Scholem may not have known it. But Jonas did. His "'Between the Times'" referred with express clarity to dialectical theology, whose mouthpiece (founded in 1922 by Barth's colleague Friedrich Gogarten) went precisely by that name.[17]

The citation is important for another reason. It alerts us to the ways in which Scholem wrote of Frank as he had once written of himself. Scholem's commentary on Frank doubled as commentary on a form of Jewish selfhood and worldhood with which he was only too familiar. Frank's nihilism was the natural corollary of his sense for God's absence; Scholem's, too. For them both, God's apparent evacuation from creation licensed a form of Jewish subjectivity that negated the actual world even as it sought, if it sought, to create its own. God's absence, in other words, opened a space for Jewish nihilism.

The parallels are startling. Here the gnostic nihilist has granted himself license to engage in acts of "self-ruling arbitrariness," or in the German original, of *selbstherrlichen Willkür*. In his diaries, Scholem spoke of the demand laid upon the Zionist—himself—to engage in acts of *selbstherrliche Gesetzgebung*, of autocratic or autonomian lawgiving.[18] In 1974, Scholem spoke of Frank as one who sought a Nietzschean "transvaluation of all values of the Jewish tradition." In 1916 he spoke of the need to write a *Judenzarathustra*. In 1974, Scholem spoke of Frank's program as the "freedom of anarchic life as an ideal" with the "discipline of the soldier as its path."[19] In early twentieth-century Germany, Scholem evinced similar hostility to the reigning forms of political and religious authority, calling for "Revolution everywhere!" In 1974, Scholem spoke of the Frankists as soldiers who "stormed the escarpments" of exile; in his diaries, he spoke of Zionists as disciplined bands of *Mauerrenner* or wall runners, who would smash headfirst the boundaries of exile.[20]

The examples could be multiplied. Together, they comprise a Jewish version of the Nietzscheanism that so exercised Scholem's friends—Jonas and Strauss—and also Hans Blumenberg, his acquaintance.[21] All three— Jonas, Blumenberg, Strauss—would have found Scholem's Frank detestable. All three would have found in Scholem's Nietzschean moods a source of considerable discomfort. Jonas would have diagnosed them as a Jewish example of a natural affinity he hoped to undo: the link between gnosticism, nihilism, and a denigration of the world. Blumenberg might have understood them as a Jewish overreaction—another example of man's efforts to assume the role of God after God's self-evacuation from the world. Strauss would have diagnosed Scholem as part of the problem he hoped to overcome. Not only would, but did: after all, Scholem's letter had confirmed for him his prior diagnosis. "Nihilistic" and "philosophic" may have been occasional synonyms for Scholem. But for Strauss they were antonyms through and through.

Scholem, too, expressed deep aversion to Frank. His writings make plain his distaste for Frankist excess. But they also betray an obvious fascination for this Jewish Manson, this ghetto prototype of the modern abject hero. For all his despotic nature, for all his "customary savagery," Frank presided over a "hidden poetic impulse." For all the negativity of his teachings, "they nonetheless contained a genuine creed of life." Even his incoherencies and grotesqueries had in them a kernel of "vigor and imagination." And whatever his discomfort with Frank, Scholem commended his followers and all the radical Sabbatians for their disdainful rejection of exile. They had cast themselves into the abyss, but their devotion compelled a measure of esteem.[22]

Whatever the dimension of Scholem's sympathies, this Jewish ethos of world-overcoming and world-abandonment does not exhaust the moods at work in his scholarship and politics. Far from it: he countenanced other forms of Jewish self-assertion, which accepted the premise of God's absence but promised a way beyond the problem diagnosed by Jonas, Blumenberg, and Strauss, the problem also at the heart of "Nihilism as a Religious Phenomenon" and "Redemption through Sin." Scholem was enough of a gnostic to know he could not simply affirm the world in which he lived. He identified enough with Kafka to register the desolation visited upon the world by God's absence. Nihilism attracted him, to the extent that it attracted him, in its honesty, in its refusal to make its peace with a world that did not deserve it. But it had also gone too far. Scholem knew this. He may have wished to walk the "fine line between religion and nihilism," as he put it in 1937 to Zalman Schocken, but he did not intend to abase himself like Frank. He did not intend to sink in the abyss.

Fortunately for Scholem, nihilism is not the only means by which to register discomfort with the world. Nihilism may bespeak a desire to destroy the modern world, as Strauss put it in 1941 to his students.[23] But it does not follow that a refusal to affirm the world or even to dispute it is *eo ipso* nihilist. Nihilism does not exhaust, neither historically nor formally, the ways in which one might speak of worldly deficiency. An alternative, discovered by Scholem in the kabbalah and diagnosed in Scholem by Strauss, points no less to the nothingness of the world, as it yokes a version of nothingness, nihil, to nature, physis. But this approach to nothingness at the heart of all being would enable Scholem to affirm the world, whatever its wants and lacks. It would enable him to leave Nietzsche behind and gravitate to an appreciation for the nothingness at once present in all being and beyond it—a mood more akin to those we discover in the thought of Martin Heidegger. Only Scholem lived out this shift in European intellectual history—or spoke it—in a Jewish idiom.

From Nihil to Physis

Strauss declined to elaborate on his equation of Scholem's nihil with the philosopher's physis. He equated them, period. Perhaps he did not think it necessary, or advisable. Whatever the case, the equation invokes a series of philosophical and religious problems of long, even ancient standing: the relation of being to nothingness, and the role of creation, both human and divine, as a bridge between the two. Two Latin maxims have come to frame the scope of debate, even if neither of the sensibilities they describe had their origin in Roman thought. *Ex nihilo nihil fit* (from nothing, nothing comes to be) does well to sum up the approach of Parmenides, who set the terms of discussion for the centuries of Greek thought to follow. Parmenides had dismissed as a false path the line of thought intent on proceeding from the being of nothing. It led not toward enlightenment but devolved into darkness and confusion, into a great "pile of indistinction" for which being and not-being were at once same and not-same. But the tautology implicit in his solution—to affirm that being quite simply is—only attested to his deeper failure, and the Parmenidean doctrine soon came in for dispute. The sophist Gorgias advanced a position, perhaps in jest, that seemed to equate non-being with nature itself. Plato argued in one of his dialogues for an inflection of being by not-being; not-being was not opposed to being so much as the source of a thoroughgoing difference internal to being.[24] The Aristotelian doctrine of *steresis* or privation appeared to extend aspects of the Platonic argument, insofar as it defined all natural things in part by that which they ought by nature have, but did not (the notion would prove especially important for Scholem). From the beginning, or what passes for it in Western thought, the question of the nothing has been bound to the question of nature.

The same holds true of Western religious thought. *Creatio ex nihilo* (creation from nothing) was a belated innovation and not a foundational doctrine. The term has textual origins in the Jewish tradition, but not in the Bible itself. Even the Hebrew evidence at hand required the help of a suspect translation or two before the notion became a mainstay of the monotheistic vocabulary. The church fathers used it to attack Greek notions of creation, whether Aristotle's doctrine of the eternity of the world, or Plato's of creation by the demiurge from preexistent matter. They also used it to distinguish the world, created from things nonexistent, from the word, understood as issuing directly from "God's nature." The distinction, however, signals also the means of its undoing. Those Christians (such as Dionysius the Areopagite and John Scotus Erigena) beholden to Neoplatonic theories of creation by emanation seized on the distinction but reversed in a fashion its terms. The world, they held, and not merely the word, had issued out of God. In a complicated operation, *ex nihilo* became *ex essentia Dei*.[25] Creation from nothing in effect meant creation from God.

The kabbalists, or many of them, arrived at similar conclusions about the problems of not-being. They too professed literal adherence to *creatio ex nihilo* even as they reversed its intent. Most of the early kabbalists taught that creation from nothing inhered in the emanation of *chochma* (divine wisdom and the second of the *sefirot*) from the first of all the divine emanations, *keter* or crown. This first emanation, however, also went by the name of *ayin gamur*, the primordial nothingness, and so creation from nothing also meant the emanation of divine wisdom, the template for all the creation to follow, from the nothingness of God. Some early kabbalists distinguished between God's nothingness and God in his purely transcendent form, the infinite or *ein-sof* that preceded this first act of creation. Others advanced a position (especially common among the early Spanish kabbalists) that equated the *ein-sof* with the *ayin*, God's infinity with his nothingness. Nearly all the early kabbalists, however, agreed with the thrust, if not the wording, of the first of our maxims, *ex nihilo nihil fit*. None could countenance a nothingness wholly independent of an otherwise complete and perfect being. All betrayed a kind of "horror for the nothingness" presumed by the orthodox understanding, and adduced a variety of ingenious interpretations to dispel it.[26]

All this may seem far removed, in time and in sensibility, from the philosophical and theological scene in interwar Europe. But Strauss did not think so and neither did Scholem, who arrived at the conclusion, if not yet the proof, at a remarkably early stage in his career. It is easy to see how the contest between *ex nihilo nihil fit* and creation *ex nihilo* could play to an interwar audience accustomed to two competing approaches to the relation of God to world. In its normative sense, that is, creation from nothing is theist to the core, since it posits an absolute distinction between creature and creator. The world is that which God has created out of a nothingness not himself. It speaks of total creative power, of a wholly voluntarist God. But the early kabbalist interpretation bordered on pantheism, since it understood nihil not as nothingness, or not merely as nothingness, but as a symbol for divine infinity, an infinity beyond rational intellection. The sharply voluntarist aspect of creation from nothing was thereby revised. So was the rigid distinction between creature and creator, since creation in a way was reduced to the self-creation of the divine. All this came to a head in Scholem's essay of 1957, "Creation from Nothing," in which he characterized the orthodox position, exemplified by Saadia Gaon and Maimonides, as an attempt to ward off the unallowed "pantheist boundary-blurring" which the kabbalists would in fact undertake shortly thereafter.[27]

All this indeed came to a head in Scholem's essay, but it began much earlier. "The difference between *Nicht* and *Nichts*," he wrote in February of 1918, "is of the greatest weight to philosophy. The kabbalah and this foundational idea: God as nothingness. On this could easily be written an entire thesis." The thesis would have to wait. Scholem would not write it for forty years. But he did mull over the problem in the months to follow, both before and during his time with Benjamin in Berne. "The Kabbalah calls God, the infinite, also nothing," Scholem observed, in the summer of that year. Asriel of Gerona, Joseph Gikatilla, Moses de Leon, and Moses Cordovero, to name the most prominent, all held to the view, and Scholem would have encountered them in the course of his reading. "This is the true path of Jewish mysticism," he understandably wrote in summary of their position. But that path, he less understandably concluded, led directly to Hermann Cohen.[28] It is odd, because Scholem had included Cohen from 1918 on among those like Saadia and Maimonides whose stance he opposed. All, he held, had failed to appreciate the Jewish potential implicit in gnostic myth and in pantheism; they should have sublimated what they sought to refute. But in one way at least, Cohen seemed to reproduce in modern form the kabbalistic approach to God's nothingness. What the kabbalists had meant by creation from nothing, Cohen meant, or so Scholem thought in 1918, by the "logic of origins."[29]

This was no accident. Cohen's approach to the question of being out of nothingness had set the terms for a host of interwar thinkers, among them Karl Barth, Martin Heidegger, and Franz Rosenzweig. All three were existentialists of sorts who repudiated the neo-Kantianism by which Cohen made his name. But all, in parallel if dissimilar ways, owed a heavy debt to Cohen as well, especially his attention to the problem of origins. Barth, for example, redivinized Cohen's notion of originary thinking—a kind of thought with origins in itself, origins not spatial or temporal but logical, and with the potency to produce the content of its thought in addition to its form—to describe a divine whose fact was prior to all human knowing.[30] Heidegger and Rosenzweig replicated the thrust of Barth's argument, even as they redirected it toward other, worldly ends. Both, as Peter Gordon has recently pointed out, sought to sever the identity of being and thought presumed—or desired—by the philosophical tradition of German idealism. Both did so by imagining a "being-prior-to-thought" that anchored human existence in the world, in the particularities of life as lived.[31]

Both Rosenzweig and Heidegger engaged Cohen specifically on the question of nothingness as well. Cohen had come to realize that originary thinking could not arrive at a "something" by recourse to another "something" prior to it, since the infinite regress it implied would only continue to beg the question. Instead, as Rosenzweig recognized and applauded, Cohen adapted mathematical reasoning—the differential of calculus in particular—to arrive at a model for which the something proceeds out of the negation of a "primal nothing" (as opposed to the mathematical nothingness of a zero). Rosenzweig allegorized what for Cohen had remained a methodological principle elaborated to ensure the identity of being and thought. He transformed Cohen's "heuristic device" into a story of the origins of God, world and man.[32] Much as Heidegger was to do, Rosenzweig also shifted the terms of discussion. Not negation, but nothingness assumed pride of place; not *nicht*, but *das Nichts*. Rosenzweig inserted *das Nichts* into the seams stitching being to thought in order to ruin the idealist scheme.

Independent of Rosenzweig, Heidegger would take Cohen to task for his failure to proceed from negation to nothingness, in a speech ("What Is Metaphysics?") delivered on the occasion of his appointment to the German professoriate. There Heidegger struck out a middle path between *ex nihilo nihil fit* and creation *ex nihilo*. He proposed *ex nihilo omne ens qua ens fit* in their stead: out of nothing all beings as beings come to be. The line took aim at the Greek scheme by granting to nothing a "creative significance," as Heidegger's student Karl Löwith would put it. But it defeated the Judeo-Christian scheme (or a belated manifestation of it) no less, since it rid divine creation from nothing of all vestige of the divine. It was a "creationism without a creator."[33] Here, the nothing is neither the privation of being or the difference internal to it, as the classic position for the most part held, nor the total void out of which God made the world. The existential sense of nothingness is revealed instead in generalized anxiety about the contingency of human existence; it is the condition for a form of freedom obtained in the affirmation of contingency, an existential condition far indeed from Cohen's methodological principle. Heidegger's essay levied a thinly veiled attack on Cohen, and concluded by discovering a form of transcendence in the world, not beyond or alongside it.[34]

Scholem's encounter with Cohen and his stance on being out of nothingness traced a Heideggerian arc. As a young man, Scholem had thrown in his lot with a nihilism he associated with Nietzsche. But in other of his moods, he proved more sensitive to nothingness than to nihilism. By 1918, for example, he had picked up on Cohen's distinction between the nothing of the zero and the negation out of which, for Cohen, originary thought could emerge. This is unsurprising. Scholem had imagined for himself a career as a mathematician, had read widely in the philosophy of math, and in some of his more effusive moments had declared mathematics the language of Zion. But Scholem also translated Cohen's distinction into the lexicon of the kabbalah: in his diaries he opposed *efes*, zero, to *ayin*, the nothingness which kabbalists such as Gikatilla could, by rearranging its letters, transform into a manifestation of God.[35]

Scholem also picked up on the other crucial aspect of Cohen's argument, and which Rosenzweig, too, had made his own: the notion of privation. To be sure, Scholem broached the issue in a way Cohen would have rejected. He concluded his essay on creation from nothing by reviving an Aristotelian approach to privation for which Cohen had little truck. Cohen worked in the tradition of modern science; the bulk of his work, in fact, had undertaken philosophically to ground it. Being from nothingness was for Cohen a logical operation, designed in the end to secure the autonomy of thought from the world, the natural world, from any "sensuous given" as Gordon has put it.[36] Cohen's stance might be cast as a denial of worldliness undertaken for the sake of science, understood by him as a self-sufficient system conceptually independent of the world it purports to describe. But modern physics had long since eclipsed its Aristotelian predecessor, and Scholem's selective recovery would certainly have baffled Cohen had he lived to witness the affront.[37]

If the move would have left Cohen mystified, however, it met almost certainly with a measure of delight on the part of Strauss: this, because to revive Aristotelian privation meant also to revive, if by implication, Aristotelian teleology. Strauss had undertaken a partial recovery of the latter category himself, most recently in *Natural Right and History*. Strauss diagnosed a similar recovery at work in Jonas in 1958, at just the time, in fact, that he read Scholem's essay. In other words, Strauss was primed, and Scholem's talk of Aristotelian privation and natural form undoubtedly attracted his interest. It was, I believe, the move that alerted Strauss to the proximity of Scholem's nihil to the physis of the philosophers.

Let us follow the train of Scholem's thought more closely. Aristotle had posited matter, form, and privation as the constituent elements of all natural things. Privation, or steresis as Aristotle called it, stipulates that a thing is limited in its becomings by the precept of its form. "A thing [at any one moment] is not yet all that it can become in accord with its nature," Scholem observed in summary. "There is a series of forms, and every form realizes something of that which matter can become. Not everything can become anything. A piece of wood cannot become iron, but rather a board or, further belabored, a carved figure. Things can only become that which lie in the laws of their form."[38] In Scholem's version of Aristotelian privation there inheres dialectically a kind of potential. A thing has already within it that which has not been realized but which its innate purposefulness implies that it yet will (or may). On the other hand, the fullness of a thing implied by privation is limited by the laws or form of being that govern its growth. Steresis, in other words, is the logical flip side of physis.

Scholem's Aristotle seems to have lost a mental move or two over the millennia that intervened. Aristotle defined privation as the lack of that which a thing ought by nature have, and not, as Scholem had it, as the lack of what it might yet become.[39] But no matter: the crucial step came next, and was Scholem's alone. The kabbalists, he argued, had transformed Aristotelian steresis by identifying its not-being with the nothingness of the divine. Scholem put it this way: "There, where the forms transform into matter, which is to say, *in every living process*, the nothingness [of God] also breaks forth."[40] God's nothingness manifests itself precisely there where a thing acts or grows in accord with its nature. Physis opens a space for a kind of revelation in (and out of) the world. In "Creation from Nothing," Scholem tells us, this mystical rendering of the Aristotelian doctrine was best formulated by Asriel of Gerona in the thirteenth century, and transmitted in an unbroken line to eighteenth-century Hasidim such as Dov Baer. Perhaps true, but the principle surfaces also in Scholem's diaries from his time in Berne, before he had turned seriously to the study of kabbalah, and as an account of the world in which he, not the kabbalists, lived.[41]

Elsewhere in the essay ("Creation from Nothing"), Scholem made recourse to another version of the principle—this time in his treatment of Lurianic kabbalah, and with more general implications. Luria had described the first act of creation as a self-contraction of the divine. This revised the scheme of those kabbalists, Cordovero especially, indebted to Neoplatonic theories of creation by emanation, or to those thinkers indebted to the Thomistic principle of *processio dei ad extra*. God compressed inward before he flowed outward, and every stage of creation thereafter, every form of being whatsoever, had this dialectic at its core. "Everywhere," Scholem wrote, "the nothingness (Nichts) that is born of the *tzimtzum* inserts itself into Being." The result: "there is no pure being and no pure not-being."[42] Some of those writing in Luria's wake understood this nothingness as an emptiness or a void, the space left by God as he beat his hasty retreat. Others, as we have seen, understood it as a kind of fullness, not-being cast as the nothingness of the divine, or even as the divine itself. The first spoke of creation out of nothingness; the second spoke of the nothingness—or the divinity—of creation. The former enabled the world. The latter, in a modest way, redeemed it.[43]

What began, then, as a reflection on privation and natural form, on the relation of steresis to physis, became something much more: a dialectic of the formlessness at work in all form, or of the active nothingness at the heart of being. It also promised a solution to a problem that had bedeviled Scholem for some time. The gnostic in him could not simply affirm the world, but neither could he negate it, for fear of sacking what he knew as God's creation after all. He could not embrace a gnostic God who was nowhere to be found, a God of salvation but not creation—but neither could he accept a pantheist divine whose omnipresence would dissolve it. In the kabbalist *Nichts*, however, he discovered—invented?—a peculiar historical example, perfectly suited to his own, contemporary needs: an affirmation of a world whose very deficit or deficiency—the abyss of nothingness present in all being—might be understood also as the presence in the world of an otherwise absent divine. It enabled him to speak both gnostic and pantheist languages of heresy at once, even if he revised and transformed them in the process. Nothingness—or as Strauss put it, Scholem's update to what the falasifa would have called physis—was Scholem's answer to nihilism, in both its gnostic and pantheist forms.

The case of Jacob Frank helps us see just how. In 1957, the year Scholem published "Creation from Nothing," he also delivered a lecture at Eranos devoted to the theme of mysticism and religious authority. The challenge of the mystic, he observed, inhered in his dissolution of the world of natural forms, as part of an attempt to build the world anew. All mystical experience was fundamentally formless, Scholem argued, but most mystics imagined the dissolution of form as a prelude to its recrudescence. A minority, however, did not. These "mystical nihilists" preferred to make of formlessness a program without return. They lacked dialectical sense. Still more, they applied this single-mindedness of purpose to the world itself, not only to their mystical experience. As Scholem put it of Frank, the mystical nihilist "descends into the abyss in which the freedom of living things is born; he passes through all the embodiments and forms that come his way, committing himself to none; and not content with rejecting and abrogating all values and laws, he tramples them underfoot and desecrates them, in order to attain the elixir of Life." This was a far cry indeed from the cosmic piety of the Greeks, that "harmonious life of all things in bond with God." It also rejected the Jewish model of creation, "a world ordered by divine law and submissive to His authority." It looked instead to the dark underbelly of nature, or, to the "anarchic promiscuity of all living things."[44]

The phrase is a potent one. It also implicated, even literalized, the distinction between nomos and physis that Strauss and Jonas had revived. Life is anarchic. It is wild and ungovernable. It defies in the end every effort to bring it to order, to subdue it to the dictates of law, any law. It is the wellspring of lawlessness, a primal earthly force. But Scholem's Frank ruined the distinction between physis and nomos also. If the stuff of life only undoes all that is ordered, then it defies not only nomos. It defies physis, too. It ignores the impulse behind the distinction—to point to the disparity between natural and conventional forms of order, whether to argue for the superiority of one or the other—by doing away with all order whatsoever. Neither law nor nature was a template for right conduct, and so Scholem's Frank far outstripped in radicalism the antinomian impulse in Jonas and Strauss. He did not merely assert the primariness of nature to law, its "beforeness." He was no mere "antenomian." He was an antinomian through and through.

None of this would have come as a surprise to Jonas, who had ascribed a similar sensibility to the gnostics of late antiquity and their modern, existentialist heirs: "That which has no nature has no norm. Only that which belongs to an order of natures—be it an order of creation, or of intelligible forms—can have a nature. Only where there is a whole is there a law." As Jonas wrote of the gnostic God, so we might say of Frank's: "no nomos emanates from him, no law for nature and thus none for human action as a part of the natural order."[45] Both Strauss and Jonas hoped to temper human excess by reacquainting man with his natural origins, by reinserting him into a natural order. Frank wanted no such thing. Scholem called him a deviation, one of the outcomes of a dialectic ignored. Mystical nihilism, after all, had little use for the nexus of nothingness and nature—the version of it—Scholem discovered elsewhere in the kabbalistic tradition.

All this begs an obvious series of questions. Was this a descriptive enterprise or a prescriptive one, a historical insight or a normative injunction? Was this a reflection on the era of the kabbalists or Scholem's own? The answer, I think, is both. Scholem, of course, was a historian. For the most part, he did not traffic in vulgar presentism or, put rather differently, in philosophy. But his friends Strauss and Jonas did, and surely it says much that they demanded in a philosophical idiom just what Scholem urged, for the most part, in a historical and theological one. Like Scholem, that is, they hoped to get beyond nihilism by charting a path between its modern forms: the perils of a gnostic existentialism and a pantheist naturalism.

Take Jonas: "The disruption between man and total reality is at the bottom of nihilism," Jonas observed, in 1952. The disruption rules, both in the gnostic embrace of a transcendent beyond and in its updated, existentialist denial. "The illogicality of the [existentialist] rupture, that is, of a dualism without metaphysics," which is to say, without otherworldly transcendence, "makes its fact no less real, nor its seeming alternative any more acceptable." The fate to which existentialism had condemned man, "the stare at isolated selfhood," may well prompt an embrace of its apparent antidote, Jonas thought, "a monistic naturalism which, along with the rupture, would abolish also the idea of man as man." It may well generate, in theological terms, a pantheism that involves the obliteration of personality, both human and divine. "Between that Scylla and this her twin Charybdis," between gnosticism and pantheism, existentialism and monistic naturalism—between them all Jonas believed the modern mind to hover. "Whether a third road is open to it— one by which the dualistic rift can be avoided and yet enough of the dualistic insight saved to uphold the humanity of man—philosophy must find out."[46] Not only philosophy, but, in the case of Scholem, Judaism too had been enjoined to set out upon that path, and it could look to the history of kabbalah for lessons in how to follow it.

It was no accident that Scholem first fastened on this set of reflections around 1918—around the time he emancipated himself from the need to write a *Zarathustra* for the Jews. That is, the kabbalist notion of the nothingness at work in all being, of the formlessness at work in every form, of the privation that contradicts every claim to plenitude—all these had corollaries in ideas Scholem advanced about modern Jewish identity, culture and statehood, ideas opposed to the positions he staked out in his early allegiance to Nietzsche, and which he later discovered in the mystical nihilism of Jacob Frank.

How so? The *Judenzarathustra* had declared the world fallen, and proposed to create a new one in its stead. But Scholem came to affirm a stance for which privation and steresis—the deficiencies of the world, its nothingness—are the traces of divine transcendence, however nebulous and faint. The *Judenzarathustra* had set out to negate the history of exile, to create a "new Jew" or an ancient Jew or both, so long as it replaced the dereliction of the old. But Scholem professed incomprehension for those, the neo-Canaanites, who hoped to do the same; he rejected a Zionism predicated on the annihilation of exile as doomed on its face, and undesirable to boot.[47] The *Judenzarathustra* had set out to create a "pure" Jew. Scholem came to recognize that there could not—and should not—be any such thing. The *Judenzarathustra* was born of nihilism; Scholem's notion of an anarchic community was one, as he put it in 1918, to be founded instead on *Nichts*.[48] The *Judenzarathustra* looked to superhuman willfulness as the answer to the debasement of the Jew; Scholem came to understand the position for the hazard it was, and hoped to get beyond the "chimera of will."[49] To put it in formulaic terms, his embrace of the nothingness in being or of the formlessness in form meant also to accept the otherness within the individual and collective Jewish self. It meant to make peace with the *ger* (or stranger) in his first name that frustrated every effort to be the *scholem* (or wholeness) of his last; it meant to accept the emptiness in the heart of Jewish plenitude. In the end, it meant to affirm Jewish identity as an act of nonidentity, too.

Franz Rosenzweig seems to have understood all this. Or rather, and more remarkably, he imagined the future advent of this "maturation" in Scholem's stance, as he wrote to his friend Rudolf Hallo in March of 1922. Hallo had written in despair of an encounter with Scholem, who on that day at least appeared as a man in tune with his inner ogre, and Rosenzweig felt obliged to comfort him:

Dear Rudi—I think it's wicked Scholem who is the cause of this long and theoretical letter (to which you, O wretched man, need not give so long an answer). Why are you debating [with him]? No debating is possible over what one *does*. And least of all with a nihilist like Scholem. The nihilist always gains his point. If someone sweeps all the pieces off the chessboard with his sleeve, obviously he's made it difficult for me to win the game. In Scholem there is the ascetic's *Ressentiment*. We are not ascetics. But we also do not want to be scoundrels, who give out more than they have. What we have is not nothing, as Scholem, thanks to his Zionist dogma, would claim—but also is not all, as you, distressed at that nothing Scholem coldly hurled at you, would like to find in me. Rather we both have only something, really and truly only something. Let us hold by it, and play our games with those who have learned to play with their fingers and not with their sleeves. Maybe Scholem too will learn that someday.[50]

Scholem never did learn to play very well with others. But he at least learned to refrain from wiping the chessboard clean. If he could not quite bring himself to accept the world on its own imperfect terms, what Rosenzweig apparently meant by the "something" which we all have, he at least came to refrain from disavowing it altogether. And he did so by defining the something that made the world a livable one as the nothingness at its heart.

CHAPTER THIRTEEN

Scholem's Golem

ONCE UPON A TIME in a city called Rehovot there lived a powerful Jewish magus. He was known as Dr. Chaim Pekeris to his colleagues and students at the Weizmann Institute of Science. But some knew Pekeris as more than a mild-mannered professor of applied mathematics. They knew him also as a master of the dark force at the heart of all creation. Steeped in the lore of Jewish creative genius, these few referred to Professor Pekeris as "Rabbi" instead, since they recognized in him a scion of Rabbi Judah Loew ben Bezalel, the Maharal, of sixteenth-century Prague. Scholar and mystic, counselor to the king, the Maharal had also made a name for himself as an applied mathematician. Like Pekeris, if several centuries before him, the Maharal had made a golem.

The golem of Prague and the golem of Rehovot had much in common, as Gershom Scholem duly noted in 1965. The old golem was born of a mystical system of signs based on the twenty-two letters of the Hebrew alphabet. The new golem was born of only two, a binary system composed of ones and zeros. "I dare say the old kabbalists would have been glad to learn of this simplification," Scholem announced. "This is progress." The old golem was made animate by the *shem ha-meforash*, the explicit name for God; the new golem, too, worked according to a series of ciphers, though of purely human origin. The old golem served his master by delivering water to the house; the new golem by computing the movement of the tides, "a more progressive type of activity," Scholem thought, "so far as water is concerned."[1]

Loew had fashioned his golem of clay, and had granted him life, or what passed for it, by slipping into his mouth a scrap of paper bearing a mystical name for God. Golem life was not human life, and most who have weighed in on the subject have refused to call it animal as well. Loew's golem could respond to orders and perform chores, but little more. He could not speak. He could not love. And he collapsed into an amorphous mass when Loew plucked the slip of paper from his mouth, as was his custom as the Sabbath queen drew nigh. Even golems, it seems, were obliged to rest, as God commanded also of their human creators.

But one week, the story goes, Loew neglected to put down his creation. The golem grew restive and recalcitrant, magically increased in size, tore through the ghetto, and proceeded to run amok. Loew rushed from his prayers at the Altneuschul and with a desperate effort subdued the golem for good as he ripped the holy name from his mouth. Another rendition of the tale ends otherwise. Set in sixteenth-century Poland, this version has the golem collapse when the first letter of the word carved into his forehead, *emeth* or truth, is erased to leave *meth*, death; except that in this case, the golem had grown so great of bulk and enormous of stature that the rabbi was killed as his creation crashed upon him. The legend has therefore served as a cautionary tale about the perils of the creative impulse. For to create a golem is in some sense to compete with God's own creation of man. "In such an act," as Scholem well knew, "the creative power of man enters into a relationship, whether of emulation or antagonism, with the creative power of God."[2]

Scholem claimed to spy a "straight line" through time joining the golems of Rehovot and Prague, notwithstanding their obvious theological disparity. It is easy to see why. Both were creatures of human artifice. Both were enjoined by their creators to help them make their way in a world of others' making. Both tapped into an earthly power only poorly understood and so tended on the one hand to falter, on the other to outstrip the capacity of their creators to control them. In both cases, the golem was less a servant of man than a creature animated by man's invocation of the autonomous power of the earth; his resistance to human control spoke to a deeper resistance of the earth to human claims upon it. This tellurian force recalls Scholem's "anarchic promiscuity of all living things." Scholem called it an "earth magic" which "awakens chaotic forces." Like the pit of promiscuity out of which all that lives comes to be, this tellurian power both gives rise to creation and undoes it. Applied to the golem, it threatened to reverse wholesale the creation of man himself. "Whereas Adam began as a gigantic cosmic golem and was reduced to the normal size of a man, this golem seems to strive, in response to the tellurian force that governs him, to regain the original stature of Adam." Set free by man, the golem proceeds to destroy him. He has "prodigious strength and grows beyond measure," Scholem tells us. "He destroys the world, or in any case does a good deal of damage."[3]

Scholem's account of the story has obvious affinities with others we have encountered. It reads much like a Jewish version of the injunctions against human creative license issued, in parallel but dissimilar form, by his friends Jonas and Strauss. It is a story of science—Jewish science in this case—gone awry. The tale resonates among us moderns, and for good reason. This version of the golem legend, in which the *product* of human creation turns on its master in the end, was in fact a late innovation. It took root in Jewish literature by the middle of the eighteenth century, but did not become thoroughly popularized until the turn of the nineteenth, as figures associated with romanticism (and for that matter, a particular brand of nihilism) made the golem and others like him a mainstay of the European cultural scene. Jakob Grimm, for example, included a version of the story in an 1808 edition of his *Journal for Hermits*.[4] Goethe's play *The Sorcerer's Apprentice* was on some accounts inspired by his visit to Prague's Altneuschul. Mary Shelley, meanwhile, had Doctor Viktor Frankenstein at work in the Bavarian town of Ingolstadt on the monster that came to bear his name. The golem gathered into himself an array of themes the romantics had made it their mission to revive. A neo-romanticism afoot in Scholem's own time aspired to something of the same.

But Scholem also set out to recover an early tradition in golem interpretation obscured by its Frankensteinian successors. This tradition stressed the dangers at work in the creative process itself, in the hazard unleashed in *man* by the act of taking license, rather than the danger posed by the product of his creation. One of the earliest extant golem texts, composed in thirteenth-century Languedoc, has Jeremiah and his son Sira at work for three years on forging their automaton, who comes to life with the words *YHWH Elohim Emeth* (God the Lord Is Truth) inscribed upon his forehead. But he comes also with a knife, with which he erases the *alef* of *emeth* to leave in its stead the phrase "God the Lord Is Dead." Confronted with the spectacle of this great clay hulk, armed with a blade and a rather disturbing message, Jeremiah and his son rend their garments in contrition. This golem speaks, and takes care to spell out the nature of their blasphemy. God had made man in his image, but now that Jeremiah and Sira had done the same, other men would proclaim: "There is no God in the world besides these two!" Horrified, the pair promptly undo their monster by writing the mystical permutation of letters backward on the earth, all the while meditating on destruction and "de-creation." The moral, as Jeremiah understood it: "Truly, one should study these things only in order to know the power and omnipotence of the Creator of this world, but not in order really to practice them."[5]

Scholem recounted just this story to Pekeris and the others assembled around the golem of Rehovot, when he helped dedicate the blinking, squawking creature in 1965. He recounted the story with only one difference: he neglected to mention the moral. Perhaps Scholem thought it impolitic. The jeremiad had after all been directed at precisely the sort of undertaking that brought the golem of Rehovot into being. Theoretical golem-making was permitted. Applied golem-making was not. The first could elicit a regard for the wonder of creation and for the power of the God who made it. The second risked idolatry. But perfunctory attention to the demands of politesse had rarely shackled Scholem before, and so it seems more likely that he left the moral out because he could not in the end condone it. Scholem drew conclusions different and more ambiguous in their thrust: "It is indeed significant," he told those gathered around him, "that Nietzsche's famous cry, 'God is dead,' should have gone up first in a Kabbalistic text warning against the making of a Golem and linking the death of God to the realization of the idea of the Golem."[6]

Scholem was neither a kabbalist nor a scientist, and while the golems of Prague and Rehovot were of interest to him, he knew they were not his own. But the Nietzschean problems he associated with both applied just as much, if not more, to himself. Scholem had also dabbled in applied golem-making. Scholem's golem was made of neither clay nor the stuff—vacuum tubes, punch cards, what have you—of the earliest computers. It could not deliver water. It could not compute the tides. But for all that it was yet more powerful than its cousins, and also more dangerous. Scholem's golem was less the product of human creation than the energy of the creative process—of the Jewish creative process—unleashed from whatever constraint had bound it. It was less technical creation than existential self-creation. It was less a Jewish work of nature than work on Jewish nature, all of it undertaken to revitalize the Jewish people, but at the risk, as he also knew, of their ruin. Scholem spent a lifetime at work on his golem. He first named him in 1944: "this terrifying giant, our history."

Scholem took his German-Jewish predecessors to task for hiding this golem from sight. They had locked him away in the synagogue attic, deaf to the entreaty of his thumps and blind to the show of his ashen face at the attic's single window. Or worse still: if they had not banished him, they had set out to domesticate him instead. They had compelled "this enormous creature, full of destructive power, made up of vitality, evil and perfection" to contract itself, to "stunt its growth and declare that it has no substance." They had clothed him, tamed him, socialized him, sterilized him, if only so that "every decent Jewish bourgeois could unashamedly bid him good-day in the streets of the city, the immaculate city of the nineteenth century." Their great error, Scholem believed, had been "to remove the irrational stinger and banish the demonic enthusiasm from Jewish history through exaggerated theologizing and spiritualizing." This had been their "decisive original sin," committed in the name of the assimilationist project. But Scholem hoped to undo all this. "This terrifying giant, our history," he proclaimed, "is called to task."[7]

But what task exactly? Scholem was oddly silent on this count. The task he neglected to specify, not in 1944 and not later. Scholem urged the Jew to "return to history" (as if he had actually left it), but was silent about what he ought to do once there. Merely to animate the golem of Jewish history seemed for him to suffice, because it meant to awaken the Jewish people to its own existential imperative. The act itself, that is, would call forth the creative and productive energies of the Jew. To return to history meant for the Jew to assert himself in a world of others' making. It meant to take responsibility for a Jewish present and Jewish future by fashioning out of the historical detritus a living Jewish past. It meant to stake a claim and to choose. Above all, it meant to affirm the historical world—not some beyond—as the scene for authentic Jewish life.

In a Jewish context, Scholem thought this meant to live a life shorn of messianic ferment. The messianic idea he considered the "anti-existentialist idea" par excellence—it denied the authenticity of this-worldly life. The pejorative says much. As an adolescent, Scholem had announced his yearning for objective and subjective redemption, a want so keen that he declared himself the messiah to expedite the process. As a scholar, he devoted great effort toward deciphering the mysteries of messianism. He sympathized with the impulse, but it would be wrong to conclude that he endorsed it. The Sabbatians, after all, earned his accolades not on account of their messianism, but because they chose to *do* something about it. The activism of the deed and the Jewish self-assertion it implied made it attractive to Zionists like Scholem who hoped for something of the same.[8]

The similarity led some to impute messianic significance to the Zionist movement. "Little wonder," as Scholem put it to an audience at Eranos in 1959, "that overtones of Messianism have accompanied the modern Jewish readiness for irrevocable action in the concrete realm, when it set out on the utopian return to Zion." But the power of the messianic idea threatened the success of the Zionist project. "Whether or not Jewish history will be able to endure this entry into the concrete realm without perishing in the crisis of the Messianic claim which has virtually been conjured up—that is the question which out of his great and dangerous past the Jew of this age poses to his present and to his future."[9]

Scholem first delivered these lines at Eranos in 1959. But he felt compelled to repeat them to a group of scholars assembled in his honor in Jerusalem at the end of 1977. The year marked a sea change in the course of Israeli history. Menachem Begin and the Likud Party had deposed Israel's socialist elite and had come to rule the country for the first time in three decades of statehood. They were aided not least by the rise of the Gush Emunim (Bloc of the Faithful), which had established its first Jewish settlements in the heart of Hebron nearly a decade before as part of an activist messianic plan, and which now found itself with an ardent ally in charge at the Knesset. For an erstwhile supporter of accommodation with the Palestinian Arabs like Scholem, all this bode ill: a revisionist Zionism with suspect roots, revanchist aspirations, and a messianic subtext had come to command the apparatus of Jewish power. To be sure, Begin concluded a peace agreement with Egypt, but only, Scholem would insist in 1980, the better to pursue his enduring messianic fantasies where they truly counted—in the biblical Land of Israel on the West Bank of the Jordan River.[10]

For Scholem to counsel decisively against the messianic idea meant to contest Begin and his ilk. But it did not necessarily mean to affirm Zionism as a movement of political rationality and pragmatism (even if he faulted Begin on both counts). It meant, rather, to defend an existential imperative: a modest but still emphatic form of Jewish self-assertion threatened by the all-or-nothing apocalyptics of the Israeli messianic right. Zionist self-assertion ought to be bound to "history," he consistently held, and not to its messianic disavowal. "Zionism is not to be regarded as a species of messianism," he explained in 1974 to an audience in Santa Barbara. "I consider it the pride of Zionism that it is not a messianic movement. It is a great error, therefore—for which Zionism may have to pay dearly—if the movement attributes to itself messianic significance. Zionism is rather a movement within the mundane, immanent process of history; Zionism does not seek the end of history, but takes responsibility within the history of an *unredeemed* and *unmessianic* world."[11] Jewish self-assertion in a thoroughly historical world was the only authentic course left to the Jew for whom God, if living, was nonetheless absent and his call, interrupted.[12]

The citation is important not only for what it says about the threat to the existential imperative that animated the "Jewish return to history." It shows us also how the sensibility that underwrote Scholem's revisions of the gnostic and pantheist languages of heresy—to preserve the relative autonomy of the world—underwrote the mature form of his Zionism also. Scholem's choices for the Jewish past—Jewish gnosticism and Jewish pantheism—thus shared much with his choices for the Jewish present. All implied in the end a commitment to present and future Jewish worldliness. By contrast, the messianic idea had for Scholem largely lost the world, and with it the ground for a finite and mortal Jewish life, positively construed.[13] It is here, I think, that he most reveals his affinity for the parallel projects of Jonas and Strauss. All had at one point courted the loss of the world. But all—in some way related to their Judaism—in the end decided to save it.

That Scholem's brief for Jewish self-assertion shared much with his Jewish revisions of the gnostic and pantheist languages of heresy should perhaps come as no surprise. He spent much of his life, after all, at work on groups of heretics, which attracted him on the strength of the spirit of self-assertion that animated them. For this reason, Scholem's existential imperative might be called a "heretical imperative" instead. The term is Peter Berger's, whose book of the same name suggests we understand the modern world as a universalization of heresy.[14] The view has much to support it. The Greek *hairesis* meant originally "to choose," and modern life confronts us with an unprecedented variety of choices about how to live our lives. Even more, we are compelled to choose, whether we like it or not. We cannot escape this imperative. It is the modern condition, our lot.

There is at least one great strength to this view. It insists that *all* forms of modern religious expression are inventions, even those that style themselves an unbroken continuation of a two-thousand-year tradition. The rise of a nominally secular public sphere, this argument goes, means that even apparently traditional and insular communities must assert themselves against their "outside," whether they recognize such self-assertion as the choice that it is or whether they cloak it, as they are wont to do, in the rhetoric of heteronomy.[15]

But framing the argument in this way undermines its greatest strength: as one alternative to our stories about the secularization of the world. In other words, the heretical forms of Jewish identity developed by Scholem and others disputes both orthodoxy *and* the conceit of a public sphere rid of the divine. The secularization thesis, in its generic form, has trouble accounting for the endurance of discourses of the divine in talk about nature, politics, or art. The thesis must describe them as dinosaurs, fossils, archaic holdovers from an earlier age from which the modern has yet to be extricated. Secularization is on this view an uncompleted project: its detractors bemoan the modern world as a partial devolution while its champions bemoan it as not quite modern enough. By contrast, a "hereticization thesis" is more adept at making its peace with the endurance and even efflorescence of talk of the divine in a world for which the divine is apparently dead.

Still, Berger does well to stress the affinity of heresy for a form of human self-assertion. He writes of his heretical imperative, in fact, in the very terms Jean-Paul Sartre had used to describe the sort of freedom he thought accorded to modern man by God's absence. Here is how Jonas put it in his famous essay on gnosticism and existentialism: "Since the transcendent is silent," he wrote of Sartre, "since 'there is no sign in the world,' man, the 'abandoned' and left-to-himself, reclaims his freedom, or rather, cannot help taking it upon himself." On this view, we have no choice but to choose. We assert ourselves because we must. Sartre's error, as Jonas saw it at least, was to equate man with the freedom that obtained for him in God's absence. "He 'is' that freedom," Jonas wrote in summary, "man being 'nothing but his own project,' and 'all that is permitted to him.'" Jonas therefore thought this mode of thought complicit with a stance of unfettered human self-creation free to do with the earth what man wills. He thought it blind to the ways in which man is patently more than his existential freedom: to his biological being that makes him a part of the world before all else, and to the purposiveness or willfulness—which Jonas supposed a form of freedom—that inheres in cellular life. Jonas's view shared much with that of Karl Löwith, another of Heidegger's Jewish "children" and a friend to Scholem too. Löwith put it this way: "Perhaps one could say that modernity begins with the dissolution of a natural and social order in which man was supposed to have a definite nature and place, while modern man 'exists,' displaced and out of place, in extreme situations on the edge of chaos."[16]

There is certainly something of all this in Scholem. He had, after all, professed his desire to walk the fine line between religion and nihilism. He spoke often of the abyss that yawned on either side of his tight and precarious path. Scholem's counsel to return to history comes off much as a Jewish version of Sartre's decisionism. It came close to a formal injunction to decide without regard to the substance of the act. It smacked of interwar "resolve." Scholem had awakened the golem of Jewish history, but had neglected to tell him what to do. He had even diagnosed an example of the self-assertive Jew gone awry in the persons of Jacob Frank and his followers, and not without sympathy. Of this he spoke with eloquence in 1936: "The Gordian knot binding the soul of the exilic Jew had been cut and a vertigo that ultimately was to be his undoing seized the newly liberated individual: genuine desires for a reconsecration of life mingled indiscriminately with all kinds of destructive and libidinal forces tossed up from the depths by an irrepressible ground swell that undulated wildly between the earthly and the divine."[17] Frank might be faulted for his excess, but not his determination.

But there are also important differences between heresy as Jewish self-assertion and a Jewish existentialism unmoored from all constraint. For one, heretical subjectivity countenances an otherness in the self in a way that Sartre's existentialism—as Scholem and Jonas understood it—did not. Scholem knew the members of his generation to stand before the law as Kafka had it, fated always to alienation and to lack. He referred to them as "men from afar," and with good reason. For many, the fact of their heresy was the only residual link to their Jewishness, and whatever Jewish identity they would manage to fashion for themselves was fated to carry with it the memory of their extra-Jewish origins. At an early point in his life, Scholem bemoaned the otherness at the heart of Jewish selfhood. But he later came to accept it (or at least some of its forms), and his attention to the problem of heresy ought to be understood as a revision of the sort of Jewish self and its relation to the world he had earlier espoused. In other words, human freedom for the heretical self is not the same as self-creation. Whatever his deviance, the heretic relates to a tradition that always comes before—the freedom of transgression is made possible by the enduring force of the norms it disputes. Sabbatian freedom may have been antinomian, for example, but it remained thoroughly nomocentric. Sabbatian theologians did not ignore the law. They studied it assiduously, if only the better to break it. For Scholem—a dialectical animal through and through—to contest tradition meant implicitly to uphold it. Not ambivalence or sublimation or even studied violation, but only indifference to Jewish tradition did he condemn as "educational murder."[18]

In one respect at least, Scholem's wager proved a wild success. Perhaps overly so: Judaism was in for trouble, were the golem of Jewish history to make his way among the *Gush Emunim*. Judaism was in for trouble, were the impulse to Jewish self-creation loosed from its constraints and yoked to a messianic program of total liberation.[19] Scholem knew this. Zionism, he conjectured, "might be deadly for the Jews." But this was a danger he was willing to court. "There is no guarantee that the State of Israel is or will be a full success in any sense," he told his audience at Santa Barbara, "but I welcome the struggle because it will call forth the productive power[s]—whatever they are—of Jews."[20] The alternative in his mind to Jewish self-assertion—Jewish victimhood or assimilation in political terms, Jewish inauthenticity in existential ones—seemed to him so much the worse. But whatever Scholem's reasons, they may well be irrelevant to us now. Whatever the rightness of his wager, even of its formulation, of the premises on which it is based—whatever all this, there can be no doubt about one thing at least. Scholem's golem lives, and the man who helped create him is no more. The creature has outlived his creator, the golem his Scholem.

The upshot: man—or in Scholem's case, the Jew—reigns in a world that was once the domain of a God now dead or missing. Jonas and Strauss had issued a similar diagnosis. As an antidote to human excess, Scholem's friends had issued also a directive. Strauss asked man to recall his natural origins, Jonas his natural ends (his *telos*). They did not ask man to disavow his autonomy from the natural world. But they did ask him, each in his way, to save the world for its own sake and as a scene for human life. Whether those who hear their call will choose to heed it—and how—is difficult to say. It also remains to be seen whether the people of Israel will decide—and will discover in itself also the capacity—to heed Scholem's final directive to the most recent incarnation of Jewish creative genius. "All my days I have been complaining that the Weizmann Institute has not mobilized the funds to build up the Institute for Experimental Demonology and Magic which I have for so long proposed to establish there," Scholem told those gathered around him in 1965, in Rehovot. "They preferred what they call Applied Mathematics and its sinister possibilities to my more direct magical approach. Little did they know, when they preferred Chaim Pekeris to me, what they were letting themselves in for." Indeed they did not. Scholem concluded his short speech with a directive issued to the creation of Pekeris and his colleagues. But it is hard to imagine that he did not also have in mind his own. "Develop peacefully," Scholem commanded the golem of Rehovot. "Develop peacefully, and don't destroy the world."[21]

Epilogue

THIS BOOK began with a question with which I would like now to bring it to a close: "Should the emancipation and secularization of the modern age, which began with a turning-away, not necessarily from God, but from a god who was the Father of men in heaven, end with an even more fateful repudiation of an Earth who was the Mother of all living creatures under the sky?"[1]

Hannah Arendt posed this question in her book *The Human Condition* (1958). Her answers were idiosyncratic, couched in a language and conceptual architecture very much her own. But the book's signal concern pulls it into the orbit of others we have encountered. It asks what it means for moderns to make, what we imagine we are doing when we make, and how, historically and philosophically, it became possible to act and think in these ways at all. It is a reflection on the history of man as a creative being. It is another version of the stories told by her sometime friends Jonas, Strauss, and Scholem, by her lover Heidegger, by her contemporary Hans Blumenberg, and by many more. Like them, she was troubled by the direction human making—*technē*—had taken in the modern era. Like them, she worried about the threat it posed to the several dimensions of worldliness—our politics, our human-built world, and our Earth, which she called the "quintessence of the human condition." And like most of them, but with unmatched economy, in the space of a single question, she located the origins of this crisis in the eclipse of God, or in the interruption of his call.

There is an enormous irony at its core. Why did the turn away from God not generate a turn toward the world? Why did the aversion of our gaze from the heaven of heavens not make visible the heavens themselves? Why did it not reveal to us the cosmos anew, both the starry skies above and the earth beneath our feet? Secularization, it would seem, has had unintended consequences. Making the world worldly has had the perverse effect of leading us to neglect it. Turned from God, we did not turn toward the world. We faced inward instead, discovered ourselves wherever we looked: the world as we have made it rather than received it, or the instruments we use to take our measure of the world—our telescopes, our seismographs, our eyes—but not the world itself. In the process, we reduced God to the projection of man and the physical world to an object for the exercise of human will. God interrupted, we did not open our ears to the "unending revelation of matter" Hans Jonas asked us to heed. The revelation of matter has been drowned by the incessant, indecipherable babble of the all-too-human voice.

It is a depressing story, but in its way an appealing one also. It plays on the ancient prejudice of the humble soul against the crime of hubris. It helps us recall what "babble" has to do with Babel: the attempt to build a world fit to compete with God's. It is a lament, a work of mourning about what we have become. It is also a call to action. Some versions of the story ask us to revive and revise ways of being once lived but lost. Some versions ask us to imagine new ways of being that will correct the deficiencies of the present. Some ask us to wait for the storm to pass. As a genre, these stories are ancient, but they are modern in their details. All are fueled by a sense that there is something wrong—even pathological—about the modern age.

But are they right? As history, there is ample reason to say no. But this may be beside the point, at least in part. Whether we find their stories compelling is probably more a matter of temperament than of fidelity to a historical record. Historical records are slippery, notoriously difficult to pin down. Somehow, they always manage to sanction new interpretations fit to compete with the old. Arendt, Jonas, Strauss, Scholem: they were social scientists, but they were also makers of myths, and the measure of a myth is not its truth but its strength. To ask whether they are right is therefore only one of the questions we must pose, and perhaps not the most important one. We must ask also: why would they have felt pressed to invent them in the first place? Are they of any use? And is there an indispensable truth to be discovered in their error?

Again, there are ample reasons to say no, and they go something like this. First, these stories are trite. They are a series of typical complaints voiced by German antimoderns who peddle nostalgia in the guise of philosophy. Second, they are condescending. To say that man runs amok is to reduce him to an adolescent incapable of self-rule and in need of higher authority. It is to say that Enlightenment, which Immanuel Kant prescribed as a release from self-incurred nonage, has in fact abetted the cultural infantilism of the mob. They are also a political hazard. Antimodernism, this argument has it, is synonymous with hostility to liberal democracy and a discomfiting fascination with authoritarian forms of social control. Last, they are simply wrong. This objection is levied above all at those who lament the twin exclusion (God, teleological nature) that inaugurated the modern age. They have forgotten the teaching and the truth of Hobbes: that the all-too-human is all there is for any set of morals worthy of the name, that to submit to the authority of God or nature is in fact—and always—to submit to other men. The twin exclusion is to be celebrated, not mourned. It meant, after all, to awaken to ourselves.

The problem raised by Hobbes plays itself out nowadays in the form of a titanic battle. There are two alternatives, we are sometimes told, about how to order our relations with one another. There is political philosophy or political theology, liberal democracy or theocracy, reason or revelation, but not much hope for something in between. There is certainly something to all this. But the examples of Jonas, Strauss, and Scholem also help us see beyond the problem as it is often framed. They help us see that the scheme is incomplete. It is an argument about only one of the twin exclusions. Our most basic options are not two, but three: there is God and man, but there is also nature, earth, or world. There is political theology and political philosophy, but there is also, for lack of a better word, political ecology too. More important still, their example suggests it may be a misnomer to call them separate options at all. They demonstrate how easy it is for one to become another, how talk of God gets displaced into talk about ourselves and our world, and the inverse of that relation too. They suggest we are destined to live with all three, all at once, all the time.

Their example also casts doubt on the very premise of Arendt's question. If nothing else, the heretical ideal of which they were sometime expressions indicates that the modern age is not, or not only, a secular one. It has produced new forms of religion, new ways of thinking about God's presence in the world, new ways of imagining that "something more" than man. Arendt may have been right that the human condition, at least for now, for some, in a part of the West, is to live with the word of God interrupted. Perhaps this signals the beginning of his end, as she herself once hoped. But if our interwar ancestors are any measure by which to judge, his interruption means only that we will invent other ways and other words by which to let him speak.

Notes

Abbreviations

AGS   Archion Gershom Scholem
HBN   Hans-Blumenberg-Nachlaß
HJA   Hans-Jonas-Archiv
LSP   Leo Strauss Papers

Note to Preface and Acknowledgments

1. Hannah Arendt, *The Human Condition* (Chicago, 1958), 2.

Notes to Introduction

1. Gidon Samt, "Pay (the Orthodox) Now, Receive Later (Maybe)" [Hebrew], *Ha'aretz* (September 8, 1985), 7.
2. Cynthia Ozick, "Sabbatai Sevi: the Mystical Messiah" (review), *New York Times Book Review* (February 24, 1974), 24.
3. The Hebrew appears in Gershom Scholem, *Mechkarim ve-Mekorot le-Toldot ha-Shabta'ut ve-Gilguleha* (Jerusalem, 1974). The English translation appears in Gershom Scholem, *The Messianic Idea in Judaism* (New York, 1971).
4. On this distinction, see especially Hans Blumenberg, *The Legitimacy of the Modern Age*, trans. Robert M. Wallace (Cambridge, Mass., 1983), 37–52.
5. Bloch used the phrase as a motto for his book *Atheismus im Christentum* (Frankfurt, 1968). Scholem invoked it as he recalled in 1975 his first encounter with Bloch at Interlaken in 1919. Gershom Scholem, "Wohnt Gott im Herzen eines Atheisten?" republished and translated in Gershom Scholem, *On the Possibility of Jewish Mysticism in Our Time*, ed. Avraham Shapira (Philadelphia, 1997), 216–23.
6. Mark Mazower, *Dark Continent: Europe's Twentieth Century* (New York, 1998), 3–40.
7. Some representative accounts: Modris Eksteins, *Rites of Spring: The Great War and the Birth of the Modern Age* (New York, 1989); and Peter Gay, *Weimar Culture* (New York, 1968).
8. Jonathan Sheehan, *The Enlightenment Bible: Translation, Scholarship, Culture* (Princeton, 2005).
9. There is a voluminous literature on the subject. Among others, see Steven Aschheim, *Brothers and Strangers: The East European Jew in German and German-Jewish Consciousness, 1800–1923* (Madison, 1982); Avraham Barkai and Paul Mendes-Flohr, *German-Jewish History in Modern Times*, vol. 4,

Renewal and Destruction 1918–1945, ed. Michael A. Meyer and Michael Brenner (New York, 1998); Michael Brenner, *The Renaissance of Jewish Culture in Weimar Germany* (New Haven, Conn., 1996); and George L. Mosse, *German Jews Beyond Judaism* (Bloomington, 1985).

10. The extent to which they succeeded is debatable. In this regard, see especially David Sorkin, *The Transformation of German Jewry, 1780–1840* (New York, 1987). To Sorkin, these Jews largely failed in their intended project, but unwittingly developed a German-Jewish subculture in its stead.

11. Franz Rosenzweig, *Briefe und Tagebücher* (The Hague, 1979), 950.

12. On the liberal adaptation, see Brenner, *The Renaissance of Jewish Culture*, 36–68.

13. For example, his arguments about digestion: Hans Jonas, *The Imperative of Responsibility: In Search of an Ethics for the Technological Age*, trans. Hans Jonas and David Herr (Chicago, 1984), 65–74.

14. See, in English, Lawrence Vogel, "Hans Jonas's Exodus: From German Existentialism to Post-Holocaust Theology," in Hans Jonas, *Mortality and Morality: A Search for the Good after Auschwitz*, ed. Lawrence Vogel (Evanston, Ill., 1996); Richard Wolin, *Heidegger's Children* (Princeton, 2001); and in German, Eric Jakob, *Martin Heidegger und Hans Jonas: Die Metaphysik der Subjektivität und die Krise der technologischen Zivilisation* (Tübingen, 1996); F. J. Wetz, *Hans Jonas zur Einführung* (Hamburg, 1994); and Wolfgang Baum, *Gnostische Elemente im Denken Martin Heideggers? Eine Studie auf der Grundlage der Religionsphilosophie von Hans Jonas* (Neuried, 1997).

15. There is a large and growing literature on Strauss. Some of the major recent statements include: Leora Batnitzky, *Leo Strauss and Emmanuel Levinas* (Cambridge, U.K., 2006); Heinrich Meier, *Leo Strauss and the Theologico-Political Problem* (Cambridge, U.K., 2006); Thomas Pangle, *Leo Strauss* (Baltimore, 2006); Eugene Sheppard, *Leo Strauss and the Politics of Exile* (Waltham, Mass., 2007); Steven Smith, *Reading Leo Strauss* (Chicago, 2007); and Daniel Tanguay, *Leo Strauss: An Intellectual Biography*, trans. Christopher Nadon (New Haven, Conn., 2007).

16. Strauss invited such confusion. He wrote at length about the esoteric dimension of philosophical writing, and this has generated a search for the message hidden within his own. I try to address the matter, first, by revealing the deep continuities that link his work predating his writings on esotericism with those that came later, and second, by using previously unpublished sources—his correspondence above all—to corroborate assertions I make about the meaning of his scholarship. I also consider what he had to say about similar topics across a variety of genres (expository writing, lectures, letters) and settings (private and public) to arrive at an interpretation that I think remains faithful to the texts and their author.

17. Philip Rieff, "The Theology of Politics: Reflections on Totalitarianism as the Burden of Our Time," *Journal of Religion* 32, 2 (April 1952), 119.

18. For a recent argument to this effect, see Mark Lilla, *The Stillborn God* (New York, 2007).

19. That life may appear as it does, of course, does not make it so in fact. Its appearance may have nothing to do with its reality, and everything to do with the

limitations of our minds, a problem confronted most famously by Immanuel Kant in *The Critique of Judgment* (1790). See also Reiner Wiehl, "Von der Teleologie zur Theologie—Sackgasse oder Weg: Zur Auseinandersetzung Kants mit Spinoza," in *Spinoza und der deutsche Idealismus*, ed. Manfred Walther (Würzburg, 1991).

20. Jacob Taubes, *The Political Theology of Paul*, trans. Dana Hollander (Stanford, 2004), 58.

Notes to Part One: Overcoming Gnosticism

1. On Culianu's remarkable life and equally remarkable death, quite probably at the hands of Romanian neo-fascists linked at one time with Culianu's own teacher and collaborator Mircea Eliade, see Ted Anton, *Eros, Magic and the Murder of Professor Culianu* (Evanston, Ill., 1990).

2. Ioan Culianu, "The Gnostic Revenge: Gnosticism and Romantic Literature," in *Gnosis und Politik*, ed. Jacob Taubes (Munich, 1984), 290–91.

3. Hans Jonas, *Gnosis und spätantiker Geist. Teil I: Die mythologische Gnosis* (Göttingen, 1934).

4. Strauss to Jonas, November 19, 1958, Hans-Jonas-Archiv (hereafter HJA) 7-13b-10.

5. See, for example, Blumenberg, *Legitimacy*; Augusto del Noce, *Secolarizzazione e crisi della modernità* (Naples, 1989); Micha Brumlik, *Die Gnostiker: der Traum von der Selbsterlösung des Menschen* (Frankfurt, 1992); Peter Sloterdijk and Thomas H. Macho, eds., *Weltrevolution der Seele. Ein Lese- und Arbeitsbuch der Gnosis von der Spätantike bis zur Gegenwart* (Gütersloh, 1991); Taubes, ed., *Gnosis und Politik*; Eric Voegelin, *The New Science of Politics* (Chicago, 1952); and Eric Voegelin, *Wissenschaft, Politik und Gnosis* (Munich, 1959).

6. Rudolf Bultmann, a teacher to Jonas and for a time an ally of Barth, described its revival this way: "The despair [prompted by Barth's theologizing], radically conceived, is the realization that natural man is trying to flee from before God and that he cannot flee because he was trying to flee before God." Bultmann, "Liberal Theology and the Latest Theological Movement," in *Faith and Understanding*, vol. 1, ed. Robert W. Funk (New York, 1969), 50.

7. As for neo-Kantian epistemology, gnosis in some ways reversed its terms. Where the former insisted on a strict distinction between knowing subject and unknown object (and in its more idealistic guise, effaced the object altogether), the latter conceived of knowledge as the event of their fusion. Where the former located knowledge within the confines of an ideal epistemological subject, a transcendental "self," the latter described it as the incursion and recognition of the transcendent other.

8. Hans Jonas and Ingo Hermann, *Erkenntnis und Verantwortung: Gespräch mit Ingo Hermann* (Göttingen, 1991), 87. By this he meant the challenge of gnostic gnosis to *theoria*, its predecessor. Like gnosis, for *theoria* knowledge coincided with the soul's attainment of the known. But the *object* of knowledge was a universal, and the relation to it the analogue of an optical one in which the

known stands apart, unaffected by its apprehension. (An earlier notion of *theoria* entailed by contrast a passionate spectacle of the suffering God, which induced a reunion of spectator and spectacle, knower and known. F. M. Cornford, *From Religion to Philosophy* [Atlantic Highlands, N.J., 1980], 200.) By contrast, gnostic knowledge was of a particular, if transcendent, divinity, and its mode of relation, initially, was auditory rather than visual. Gnosis as event was precipitated by a "call" from the beyond. Also, gnosis once enacted entailed a mutual knowing: for the (human) subject to know is also to be known (by God); at the same time, God's apprehension by man involves purposive self-divulgence. Gnosis implied a new kind of relation: not of subject to object, but of subject to subject, or at least to an other so imagined.

9. See Michael Allen Williams, *Rethinking "Gnosticism"* (Princeton, 1996). See also Karen L. King, *What Is Gnosticism?* (Cambridge, Mass., 2003).

10. These are elaborated in *The Phenomenon of Life* (New York, 1966); in *Philosophical Essays: From Ancient Creed to Technological Man* (Englewood Cliffs, N.J., 1974); and in *The Imperative of Responsibility: In Search of an Ethics for the Technological Age*, trans. Hans Jonas and David Herr (Chicago, 1984).

NOTES TO CHAPTER ONE: THE GNOSTIC RETURN

1. By some accounts, the publication of the Nag Hammadi texts has failed to revolutionize understandings of gnosticism, despite initial expectations. See, for example, Sloterdijk and Macho, *Weltrevolution der Seele*, 21.

2. Hans Jonas, *The Gnostic Religion* (Boston, 1958), 32.

3. Ferdinand Christian Baur, *Die christliche Gnosis oder die christliche Religionsphilosophie in ihrer geschichtlichen Entwicklung* (Tübingen, 1835).

4. Heinrich Graetz, *Gnosticismus und Judentum* (Krotoschin, 1846), vi–vii. Michael Brenner argues otherwise in "Gnosis and History: Polemics of German-Jewish Identity from Graetz to Scholem," *New German Critique* 77 (Winter 1999), 46–47.

5. Moriz Friedländer, *Der vorchristliche jüdische Gnosticismus* (Göttingen, 1898). Though rejected at the time, his thesis has enjoyed a revival in the last fifty years, led by the Dutch scholar Gilles Quispel and the American Birger Pearson. Quispel, "Der gnostische Anthropos und die jüdische Tradition," *Eranos-Jahrbuch* 12 (1954), 195–234; and Pearson, "Friedländer Revisited," *Studia Philonica* 2 (1973), 23–39.

6. Of his many, many writings, see especially, Rudolf Steiner, *Der Orient im Lichte des Occidents. Die Kinder des Luzifer und die Brüder Christi. Vortragscyklus von Dr. Rudolf Steiner in München vom 23. bis 31. August 1909.* There Steiner developed a theology that made a norm out of redemption through sin. He hailed the Christian who has traversed the devil's realm, and denounced those who believe themselves the best Christians of the day as in fact the most potent eradicators of the Christian spirit.

7. Many of his critics considered him a latter-day gnostic as well, though in this charge they sometimes revealed themselves as deeply confused. For example:

Anna Louise Matzka, "Der Neu-Gnostizismus unserer Tage. Grundsätzliche und vergleichende Gedanken über Theosophie und Anthroposophie," *Der Fels* 27, 6 (1932/33), 224–29. For an exhaustive if aggressive treatment of Steiner's gnosticism, see Richard Geisen, *Anthroposophie und Gnostizismus* (Paderborn, 1992). See also Johannes Müller, *Theosophie* (Elmau, 1916); Friedrich Laun, *Moderne Theosophie und katholisches Christentum* (Rottenburg, 1920); Max Kully, *Die Geheimnisse des Tempels von Dornach* (Basel, 1920); and R. H. Grützmacher, *Kritiker und Neuschöpfer der Religion im zwanzigsten Jahrhundert* (Leipzig, 1921). Steiner's movement occupied center stage in the occult world theater, but hundreds of bit players did their own part in spreading a self-styled gnostic gospel. For two examples, see Fra. Gregorius, "Menschheitsepochen und Astrologie," *Saturn Gnosis* 1, 3 (1928), 124–34; and Fra. Pacitius, "Der Sternenmensch," *Saturn Gnosis* 1, 2 (1928), 57–67.

8. Harnack was not the first in the interwar period to situate Marcion on the cultural map. This distinction belonged to the young Ernst Bloch, who inaugurated a prominent tendency among Marcion exegetes: to ask after Marcion's "modernity." Bloch discovered in Marcion a precursor to his own utopianism, which did not seek a return to a homeland so much as it strove toward one not yet—always not yet—attained (Bloch, *Geist der Utopie* [Munich, 1918], 330). Later, Bloch discovered the origins of Marcion's God in the Exodus story itself: "Marcion descends not only from Paul, he descends just as much from Moses; the true or foreign God dawns in the God of Exodus, between Egypt and Canaan." (Bloch, *Das Prinzip Hoffnung* [Frankfurt, 1959], 1500. See also *Atheismus im Christentum* 241).

9. Adolf von Harnack, *Marcion: das Evangelium vom fremden Gott* (Leipzig, 1921), 20.

10. Harnack, *Marcion,* 142.

11. Harnack, *Marcion,* 144, 145.

12. Though hostile to the neo-Marcionite spirit, Buber recognized it as the spirit of his age. See Paul Mendes-Flohr, "Buber and the Metaphysicians of Contempt," in *Divided Passions* (Detroit, 1991).

13. Erich Foerster, "Marcionitisches Christentum," *Die christliche Welt* 35, 45 (1921), 811.

14. Arnold Hein, "Moderner Marcionitismus und praktische Theologie," *Theologische Blätter* 32, 6–7 (1922), 148. On the other hand, Marcion could be assimilated to an aggressive, anti-liberal Protestantism. Given his reputation as the primordial antagonist of the Catholic Church, the one against whom the church first cohered as an institution, Marcion could be—and was—yoked into the service of anti-Catholic and anti-Jewish polemic. See Alfred Falb, *Luther und Marcion gegen das Alte Testament* (Leipzig, 1923).

15. Hein, "Moderner Marcionitismus," 147.

16. Foerster, "Marcionitisches Christentum," 813.

17. Karl Barth, *The Epistle to the Romans,* trans. Edwyn C. Hoskyns (Oxford, 1968), 238, 244.

18. Barth, *Romans,* 13. Gogarten also took charges of his "gnosticism" seriously. In his classic work of 1953, *Verhängnis und Hoffnung der Neuzeit,*

Gogarten set out to deflect the gnostic implications of assertions like the following: "In opposition to all previous thought, both gnosticism and the Christian faith understand man as a being which is not from the world, which owes its existence not to the fact that it is enclosed by the world and embedded in its orders, but to its not-being-from-the-world." Whether Gogarten succeeded in his endeavor, by means of a distinction between secularization (Christianity) and secularism (technocratic dystopias, ideologies or nihilism), the fact that he did so attests to a twofold sensitivity: the charges of gnosticism levied against dialectical theology, and the sense that such theologizing abetted a natural-scientific approach to the world that rid it of value. It attests also to the challenge posed by Jonas, whose work comprises the subtext of the book's first chapter. *Verhängnis* appeared in English as *Despair and Hope for Our Time*, trans. Thomas Wieser (Philadelphia, 1970), here at 13 and 17.

19. Barth, *Romans*, 250, 253. Barbara Aland is the foremost representative of the gnostic love thesis. See "Was ist Gnosis?" in Taubes, ed., *Gnosis und Politik*, 54–65.

20. Hans Jonas, "Das geistesgeschichtliche Milieu," 73. HJA 10-21-2. Italics added.

21. Williams, *Rethinking "Gnosticism,"* 216. See also Carl Kraeling, *Anthropos and Son of Man* (New York, 1927); and Carsten Colpe, *Die religionsgeschichtliche Schule: Darstellung und Kritik ihres Bildes vom gnostischen Erlösermythos* (Göttingen, 1961).

22. Hans Leisegang, *Die Gnosis* (Leipzig, 1924). Scholem rejected Leisegang also. Gershom Scholem, "Hans Leisegang, *Die Gnosis,*" (review) *Kiryat Sefer* 1 (1924/25), 206–7.

23. Wilhelm Bousset, *Hauptprobleme der Gnosis* (Göttingen, 1907). For Jonas on Bousset, see *Gnosis I*, 15–48.

24. Jonas, *Gnostic Religion*, 36; Jonas, "Das geistesgeschichtliche Milieu," 4. HJA 10-21-2; Jonas, "Methodologische Einleitung," 4. HJA 13-16-1.

25. Von Loewenich, "Gnosis in spätantiker Geist," *Theologie der Gegenwart* 1 (1935), 8.

26. Strauss continued: "I therefore believe that you have taken a decisive step, possibly *the* decisive step towards the illumination of the darkness that has [until now] separated Epicurus and Zeno on the one side, the era of high scholasticism on the other." Strauss to Jonas, June 13, 1935. LSP, Box 4, Folder 10.

27. Hans Blumenberg, "Epochenschwelle und Rezeption," *Philosophische Rundschau* 6 (1958), 107.

28. To this his disagreements with Scholem attest. See Jonas, *Philosophical Essays*, 287–88. Toward the end of his life, Scholem summed up their differences in a letter: "Your definition of gnosis is not mine, and to discuss it would make no sense. For me, gnosis is a structure in religious thought that reproduces itself again and again. For you it is a singular historical-philosophical phenomenon." Scholem to Jonas, November 14, 1977, in Gershom Scholem, *Briefe III 1971–1982*, ed. Itta Shedletzky (Munich, 1999), 160.

29. Martin Heidegger, "Die Selbstbehauptung der deutschen Universität," in Heidegger, *Gesamtausgabe*, vol. 16 (Frankfurt, 1976), 107–17. A translation

appears in *The Heidegger Controversy*, ed. Richard Wolin (Cambridge, Mass., 1992).

30. Hans Jonas, *Erinnerungen* (Frankfurt, 2003), 109.

31. Jonas, *Erinnerungen*, 299–300.

32. Mark Lilla asks after the fitness of intellectuals (Heidegger among them) for politics in *The Reckless Mind* (New York, 2001).

33. Jonas, "Gnosticism and Modern Nihilism," *Social Research* 19 (1952), 452ff., emended and republished as an epilogue to *The Gnostic Religion*, 320–40.

34. His interpretation is idiosyncratic and debatable. Heidegger had a reputation as an *opponent* of dualism, as one who pined for an age prior to the split between subject and object; Jonas diagnosed his thought as nevertheless a form of it. Heidegger's notion of *Geworfenheit* (thrown-ness), whose avatar Jonas found among the gnostics, was thought to smuggle into existentialist thought a dualism of man against world (Jonas, *Gnostic Religion*, 339). On the equation of *Geworfenheit* with gnostic tenets, see also Jonas and Hermann, *Erkenntnis und Verantwortung*, 96. For examples of accounts that describe the attacks on Heidegger and on gnosticism as battles in a wider war against nihilism, see, in English, Vogel, "Hans Jonas's Exodus," 7; and in German, Jakob, *Martin Heidegger und Hans Jonas*; Wetz, *Hans Jonas*; and Baum, *Gnostische Elemente*.

NOTES TO CHAPTER TWO: ROMANS IN WEIMAR

1. Hans Jonas, *Augustin und das paulinische Freiheitsproblem* (Göttingen, 1930).

2. Gustav Krüger, "*Augustin und das paulinische Freiheitsproblem*," (review) *Zeitschrift für Kirchengeschichte* 49 (1930), 500.

3. Hugo Koch, "*Augustin und das paulinische Freiheitsproblem*," (review) *Theologische Literaturzeitung* 20 (1930), 469–70. Jonas seems to have imputed the vitriol of these reviews in part to anti-Semitism as well. Interview with Lore Jonas, January 9, 2000. For Jonas's recollections of the saga, see Jonas, *Erinnerungen*, 238–40.

4. See Bultmann's foreword to *Gnosis und spätantiker Geist*, and Jonas's recollections in *Erinnerungen*, 239. Writing to Scholem from London in 1933, Jonas hoped to enlist Scholem's aid in securing professional affiliation with the Hebrew University. He thought an "apology" in order for the stylistic infelicity of his study. Jonas to Scholem, December 14, 1933. Archion Gershom Scholem (hereafter AGS).

5. The outline for the program came in an appendix, "On the Hermeneutic Structure of Dogma." It appears inspired in part by Heideggerian hermeneutics and was likely modeled on the Heideggerian project of *Destruktion*. See, for example, James M. Robinson, "Interpretation in Contemporary Theology. VIII. The Pre-history of Demythologization," which serves as the introduction to the second edition (1966) of Jonas's *Augustin* book, 65–77.

6. Hans Jonas, "Philosophische Meditation über Paulus, Römerbrief, Kapitel 7," in *Zeit und Geschichte* (Tübingen, 1964), 559, later translated and published as "Abyss of the Will" in Jonas, *Philosophical Essays*.

7. On Heidegger's reception of Barth and Gogarten, see Charles R. Bambach, *Heidegger, Dilthey, and the Crisis of Historicism* (Ithaca, 1995), 187–93.

8. Hans Georg Gadamer, "Martin Heidegger und die marburger Theologie," in *Zeit und Geschichte* (Tübingen, 1964), 480. Gadamer also knew Jonas from his time in Marburg, and had "marveled at his precociousness." Gadamer to Brigitte Uhlemann, April 27, 1998, HJA.

9. For the Bultmann text, see *Theologische Blätter* 3 (1924), 73–86, and in English, Bultmann, "Liberal Theology and the Latest Theological Movement," 28–52. For a discussion, see James M. Robinson, *The Future of Our Religious Past* (London, 1971).

10. Jonas, *Augustin*, 7.

11. Jonas, *Augustin*, 26–29.

12. Jonas, *Augustin*, 36, 42. For this reason Jonas found in the Pelagians the religious origins of the idea of progress, a notion seconded, to an extent, by Blumenberg in *Legitimacy*, 54.

13. Jonas, *Augustin*, 48–9.

14. Barth, *Romans*, 228.

15. Barth, *Romans*, 250.

16. Barth, *Romans*, 242.

17. Barth, *Romans*, 241.

18. Barth, *Romans*, 85, 255.

19. Barth, *Romans*, 234.

20. Jonas, "Das geistesgeschichtliche Milieu," 15. HJA 10-21-2.

21. Barth, *Romans*, 235, 263.

22. Barth, *Romans*, 244.

23. Jonas, *Phenomenon of Life*, 4.

24. "Methodologische Einleitung: Zur Hermeneutik religiöser Phänomene." HJA 13-16-1, 4, 5, 15, 16. Its continuation is HJA 3-11-1. See also the first chapter of his dissertation, "Das geistesgeschichtliche Milieu," 15fn. HJA 10-21-2.

25. Jonas, *Philosophical Essays*, 337.

26. Jonas, *Philosophical Essays*, 340.

27. Jonas, *Philosophical Essays*, 341, 345.

28. In this, Jonas departed from a common move at the time—to use Paul as a vehicle for antagonism toward Kant. Barth, for example, did just this, as did the son of the great neo-Kantian Ernst Cassirer. Heinz Cassirer found Paul at age fifty, and had himself baptized shortly thereafter. See Cassirer, *Grace and Law: St. Paul, Kant and the Hebrew Prophets* (Grand Rapids, Mich., 1988).

29. Jonas, *Philosophical Essays*, 342, 345.

30. Jonas, *Philosophical Essays*, 341. Compare also Jonas, "Zur Hermeneutik religiöser Phänomene," 29. HJA 3-11-1.

31. Jonas, *Philosophical Essays*, 346–48.

32. "Existential self-knowledge belongs to the complete wholeness of the Pharisee." Jonas, *Philosophical Essays*, 346–48.

33. HJA 3-11-2.

34. One might surmise that their similarities derive not from proximity or influence, but from the fact that Barth and Jonas direct their energies to the same passages. It is therefore important to point out that their anthropological reading of Paul was not—is not—the only possible one, nor the only one available at the time. Gottlieb Klein's *Studien über Paulus* (1918) understood Romans to refer to historically specific periods in Paul's own life. Romans was reduced to autobiography, the conversion experience to psychology. Max Wertheimer had little use for Paul, anthropological or otherwise; he denied the actuality of Paul as a historical figure altogether (Max Wertheimer, *Das Mysterienjudentum und der Heidenapostel Saulus-Paulus* [Wien, 1928]). Hans-Joachim Schoeps disavowed the anthropological reading of Paul sometime after Jonas, and this despite the considerable influence exerted upon him by Barth's theology. (Schoeps associated the anthropological move in the history of religions with Heidegger, and bemoaned what he called the "Heideggerization" of the discipline. See Schoeps, *Urgemeinde, Judenchristentum, Gnosis* [Tübingen, 1956], 35. For a critique of Schoeps's reception of Barth, see Gershom Scholem's important letter, "Offener Brief an den Verfasser der Schrift 'Jüdischer Glaube in dieser Zeit,'" *Bayerische Israelitische Gemeindezeitung* 8, 16 [August 15, 1932], 241–44. Schoeps considered Scholem his most astute critic. Schoeps, *Rückblicke* [Berlin, 1963], 73.) On the scholarly stage, then, the philosophical anthropologist was one of Paul's more infrequent roles. But only until Jonas: three years later, in 1932, Bultmann would publish his own interpretation of Romans 7, and in the terms of philosophical anthropology: Rudolf Bultmann, "Römer 7 und die Anthropologie des Paulus," *Imago Dei* (1932), 57ff. Others would pick up on his lead: Günther Bornkamm, *Das Ende des Gesetzes: Paulusstudien* (München, 1952), 51–69.

35. Barth, *Romans*, 245.

36. See Harnack, *Das Wesen des Christentums* (Leipzig, 1902), a series of lectures published to wild acclaim.

37. HJA 13-16-1, 14.

38. Jonas, *Gnostic Religion*, 321.

39. Rudolf Bultmann approved, in "Liberal Theology."

40. Translations of Heidegger's contributions to the conference appear in John D. Caputo, ed., *The Religious* (Malden, Mass., 2002). For Ott on the issue, see *Denken und Sein: Der Weg Martin Heideggers und der Weg der Theologie* (Zollikon, 1959).

41. Jonas, *Erinnerungen*, 305.

42. Jonas, *Erinnerungen*, 304.

43. Jonas, *Phenomenon of Life*, 248.

44. Jonas here reproduced almost verbatim a passage from his dissertation. Jonas, "Methodologische Einleitung," 28. HJA 13-11-1.

45. Jonas, *Phenomenon of Life*, 261.

46. Jonas, *Phenomenon of Life*, 254, 258. For some responses to the talk, see William J. Richardson, "Heidegger and God—and Professor Jonas," *Thought* 15 (1965), 13–40; Gerhard Noller, ed., *Heidegger und die Theologie. Beginn und Fortgang der Diskussion* (Munich, 1967). More recently on the theme, Pero Brkic,

Martin Heidegger und die Theologie. Ein Thema in dreifacher Fragestellung (Mainz, 1994).

NOTES TO CHAPTER THREE: OVERCOMING GNOSTICISM

1. Blumenberg wrote all this in a text-fragment one page in length, called "Hans Jonas: Prognostiker der wiedergefundenen Gnosis," but without date. Hans-Blumenberg-Nachlaß (hereafter HBN).

2. Blumenberg, "Epochenschwelle und Rezeption," 107.

3. Blumenberg, "Hans Jonas." HBN.

4. As Blumenberg told it twenty-five years later. Blumenberg to Jonas, May 6, 1978. HBN.

5. Blumenberg to Jonas, November 12, 1955. HJA 4-3-25.

6. Jonas to Blumenberg, December 28, 1973. HBN. Jonas to Blumenberg, May 7, 1976. HJA 4-3-40.

7. Jonas, "Das geistesgeschichtliche Milieu," 22. HJA 10-21-2. For a full elaboration of *Entweltlichung* as a primary gnostic mood, see Jonas, *Gnosis und spätantiker Geist, Teil II, 1* (Göttingen, 1954), 1–23.

8. For "secularization" German has at its disposal both *Verweltlichung* and *Säkularisierung*.

9. Blumenberg, *Legitimacy*, 5.

10. Blumenberg may have had in mind Gogarten's book of 1953, *Verhängnis und Hoffnung der Neuzeit*, which insisted on a notion of faith that took as its corollary a world that was "merely world," divested altogether of enchantment.

11. Blumenberg, *Legitimacy*, 54, 133–35. Augustine in fact made his first substantial appearance in *Legitimacy* in the form of a citation from Jonas's study.

12. Blumenberg, *Legitimacy*, 135, 136.

13. Jonas, "Das geistesgeschichtliche Milieu," 31–33. HJA 10-21-2.

14. Blumenberg, *Legitimacy*, 384, 389.

15. Strauss to Jonas, November 19, 1958. HJA 7-13b-10.

16. Jonas to Strauss, December 28, 1958. HJA 7-13b-10.

17. Fritz Heinemann, *Nomos und Physis* (Basel, 1945). Physis was not always privileged in the pair. The Sophists, for example, occasionally elevated nomos above nature. G. B. Kerferd, "Physis and Nomos," in *The Encyclopedia of Philosophy*, vols. 5–6, ed. Paul Edwards (New York, 1967), 305. See also Carl Schmitt, "Nomos-Nahme-Name," in Siegfried Behn, ed., *Der beständige Aufbruch* (Nürnberg, 1959), 92–105.

18. Blumenberg, *Legitimacy*, 383.

19. Blumenberg would have contested him: "The final overcoming of the Gnostic inheritance cannot restore the cosmos because the function of the idea of the cosmos is reassurance about the world and in the world, because it has as its correlate the theoretical ideal and the theoretical leisure that had been associated with the idea of the cosmos from the time of the Greeks. The world cannot be

made 'good' in itself once more by a mere change of sign because it would then cease to be man's irritation and provocation." *Legitimacy*, 140.

20. Recent scholarship has revised understanding of the scientific revolution as fundamentally anti-Aristotelian in emphasis. See Peter Dear, *Discipline and Experience: The Mathematical Way in the Scientific Revolution* (Chicago, 1995); Peter Dear, *Mersenne and the Learning of the Schools* (Ithaca, 1988); and Steven Shapin, *The Scientific Revolution* (Chicago, 1996). Even Bacon has been "reunited" with his Aristotelian roots. Antonio Pérez-Ramos, *Francis Bacon's Idea of Science and the Maker's Knowledge Tradition* (Oxford, 1988).

21. Jonas, *Phenomenon of Life*, 7, 34–35.

22. Jonas recommended not quietism but power to counteract the power of human self-assertion made impotent to end its doings by its very success. He described it in decidedly illiberal terms, as "a maximum of politically imposed social discipline." He had little faith that the liberal democracies of the West would subordinate present advantage to future exigency. In the late '70s Jonas could look to Marxism—which in his view yoked the Baconian ideal to a vision of a classless society—as the only source, however unlikely, of a solution. *Imperative of Responsibility*, 2, 8, 71, 75, 141–42. But by the end of his life, with the Eastern bloc's dismal environmental record bared to the world, he recognized that tentative hope for the delusion it was. Hans Jonas, *Ethik für die Zukunft: Im Diskurs mit Hans Jonas*, ed. Dietrich Böhler and Ingrid Hoppe (Munich, 1994), 41–42.

23. Jonas, *Phenomenon of Life*, xii. For similar secondary accounts, see Vogel, "Hans Jonas's Exodus," 1; Wetz, *Hans Jonas*; and Jakob, *Martin Heidegger und Hans Jonas*. Like Franz Rosenzweig, Jonas outlined his ideas in a series of letters (*Lehrbriefe*) sent home from the front. They are lovely, stunning meditations on the series of cosmic accidents that gave birth to life, and since published by Christian Wiese in Jonas, *Erinnerungen*, 348–83.

24. Jakob, *Martin Heidegger und Hans Jonas*; and Ioan Culianu, "From Gnosticism to the Dangers of Technology: An Interview with Hans Jonas," in Culianu, *Gnosticismo e pensiero moderno: Hans Jonas* (Rome, 1985).

25. Jonas, "Das geistesgeschichtliche Milieu," 73–74. HJA 10-21-2.

26. Jonas, *Gnostic Religion*, 324–25.

27. Cf. Friedrich Nietzsche, *Beyond Good and Evil*, trans. Walter Kaufmann (New York, 1966), 21.

28. Cited in Blumenberg, *Legitimacy*, 140, 143.

29. Blumenberg, *Legitimacy*, 138.

30. Or as Blumenberg would put it in a later essay: "It makes a crucial difference whether we *put up with* reality as unchangeable or if we rediscover it as the core of what is evident in the free play of the infinite possibilities and are able to consent freely to *recognize* it—if we are capable, finally, of 'making the accidental essential.'" Blumenberg, "'Imitation of Nature': Toward a Prehistory of the Idea of Creative Being," trans. Anna Wertz, *Qui Parle* 12, 1 (Spring/Summer 2000), 48.

31. This may be the singular theme of his doubled attack on Heidegger. It played prominently, for example, in his 1964 speech: "For let this be said now: the

subject-object relation, which presupposes, holds open, and stands through the duality, is not a lapse but a privilege, burden and duty of man. Not Plato is responsible for it but the human condition, its limits and nobility under the order of creation. . . . [I]t is the condition of man *meant* in the Bible, imposed by his createdness, to be accepted, acted through—and transcended only in certain encounters with fellow beings and god, i.e., in existential relations of a very special kind." Jonas, *Phenomenon of Life*, 258.

32. This text has neither date nor title. It begins with a citation of which the first words are "Die Welt sei noch zu retten." HBN.

33. Avi Katzman, "Le-Achar Hitnakrut Memushechet [After a Prolonged Estrangement]," *Ha'aretz* (weekly supplement), January 17, 1992, 16. This was not his only mood. Elsewhere, and at about the same time, he could state flatly that "the world has never been for me a hostile place." Jonas, *Erinnerungen*, 181.

NOTES TO CHAPTER FOUR: AFTER AUSCHWITZ, EARTH

1. Jonas, *Mortality*, 140.
2. Jonas, *Mortality*, 141, 142–43.
3. See Vogel, "Hans Jonas's Exodus," in Jonas, *Mortality*; and more recently, his foreword to the republication of *The Phenomenon of Life* (Evanston, Ill., 2001). While insightful, this view diverts our attention from the ways in which his philosophical interventions had their ground in interwar theological debates, how Jonas displaced modes of thought culled from theology into his philosophy, how talk of God could be—and was—adapted for talk of the natural world, and how the displacement worked in the other direction as well.
4. This aspect of his myth radicalizes some tendencies in post-Holocaust Jewish theology. See Eliezer Berkovits, *Faith after the Holocaust* (New York, 1973); and Richard Rubinstein, *After Auschwitz* (Indianapolis, 1966). But it pits Jonas *against* Emil Fackenheim, for some time the leading figure in the field. Fackenheim discovered in Auschwitz a negative divine command, but a revelation nonetheless: that Jews should not grant Hitler a posthumous victory, whether by opting out of the Jewish nation or by disavowing faith in God as Lord of History. Fackenheim therefore elevated to ontology the fact of resistance to Nazism, and declared "After Auschwitz, Jerusalem" an appropriate response. A less charitable interpretation might call this—with some justice—a theology of spite. See Fackenheim, *God's Presence in History* (New York, 1970); *To Mend the World* (New York, 1982); and "After Auschwitz, Jerusalem," *Judaism* 50 (Winter 2001), 53–60. For a very useful discussion, see Vogel, "Hans Jonas' Exodus."
5. Jonas, *Mortality*, 134, 142.
6. Jonas, *Mortality*, 134.
7. Jonas, *Mortality*, 136.
8. Jonas, *Mortality*, 134, 136.
9. Blumenberg, "Die Welt sei noch zu retten." HBN.
10. Jonas, *Mortality*, 201.
11. Jonas, *Mortality*, 202.

NOTES TO PART TWO: THE PANTHEISM CONTROVERSY

1. "These are the abominable doctrines and hideous errors which this shallow Jewish philosopher has (if I may say so) shit into the world." Anonymous, *Fürstellung Vier Neuer Welt-Weisen* (1702).

2. Hans Hartmann, "Der Spinozakongreß 1932," *Philosophisches Jahrbuch der Görres-Gesellschaft* 45, 4 (1932), 530–34. On the French reception, see Raoul Lantzenberg, "Le tricentenaire de la naissance de Spinoza," *La Nouvelle Revue* 54, 121 (September 1932), 29–32. The French philosophical society convened two months later as a follow-up to the congress, held from September 5 through 12. For a transcript of the meeting, see "Commémoration du troisième centenaire de la naissance de Spinoza," *Bulletin de la Société française de Philosophie* (1932), 153–81.

3. It is difficult to imagine Aquinas as a covert Spinozist (four centuries before it became historically possible). To be sure, Aquinas had stressed the rationality and intelligibility of creation over the predicates of absolute power and freedom accorded God by his nominalist usurpers. Neither did Aquinas share the natural corollary, the nominalist notion of the *deus absconditus*, of the absent and inscrutable God so revered by the gnostics. So, too, had he accepted the Aristotelian proof of the world's uniqueness, regarded by nominalists like Ockham as an odious restriction on God's omnipotence. But none of this suggests that he would have abided Spinoza's "conflation" of God with world. For an account of the shift from scholasticism to nominalism and its consequences, see Blumenberg, *Legitimacy*, 160–61.

4. Hartmann, 530–34. The link between Spinoza and Schleiermacher had been by then well established. See, for example, Theodor Camerer, *Spinoza und Schleiermacher: die kritische Lösung des von Spinoza hinterlassenen Problems* (Stuttgart, 1903); and Paul Schmidt, *Spinoza und Schleiermacher: die Geschichte ihrer Systeme und ihr gegenseitiges Verhältnis* (Berlin, 1868). Barth recognized their affinities also.

5. Franz Rosenzweig, *The Star of Redemption*, 2nd ed., trans. William W. Hallo (New York, 1971), 17.

6. For a similar assessment, see K. Muth, "Spinoza-Renaissance," in the Catholic journal *Hochland* 30, 4 (1933), 346–51.

7. Yirmiyahu Yovel echoes Gebhardt in *Spinoza and Other Heretics*, 2 vols. (Princeton, 1992).

8. Amos Funkenstein writes of their relation in *Perceptions of Jewish History* (Berkeley, 1993), 297. For an analysis by a contemporary, see Alexander Altmann, "Zur Auseinandersetzung mit der 'dialektischen Theologie,'" *Monatsschrift für Geschichte und Wissenschaft des Judentums* (hereafter *MGWJ*) 79 (1935), 345–61. Altmann recognized in Barth a more radical version of Rosenzweig, who affirmed creation in a way Barth did not. See also Samuel Moyn's discussion in *Origins of the Other: Emmanuel Levinas Between Revelation and Ethics* (Ithaca, 2005).

9. The "reawakening of theology" in interwar Europe was for Strauss "marked by the names Karl Barth and Franz Rosenzweig." See the preface to *Hobbes*

Politische Wissenschaft (Berlin, 1965), and for its English translation, see Strauss, *Jewish Philosophy and the Crisis of Modernity*, ed. Kenneth Hart Green (Albany, 1997), 453.

10. Emil Fackenheim makes this point at some length in his work of post-Holocaust theology, *To Mend the World*.

Notes to Chapter Five: Pantheism Revisited

1. For a historical review of the term, see Christoph Jamme, "Pantheismus II," *Theologische Realenzyklopädie* (Berlin, 1995), 630.

2. Citations from Jamme. For Leibniz's response of April 30, 1709, see Toland, *A Collection of Several Pieces* (London, 1726). For the early French reception, see E. Benoist, *Mélange de remarques . . . sur les deux dissertations de M. Toland* (Delft, 1712).

3. Whereas the theist model was invoked to justify the divine right of kings, pantheism seemed to vindicate an egalitarian sensibility, since God was thought to inhabit everyone, and to an equal degree. See Frederick C. Beiser, *The Sovereignty of Reason* (Princeton, 1996), 229.

4. W. Schröder, "Pantheismus I," *Historisches Wörterbuch der Philosophie* 7 (Darmstadt, 1989), 59. Its religious overtones led eighteenth-century commentators such as J. C. Adelung (*Geschichte der menschlichen Narrheit*, 1785) to disparage pantheist teachings as "philosophical *Schwärmerey*."

5. Benedict de Spinoza, *The Ethics*, trans. R.H.M. Elwes (New York, 1955), 45.

6. For a useful discussion of Hegel's distinction between pantheism and acosmism, and for a qualified defense of Spinoza, see G.H.R. Parkinson, "Hegel, Pantheism and Spinoza," *Journal of the History of Ideas* 38, 3 (1977), 450.

7. Citations from B. A. Gerrish, *Continuing the Reformation* (Chicago, 1993), 112.

8. In English, as a "theist and a Christian of highest degree." Gerrish, *Continuing the Reformation*, 112. On Hegel, see Terry Pinkard, *Hegel* (New York, 2000), 31–32. See otherwise, Frederick Beiser, *The Fate of Reason: German Philosophy from Kant to Fichte* (Cambridge, Mass., 1987); Olivier Bloch, ed., *Spinoza au XVIIIe Siècle* (Paris, 1990); Hans Blumenberg, *Work on Myth*, trans. Robert M. Wallace (Cambridge, Mass., 1985); Warren Breckman, *Marx, the Young Hegelians and the Origins of Radical Social Theory* (Cambridge, U.K., 1999); Max Grunwald, *Spinoza in Deutschland* (Berlin, 1897); Heinrich Scholz, *Die Hauptschriften zum Pantheismusstreit zwischen Jacobi und Mendelssohn* (Berlin, 1916), xi–cxxviii; Hermann Timm, *Gott und die Freiheit* (Frankfurt, 1974); and John Zammito, *The Genesis of Kant's Critique of Judgment* (Chicago, 1992).

9. Heinrich Heine, *Zur Geschichte der Religion und Philosophie in Deutschland* (Stuttgart, 1997), 69.

10. Friedrich Schleiermacher, *On Religion: Speeches to Its Cultured Despisers*, trans. Richard Crouter (New York, 1988). For a discussion, see Erwin

H. U. Quapp, "Pantheismus III," *Theologische Realenzyklopädie* (Berlin, 1995), 638–41.

11. Graetz, *Gnosticismus und Judenthum*, vi–vii.

12. Carl Gebhardt, "Der Name Spinoza," *Chronicon Spinozanum* 1 (1921), 272–76; Leon Roth, "The Name Spinoza," *Chronicon Spinozanum* 3 (1923), 348.

13. Carl Gebhardt, "Spinoza und der Platonismus," *Chronicon Spinozanum* 1 (1921), 182.

14. Carl Gebhardt, ed. and trans., *Die Schriften des Uriel da Costa* (Heidelberg, 1922), xix–xxvi. The thesis has enjoyed of late a newfound popularity, thanks to Yirmiyahu Yovel's book, *Spinoza and Other Heretics*.

15. Spinoza, *Opera*, ed. Carl Gebhardt, 4 vols. (Heidelberg, 1924); and Carl Gebhardt, ed., *Leone Ebreo: Dialoghi d'Amore* (Heidelberg, 1929).

16. Adolph Oko, "In Memoriam. Carl Gebhardt," *Philosophia* 1 (1936), 21. See also Rudolph Geck, "Carl Gebhardt," *Frankfurter Zeitung* 383, 31 (July 1934).

17. Carl Gebhardt, "Spinozas Bann," *Der Morgen* 3 (1927), 144–48.

18. Gebhardt, *Spinoza: Vier Reden*, 12–13.

19. Gebhardt, "Spinoza und der Platonismus," 233–34, italics added. See also Gebhardt's introduction to the writings of Uriel da Costa, xl.

20. Among others, see B. Alexander, "Spinoza und die Psychoanalyse," in *Almanach für 1929 Internationaler Psychoanalytischer Verlag*, 94–103; Richard Eickhoff, "Spinoza und wir," *Deutsche Revue* 45, 2 (February 1920), 187; R. Herbertz, "Spinoza als Vorläufer Einsteins," *Das Weltall: Bildgeschmuckte Zeitschrift für Astronomie und verwandte Gebiete* 25, 2 (1925), 24–26; Wilhelm Sauer, "Spinoza. Eine juristische Betrachtung zu seinem 250. Todestag (21. Febr. 1927)," *Deutsche Juristen-Zeitung* 32, 4 (1927), 297–98; and E. Linder, "Das Erbe Spinozas," *Volksschullehrerinnen-Zeitung* (1933), 242.

21. See, for example, H. W. Weissenborn, "Philosophische Lebenshaltung (Spinoza)," *Das Goetheanum. Wochenschrift für Anthroposophie und Dreigliederung* 14, 36 (1935), 285. For a scholarly account of Spinoza's role in early nineteenth-century German *Naturphilosophie*, see Klaus-Jürgen Grün, *Das Erwachen der Materie* (Hildesheim, 1993).

22. Ernst Müller, "Die Probleme der Freiheit und der Realität in der Philosophie Spinozas," *Das Goetheanum*. 14, 26 (1935), 211–14. But not even the men from Dornach could compete with the ardor of their compatriots to the east, the Freemasons of Vienna. See Adolf Kapralik, "Arbeiten aus Wiener Logen. Spinoza. (1632–1667)," *Wiener Freimaurer-Zeitung* 10, 5 (May 1928), 25.

23. Bultmann, "Liberal Theology," 35.

24. So was the Jesuit Stanislaus von Dunin-Borkowski. For a review of Borkowski's work that attends to the stakes for Catholicism in his encounter with Spinoza, see Muth, "Spinoza-Renaissance," and for a positive assessment of the Catholic encounter more generally, Carl Gebhardt, "Spinoza in unserer Zeit," *Frankfurter Zeitung* (October 8, 1932).

25. Hartmann, "Der Spinozismus. Zugleich eine Betrachtung zum internationalen Spinozakongreß," *Preußische Jahrbücher* 231, 1 (1933), 39, 40.

26. Crisis theology had adopted as a leading theme the notion of *Entscheidung* or decision, made available in part by the revival of Kierkegaard in interwar thought. See Moyn, *Origins of the Other*, 164–94.

27. Hartmann, "Der Spinozismus," 47. Carl Schmitt, *Roman Catholicism and Political Form*, trans. G. L. Ulmen (Westport, Conn., 1996), 7.

28. Gopal Balakrishnan, *The Enemy: An Intellectual Portrait of Carl Schmitt* (London, 2000), 53–65.

29. G. L. Ulmen, Introduction to Schmitt, *Roman Catholicism*, xii. John McCormick offers a useful discussion in *Carl Schmitt's Critique of Liberalism: Against Politics as Technology* (Cambridge, U.K., 1999).

30. Schmitt, "The Visibility of the Church," in Schmitt, *Roman Catholicism*, 47, 54, 57, 58. Dieter Schellong sets Schmitt in comparison with dialectical theology: "Jenseits von politischer und unpolitischer Theologie," in Jacob Taubes, ed., *Der Fürst dieser Welt. Carl Schmitt und die Folgen: Religionstheorie und politische Theologie*, vol. 1 (München, 1983), 292–315. Barth would certainly have condemned Schmitt's contention that the Catholic Church mediates the divine to the world, represents it, as an unallowed reification. Likewise, he would have rejected Schmitt's later theological grounding of the friend/foe distinction, and more generally, Schmitt's theologized notion of political man.

31. Schmitt, *Roman Catholicism*, 10–11.

32. See Manfred Walther, "Carl Schmitt et Baruch Spinoza, ou les aventures du concept du politique," in Olivier Bloch, ed., *Spinoza au XXe siècle* (Paris, 1993), 361–72. Still, Schmitt did find in Spinoza a strong statement for the isomorphism of politics and theology, of the existence, that is, of a "political theology." And it was in the second edition of *Political Theology*, published in 1934, that Schmitt again took aim at the gnostic spirit of the day. "To be sure," he wrote, "Protestant theology presents a different, supposedly unpolitical doctrine, conceiving of God as the 'wholly other,' just as in political liberalism the state and politics are conceived of as the 'wholly other.' We have come to recognize that the political is the total, and as a result we know that any decision about whether something is *unpolitical* is always a *political* decision." Schmitt's royal "we" here was no figure of speech, or at least not merely a figure of speech—for it referred in covert fashion to his Jewish interlocutor Leo Strauss, who first suggested to Schmitt the line of thought that posited the political as a totality sufficient unto itself. See Heinrich Meier, *Carl Schmitt and Leo Strauss: The Hidden Dialogue*, trans. J. Harvery Lomax (Chicago, 1995).

33. In *Political Theology*, Schmitt described the miracle as the theological analogue of the political *Ausnahmezustand*. Schmitt, *Political Theology*, 36.

34. F. Schlerath, "Die Spinozafeier im Haag," *Der Morgen* 3 (1927), 120.

35. Siegfried Hessing, "Salve Spinoza!" in Hessing, ed. *Spinoza-Festschrift*, viii–x.

36. David Baumgardt Archive, Box 10, Folder 10, Leo Baeck Institute.

37. David Baumgardt, "Spinoza und der deutsche Spinozismus," *Kantstudien* 32, 1 (1927), 191–92. H. Slochower, also, recognized certain affinities in his article "Spinoza und Nietzsche," *Geisteskultur* 37 (1928), 16–24.

38. Joseph Klausner, *Yeshu Ha-Nozri. Zmano, Chayav ve-Torato* (Jerusalem, 1922). He later published a second work on a similar theme, *Mi-Yeshu ad Paulus* (Jerusalem, 1939).

39. The status of the *herem* has long been the object of debate. Siegfried Hessing insists that the writ of excommunication had no validity because it had gone unsigned, that it lacked authority since it had been issued not by a rabbinical council but by the "big mochers"—that is, the financial pillars—of the Amsterdam community, and that whatever authority it might have had ended with Spinoza's death, since Jewish excommunication did not admit of "anathema for ever and ever" (see the Hessing correspondence to Scholem in AGS 4°1599). All these points are debatable. Hessing may have been right about the lack of signatures (but compare the entry on Spinoza in *Encyclopedia Judaica* 15 [Jerusalem, 1971], 276). Hessing seems wrong on the question of authority; see H. Méchoulan, "Le *herem* à Amsterdam et 'l'excommunication' de Spinoza," *Cahiers Spinoza* 3 (1979/80), 117–34. So does his unequivocal statement on punishment seem premature; see Alexander Altmann, "Eternality of Punishment: A Theological Controversy within the Amsterdam Rabbinate in the Thirties of the Seventeenth Century," *Proceedings of the American Academy for Jewish Research* 40 (1972), 1–88. For an exhaustive survey of these issues, see Asa Kasher and Shlomo Biderman, "Why Was Spinoza Excommunicated?" in *Sceptics, Millenarians and Jews*, ed. David S. Katz and Jonathan I. Israel (Leiden, 1990), 98–141. Richard Popkin offers a more entertaining account in "Notes from Underground," *New Republic* (May 21, 1990), 35–41. Most recently, see Steven Nadler, *Spinoza's Heresy: Immortality and the Jewish Mind* (Oxford, 2004).

40. Scholem made the comment in notes composed on the occasion of Klausner's death. AGS 4°1599II/19.

41. His speeches on Spinoza were later collected in his book *Me-Aplaton ad Shpinoza* (Jerusalem, 1955), 283–344, here at 284 and 329. Others in Palestine contested the penchant to return Spinoza to the fold. See for example H. I. Roth, "Mishnato shel Shpinoza be-Yahadut," *Moznaim* 4, 26 (1933), 3–7.

42. Rosenzweig is complicated on the question of transcendence, at least if we follow Peter Gordon's advice and understand him as elaborating a form of "redemption-in-the-world." Gordon, *Rosenzweig and Heidegger: Between Judaism and German Philosophy* (Berkeley, 2003). Whatever his affinities with Heidegger, Rosenzweig also considered himself a "mehrjähriger Barthianer" (a Barthian for multiple years).

43. First published in *Der Jude. Eine Monatsschrift* 8, 5/6 (1924), 295–314; and reproduced in Leo Strauss, *Gesammelte Schriften* (hereafter *GS*) I, ed. Heinrich Meier (Stuttgart, 2001), 363–86.

44. Franz Rosenzweig, "Über den Vortrag Hermann Cohens 'Das Verhältnis Spinozas zum Judentum,' " in *Kleinere Schriften* (Berlin, 1937), 352–53.

45. Hermann Cohen, *Ethik des reinen Willens* (Berlin, 1921), 465.

46. Hermann Cohen, "Spinoza über Staat und Religion, Judentum und Christentum," in *Jüdische Schriften* III, 372. Ernst Simon offers an excellent summary of Cohen's evolving position on Spinoza, and a critical take on Cohen's

failed messianism: "Zu Hermann Cohens Spinoza-Auffassung," *MGWJ* 79, 2 (1935), 181–94.

47. Cohen, "Spinoza über Staat und Religion, Judentum und Christentum," 360–61, 363–64, 371.

48. As Rosenzweig writes in his introduction to Cohen's talk, reprinted in his *Kleinere Schriften* (Berlin, 1937), 352.

49. Spinoza could hardly be faulted, for example, for his failure to appreciate the noachide commands as did Cohen. In Spinoza's own time, so Strauss, Maimonides was more often than not invoked to *contest* the view attributed to him by Cohen. Strauss, *GS* I, 42.

50. Strauss, "Cohens Analyse," 382.

51. Strauss, "Das Testament Spinozas," *Bayerische Israelitische Gemeindezeitung* 8, 21 (November, 1937), 322–26; reprinted in Strauss *GS* I, 415–22.

52. As evinced, for example, by the studied neutrality of Jacob Freudenthal, *Die Lebensgeschichte Spinozas* (Leipzig, 1899).

53. Strauss, "Das Testament Spinozas," 417.

54. Strauss, "Das Testament Spinozas," 417.

55. Strauss, "Das Testament Spinozas," 418.

56. Benedict de Spinoza, *A Theologico-Political Treatise*, trans. R.H.M. Elwes (New York, 1951), 56.

57. Strauss, "Das Testament Spinozas," 420.

58. Strauss, "Das Testament Spinozas," 419.

59. Strauss, "Das Testament Spinozas," 422.

60. The distinction is problematic. As Strauss pointed out, the choice is philosophically undecidable, and is therefore, in a way, a non-choice. From another perspective it is the purest of choices, since to opt for one or the other is neither more nor less than the assertion of will. From yet another perspective—the most salient one—Strauss had much invested in its undecidability.

61. As Strauss would write much later, "[T]here are many people who believe that there can be a happy synthesis which is superior to the isolated elements: Bible on the one hand, and philosophy on the other. This is impossible. Syntheses always sacrifice the decisive claim of one of the two elements," if not both. See Strauss, "On the Interpretation of Genesis," in Strauss, *Jewish Philosophy*, 373; printed originally in *L'Homme: revue française d'anthropologie* 21 (1981), 5–36.

NOTES TO CHAPTER SIX: THE PANTHEISM CONTROVERSY

1. Leo Strauss, "A Giving of Accounts," *The College* [St. John's Review] 22, 1 (April 1970), reproduced in Strauss, *Jewish Philosophy*, 460–61. On Strauss and Barth, see also David Myers, *Resisting History* (Princeton, 2003).

2. Strauss edited the volume of Mendelssohn's papers (vol. 3, part 2) specifically devoted to the pantheism controversy. The volume appeared in 1974, but he had completed the work by 1937, as he wrote to Julius Guttmann (Strauss to Guttmann, May 31, 1937, LSP, Box 4, Folder 8), and possibly already by 1932, as he wrote to Gerhard Krüger (Strauss to Krüger, August 21, 1932), in

Strauss, *GS* III, 400. Unpublished materials bear out the import for Strauss of the pantheism controversy still further. In 1946 Strauss proposed to write a book called *Philosophy and the Law: Historical Essays*. Strauss planned for the book's end a discussion of Lessing and the pantheism controversy, intended to elucidate its meaning for modern Jewry and based on "unknown material" he unearthed in the course of his work on Mendelssohn. The plan is in LSP Box 11, Folder 11, reproduced in Strauss, *Jewish Philosophy*, 470.

3. He wrote it in Hamburg under the philosopher Ernst Cassirer. Leo Strauss, "A Giving of Accounts," in Strauss, *Jewish Philosophy*, 460.

4. According to his friend Jonas, financial concerns compelled Strauss to finish in haste. Jonas, *Erinnerungen*, 94.

5. Cited in Philip Almond, *Rudolf Otto: An Introduction to his Philosophical Theology* (Chapel Hill, 1984), 1. Rudolf Bultmann echoed and affirmed Barth's assessment in his 1924 essay, "Liberal Theology and the Latest Theological Movement," 49. On Otto, see also his *Autobiographical Essays* (Berlin, 1996), and for two excellent discussions, see Martin Jay, *Songs of Experience* (Berkeley, 2005), and Moyn, *Origins of the Other*.

6. Leo Strauss, "Das Heilige," *Der Jude* 7, 4 (1923), 240–42; reprinted in Strauss, *GS* II, 307–10.

7. Strauss, *GS* II, 307–10.

8. Strauss, *GS* II, 251–52. Otto's stance ought not be reduced to the others— his commitments to neo-Kantianism especially. See also Samuel Moyn, "From Experience to Law: Leo Strauss and the Weimar Crisis of the Philosophy of Religion," *History of European Ideas* 33, 2 (June 2007), 174–94.

9. Strauss, *GS* II, 255.

10. Strauss, *GS* II, 274.

11. Barth, *Romans*, 27.

12. Herder addressed him as such in a letter of February 6, 1784. See David Bell, *Spinoza in Germany from 1670 to the Age of Goethe* (London, 1984), 115.

13. Hans Blumenberg, *The Genesis of the Copernican World*, trans. Robert M. Wallace (Cambridge, Mass., 1987), 380.

14. As Blumenberg put it in his *Work on Myth* (Cambridge, Mass., 1985), 422: "Pantheism is the unavoidable consequence of combining the concept of creation with the attribute of infinity."

15. Jacobi seemed to think that only a finite world could "leave the 'space' vacant for a spirit and a will that were superior to it." In this his thinking was "still, or once again, medieval," at least as Hans Blumenberg describes it in *The Genesis of the Copernican World*, 380–81.

16. Strauss rehearsed Jacobi's position in his critique of Martin Buber's philosophy of dialogue. Buber erred, Strauss thought, in mistaking a monologue between self and a merely imagined other for a true dialogue between human and divine. Given his affiliation with Jacobi and with Barth, it comes as little surprise that he would attack Buber's philosophy as a kind of self-idolatry. See his letter to Scholem of October 18, 1957. Strauss, *GS* III, 737.

17. David Baumgardt, *Der Kampf um den Lebenssinn unter den Vorläufern der modernen Ethik* (Leipzig, 1933), 365.

18. I refer to Frederick Beiser's excellent account of the *Pantheismusstreit* in his book *The Fate of Reason: German Philosophy from Kant to Fichte* (Cambridge, Mass., 1987).

19. *The Spinoza Conversations Between Lessing and Jacobi*, trans. G. Vallee et al. (New York, 1988), 95.

20. For a similar argument elaborated in the interwar period, see Hans Hölters, *Der spinozistische Gottesbegriff* (Emsdetten, 1938).

21. Strauss, "A Giving of Accounts," in Strauss, *Jewish Philosophy*, 463.

22. Strauss, *Spinoza's Critique*, 15.

23. *Detroit Jewish News* (August 26, 1966).

24. The philosopher Jean-François Lyotard would have called it a differend.

25. M. Guttmann, *Mafteach Ha-Talmud*, vol. 3, part 2 (1930), 9–14; "Apikorus," *Encyclopedia Judaica* 1 (Jerusalem, 1972), 177.

26. Strauss, *Spinoza's Critique*, 41.

27. Barth, *Romans*, 253.

28. Rosenzweig, *Star of Redemption*, 93.

29. Perhaps most famously, Carl Schmitt invoked the miracle as the theological analogue to the decision of the sovereign in the political "state of emergency." Schmitt, *Political Theology*, 36. On the Jewish discourse of the miracle, see, besides Rosenzweig, Max Brod, "Das Diesseitswunder," in *Judentum, Heidentum, Christentum* (Munich, 1921); Joseph Carlebach, "Naturwissenschaft und Wunder," *Der Morgen* 8, 2 (1932), 96–105; Chaim Neuburger, *Das Wesen des Gesetzes in der Philosophie des Maimonides* (Breslau, 1933); Oskar Goldberg, "Die Götter der Griechen," *Mass und Wert* 1, 2 (1937), 163–91; and Erich Unger, "Oskar Goldberg: Maimonides," *Der Morgen* 12, 3 (1936), 130–34. On its Christian variant, see Walter Künneth, *Das Wunder als apologetisch-theologisches Problem* (Gütersloh, 1931); Wilhelm Möller, *Über das Wunder in der heiligen Schrift* (Lüjtenburg, 1925); and Kurt Stavenhagen, "Die Idee des religiösen Wunders," *Zeitschrift für Theologie und Kirche* (1928), 1–27, 130–39. For a representative sample of the occult discourse, see Bruno Grabinski, *Wunder, Stigmatisation und Besessenheit in der Gegenwart* (Hildesheim, 1924); S. Hartmann, "Das Wunder. Parteilose Gedanken eines Naturwissenschaftlers," *Das Wunder* 1 (1928), 18–20; and Franz Koehler, *Geist und Wunder. Eine Auseinandersetzung zwischen Glaubenschaft und Wissenschaft* (Berlin, 1927).

30. Strauss, *Spinoza's Critique*, 136.

31. Rosenzweig, *Star of Redemption*, 104, 106. On Strauss and Rosenzweig, see also Batnitzky, *Leo Strauss and Emmanuel Levinas*.

32. Rosenzweig, *Star of Redemption*, 108.

33. Strauss, *Spinoza's Critique*, 113, 116, 133.

34. Strauss, *Spinoza's Critique*, 181.

35. Does there exist, Strauss went on to ask, "apart from all humanly constituted law, a law plainly imposed on all men, and of which transgression is sin? Is there human action which contravenes the will of God? For Spinoza, *this* is the question regarding the *lex divina* and to the question understood in this sense his answer is No." Strauss, *Spinoza's Critique*, 164, 171–72.

36. See, for example, Gogarten's discussion in *Verhängnis und Hoffnung der Neuzeit*. Gogarten would have diagnosed Strauss's approach as afflicted with "secularism," a deviant and radicalized form of a properly Christian seculariza-tion of the world that reversed the Christian desacralization of worldliness with a form of world-idolatry.

37. Strauss to Krüger, October 3, 1931, italics added. Strauss, *GS* III, 393.

38. Leo Strauss, "Einleitung zu 'Morgenstunden' und 'An die Freunde Lessings,'" in Moses Mendelssohn, *Gesammelte Schriften. Jubiläumsausgabe* III, 2 (Stuttgart, 1974), xi–xcv.

39. Kenneth Hart Green is an exception: "'In the Grip of the Theological-Political Predicament': The Turn to Maimonides in the Jewish Thought of Leo Strauss," in *Leo Strauss's Thought*, ed. Alan Udoff (Boulder, 1991). See also David Janssens, "The Problem of the Enlightenment: Strauss, Jacobi and the Pantheism Controversy," *Review of Metaphysics* (March 2003), 605–31.

40. On Mendelssohn's reception of the Wolffians, see David Sorkin, *Moses Mendelssohn and the Religious Enlightenment* (Berkeley, 1996).

41. Moses Mendelssohn, "Philosophische Gespräche," in *Gesammelte Schriften. Jubiläumsausgabe* I, 344–50. For a useful summary, see Alexander Altmann, "Moses Mendelssohn on Leibniz and Spinoza," in *Studies in Rationalism, Judaism and Universalism*, ed. Raphael Loewe (London, 1966), 13–45.

42. Altmann, "Moses Mendelssohn," 17.

43. Hans Blumenberg, *The Genesis of the Copernican World*, 380.

44. Strauss, "Einleitung," lxii.

45. Strauss purified *Jacobi's* arguments instead. Jacobi had occasionally invoked historical arguments in his critique of the Enlightenment, and with them, had adopted a language that unwittingly subordinated belief to the "horizon of the historical concept." This Strauss disallowed. Had Jacobi "held fast to his critique of Spinoza to the end," he would have eschewed such lan-guage. Strauss insisted on a dehistoricized notion of belief that Jacobi himself had not, or at least not with such rigor, and so retrojected on to Jacobi a line of thinking to which he had already professed allegiance. Strauss, "Einleitung," lxiii, lxxvi.

46. Strauss, "Einleitung," xcv, lxxix, lxxvii.

NOTES TO CHAPTER SEVEN: FROM GOD TO NATURE

1. On Herder's intervention in the pantheism controversy, see Beiser, *The Fate of Reason*, chap. 5; Bell, *Spinoza in Germany*, especially 115ff.; Gerrish, *Continuing the Reformation*, 115–26; and Zammito, *The Genesis of Kant's Critique of Judgment*.

2. Like Herder several centuries before, Jonas resolved the pantheism controversy of his time by recovering the category of the organism, and like Herder, did so in part by reading Spinoza against the grain. For Jonas on Spinoza, see "Spinoza and the Theory of Organism," *Journal of the History of Philosophy*

3 (1965), 43–57. See also his remarks to Harvey Scodel, "An Interview with Professor Hans Jonas," *Social Research* 70, 2 (Summer 2003), 353–54.

3. Strauss to Jonas, November 19, 1958. HJA 7-13b-10.

4. See Strauss, "Disposition: Die politische Wissenschaft des Hobbes. Eine Einführung in das Naturrecht (1931)," "Vorwort zu einem geplanten Buch über Hobbes (1931)," "Anmerkungen zu Carl Schmitt, Der Begriff des Politischen (1932)," "Einige Anmerkungen über die politische Wissenschaft des Hobbes (1933)," "Die Religionskritik des Hobbes: ein Beitrag zum Verständnis der Aufklärung (1933/1934)," collected in *GS* III, 3–374, and Strauss, *The Political Philosophy of Hobbes: Its Basis and Its Genesis*, trans. Elsa M. Sinclair (Oxford, 1936). His notes and an outline for the natural right project are to be found in LSP Box 10, Folder 15.

5. Strauss, *The Political Philosophy of Hobbes*, 107.

6. Cited in Meier, *GS* III, x.

7. Strauss, *GS* III, 368–69.

8. Strauss, *GS* III, 369.

9. Strauss, "Die Religionskritik des Hobbes," 270.

10. Carl Schmitt, *The Concept of the Political*, trans. George Schwab (Chicago, 1996), 76.

11. Schmitt, *Concept of the Political*, 57.

12. An approach recently staked out by Victoria Kahn helps account for this conundrum. See Kahn, *Wayward Contracts: the Crisis of Political Obligation in England, 1640–1674* (Princeton, 2004).

13. Leo Strauss, "Notes on Carl Schmitt, *The Concept of the Political*," reprinted in Schmitt, *Concept of the Political*, 88–89.

14. Strauss, "Notes on Carl Schmitt," 105–7.

15. Steven Smith has advanced the most elaborate version of this argument, by discovering a liberal spirit at work in the manner of Strauss's philosophizing, in *Reading Leo Strauss*.

16. Strauss, *GS* III, 625. Translation adapted from Richard Wolin, "Leo Strauss, Judaism and Liberalism," *Chronicle of Higher Education* 52, 32 (April 14, 2006) B13–14.

17. To make this point, it must be emphasized, is first and foremost to understand Strauss in his historical context. If it is problematic to retroject a liberalism on to the Strauss of the early 1930s, it is no more defensible to equate without evidence the Strauss of the early 1930s with the Strauss of the 1940s, '50s or '60s. Perhaps it was simply the case that Strauss held to an assessment of the interwar scene described more recently by the historian Mark Mazower: that by the middle of the 1930s the crucial ideological battles were fought not between right and left, but were taking place "within the Right [itself]." (Mazower, 28) Many interwar observers held that the intellectual center and left had gone moribund. Strauss seems to have been one of them, and we might as well face up to the fact. At least one of Strauss's prominent students, Werner Dannhauser, has come to similar conclusions. He offers the most sensitive interpretation of Strauss's letter I have encountered to date: "The reading of such a passage causes pain. It is true that the fascism to which Strauss alludes is that of Mussolini and

not of Hitler. It is true that in the same letter, in the same breath as it were, he leaves no doubt about his loathing of National Socialism. It is also true that at times he takes a slightly unseemly pleasure in taunting Löwith, or at least in being hyperbolically provocative toward him. And yet, and yet. We must admit that the young Strauss, not yet thirty-five at the time, was more reactionary than we might wish him to be. For that matter, he was slightly more reactionary than many of us students wished him to be in 1964 when he decided to vote for Barry Goldwater. But we had learned properly to weight such facts against the whole, even as we now hope that readers of the letters will subscribe to the principles of weighting I have tried to articulate above." Werner J. Dannhauser, "Leo Strauss in His Letters," in Svetozar Minkov, ed., *Enlightening Revolutions: Essays in Honor of Ralph Lerner* (Lanham, MD, 2006), 359. For a more detailed consideration of the thesis of a Straussian liberalism, see Benjamin Lazier, "Natural Right and Liberalism: Leo Strauss for Our Time," *Modern Intellectual History* (forthcoming, April 2009).

18. Julius Guttmann, "Philosophie der Religion oder Philosophie des Gesetzes?" *Proceedings of the Israel Academy of Sciences and Humanities* 6 (1974), 6. For the Löwith correspondence, see *Independent Journal of Philosophy* 5/6 (1988), 180, 185. The citation from the Klein letter appears courtesy of Heinrich Meier in Strauss *GS* II, xxvii. The Scholem letter, of March 29, 1935, appears in Gershom Scholem, ed., *The Correspondence of Walter Benjamin and Gershom Scholem, 1932–1940*, trans. Gary Smith and Andre Lefevere (New York, 1989), 156–57.

19. Julius Guttmann, *Die Philosophie des Judentums* (Munich, 1933).

20. Strauss, *Philosophy and Law*, 42.

21. His arguments against Guttmann rehearsed the ones he directed in 1923 toward Rudolf Otto's book *Das Heilige*. Strauss found in Guttmann (as in Otto) a partial departure from Schleiermacher's stress on the human experience of the divine. And like Otto, Guttmann had recognized the disease but lacked the fortitude for the radical self-surgery required by its cure. Strauss, *Philosophy and Law*, 47.

22. Strauss, *Philosophy and Law*, 47–49.

23. For this reason, Altmann declared them unpalatable to Jewish sensibilities, and adduced the case of Rosenzweig as his proof. Altmann, "Zur Auseinandersetzung mit der 'dialektischen Theologie,'" 345–61.

24. Strauss, *Philosophy and Law*, 47–49.

25. Strauss, *Philosophy and Law*, 32, 135; Strauss, "On the Interpretation of Genesis," in Strauss, *Jewish Philosophy*, 369.

26. Strauss, *Philosophy and Law*, 32.

27. Strauss to Jonas, June 13, 1935. LSP, Box 4, Folder 10.

28. His correspondence with Löwith from 1935 has been translated and published as "Correspondence. Karl Löwith and Leo Strauss," *Independent Journal of Philosophy* 5/6 (1988), 177–92, here at 183–84.

29. Strauss wrote all this in a letter to Helmut Kuhn, who reviewed *Natural Right* in German translation. The review, along with the response, appears as "Naturrecht und Historismus" and "Letter to Helmut Kuhn," in the *Independent Journal of Philosophy* 2 (1978), 13–26, here at 24.

30. The lecture, "German Nihilism," Strauss delivered on February 26, 1941. LSP, Box 8, Folder 15. In *Prinzip Verantwortung* Jonas looked to digestion as the limit case for the willful activity of unconscious organism, perhaps the finest philosophical moment stomach juice has ever enjoyed. The Straussian criterion, meanwhile, shares much with the friend/enemy distinction advanced by Carl Schmitt.

31. Leo Strauss and Karl Löwith, "Correspondence Concerning Modernity," *Independent Journal of Philosophy* 4 (1983), 107–8.

32. Strauss and Löwith, "Correspondence Concerning Modernity," 110, 112–13.

33. This is a point of bitter controversy, above all in debates about the Straussian influence on neoconservatives eager to intervene in Iraq. Much in these debates is silly, some serious. For recent works that address the issue, if with radically disparate conclusions, see Smith, *Reading Leo Strauss*, and Anne Norton, *Leo Strauss and the Politics of American Empire* (New Haven, Conn., 2005). Citations from Allan Bloom, *The Closing of the American Mind* (New York, 1987), 184; and Leon Kass, *The Beginning of Wisdom: Reading Genesis* (New York, 2003), 294–95. For a discussion, see Lawrence Vogel, "Natural-Law Judaism? The Genesis of Bio-Ethics in Hans Jonas, Leo Strauss and Leon Kass," in *Humanity under God: Contemporary Faces of Jewish, Christian and Islamic Ethics*, ed. William Schweiker (Chicago, 2005).

NOTES TO CHAPTER EIGHT: NATURAL RIGHT AND JUDAISM

1. Steven Smith's recent book represents a partial departure from this bifurcation. Smith, *Reading Leo Strauss*.

2. Strauss, *Natural Right*, vii.

3. To yoke them together in this way occludes a distinction of long standing in Jewish thought. See Erwin Rosenthal, "Torah and Nomos in Medieval Jewish Philosophy," in *Studies in Rationalism, Judaism and Universalism*, 215–30. Also Gerhard Wallis, "Torah und Nomos. Zur Frage nach Gesetz und Heil," *Theologische Literaturzeitung* 105, 5 (1980), 321–32; Stephen Westerholm, "Torah, Nomos and Law: A Question of Meaning," *Studies in Religion* 15, 3 (1986), 327–36; and Andre LaCocque, "Torah-Nomos," in *The Life of Covenant*, ed. Joseph Edelheit (Chicago, 1986), 85–95. On the *theios nomos* in Strauss's thought, see Meier, *Leo Strauss and the Theologico-Political Problem*, 40–41.

4. Strauss to Scholem, March 23, 1959. *GS* III, 738–39.

5. His earliest formulations of the issue understandably gave rise to later confusion. In his Hobbes book (penned in the early 1930s) Strauss tended to use the two—natural right and natural law—interchangeably, and instead distinguished between modern and traditional forms of natural law. See, for example, Strauss, *Political Philosophy of Hobbes*, vii.

6. Strauss, *Natural Right*, 146–47.

7. Leo Strauss to David Lowenthal, March 8, 1954, LSP, Box 4, Folder 12; Strauss, "Letter to Helmut Kuhn," 24.

8. Strauss to Scholem, November 22, 1960. Strauss, *GS* III, 742.

9. Leo Strauss, "The Mutual Influence of Theology and Philosophy," *Independent Journal of Philosophy* 3 (1979), 117–18. First published in Hebrew in *Iyyun* 5, 1 (January 1954), 110–26. A highly similar passage is to be found in *Natural Right*, 75.

10. Joseph Cropsey, "Leo Strauss at the University of Chicago," in *Leo Strauss, the Straussians, and the American Regime*, ed. Kenneth L. Deutsch and John A. Murley (Lanham, Md., 1999), 39.

11. Strauss, "Mutual Influence," 118.

12. See Rosenzweig's 1914 essay, "Atheistische Theologie," reprinted in his *Kleinere Schriften* (Berlin, 1937), 278–90.

13. Lecture on natural right delivered January 9, 1946, to the graduate seminar at the New School for Social Research. LSP, Box 9, Folder 2.

14. See Baumgardt, *Der Kampf um den Lebenssinn unter den Vorläufern der modernen Ethik* (Leipzig, 1933); and Baumgardt, *Bentham and the Ethics of Today* (Princeton, 1952). For a discussion, see Ze'ev Levy, *David Baumgardt and Ethical Hedonism* (Hoboken, N.J., 1989).

15. David Baumgardt Papers, Leo Baeck Institute, New York, Box 15, Folder 14.

16. As Strauss once put it to Krüger: "The original fact is a *given* law, which even psychoanalysis unwillingly confirms, a law that does not first need to be sought out. Sometime, somewhere on the earth there were men who saw themselves robbed of this law and *asked* therefore after a law, that is, after a *natural* law valid for *man* as such. Since then there is philosophy; for precisely this: the falling-away of the given law and the search for *the* law [which ensues] signifies, it seems to me, philosophy itself." *GS* III, 417.

17. Strauss, *GS* III, 424.

18. Jonas, *Erinnerungen*, 93.

19. Strauss to Scholem, October 17, 1973. Strauss, *GS* III, 771.

NOTES TO PART THREE: REDEMPTION THROUGH SIN

1. Scholem first recounted the story in his essay "Zur sozialen Psychologie der Juden in Deutschland, 1900–1930," in *Die Krise des Liberalismus zwischen den Weltkriegen*, ed. Rudolf von Thadden (Göttingen, 1978), 256–77, later reproduced with some modification and embellishment in Gershom Scholem, *Judaica* 4 (Frankfurt, 1984). Christoph Schmidt offers an interesting gloss on the story in *Der häretische Imperativ* (Tübingen, 2000), 113.

2. Strauss to Scholem, August 11, 1960, in Strauss *GS* III, 743.

3. This vocabulary also underwrote what David Biale and Amos Funkenstein have called a "counter-history." David Biale, *Gershom Scholem: Kabbalah and Counter-History* (Cambridge, Mass., 1979); and Amos Funkenstein, "History,

Counterhistory and Narrative," in *Probing the Limits of Representation*, ed. Saul Friedlander (Cambridge, Mass., 1992), 66–81.

Notes to Chapter Nine: Redemption through Sin

1. Jonas, *Gnostic Religion*, xiii–xiv.

2. Jean Baptiste de Rocoles, for example, could include Sabbatai Sevi in his history of famous imposters, *Les imposteurs insignes*, published in Amsterdam in 1683.

3. Scholem, "Redemption through Sin," 78–141. On Hasidism as a "neutralization" of Sabbatian excess, see Scholem's essay, "The Neutralization of the Messianic Element in Early Hasidism," in Scholem, *The Messianic Idea in Judaism*, 176–202.

4. Zalman Rubashov, "Yom Sabbatai Sevi," *Davar* (July 29, 1925), partially reprinted in Nathan Rotenstreich, "Al Madat ha-Hizdahut: Zalman Shaźar ben ha-Shiv'im," *Molad* 17 (1959), 610.

5. Benedictus de Spinoza, *Spinoza Redivivus: Eine Fibel für Anfänger und Verächter der Philosophie* (Halle, 1919).

6. On the Sabbatians in the age of Enlightenment, see Shmuel Verses, *Haskalah ve-Shabta'ut. Toldotav shel Ma'avak* (Jerusalem, 1988). Examples of scholarship from the nineteenth through twentieth centuries: Meir Balaban, *Le-Toldot ha-Tenuah ha-Frankit*, 2 vols. (Tel-Aviv, 1934–1935); Nahum Brilel, *Toldot Shabtai Sevi* (Vilna, 1879); Abraham Danon, *Etudes Sabbatiennes* (Paris, 1910); Avraham Elimeliach, *Shabtai Sevi. Ktovav, be-Sidrei Tenuato ha-Meshichit be-Yameinu Ele* (Jerusalem, 1927); Aharon Fraimann, *Inyene Shabtai Tsevi* (Berlin, 1912); Abraham Galante, *Nouveaux Documents sur Sabbatai Sevi* (Constantinople, 1935); Heinrich Graetz, *Frank und die Frankisten. Eine Sekten-Geschichte aus der letzten Hälfte des vorigen Jahrhunderts* (Breslau, 1868); David Kohn, *Toldot ha-Mekubalim, ha-Shabta'im ve-ha-Hasidim*, 2 vols. (Odessa, 1913); Alexander Kraushar, *Frank i frankisci polscy, 1726–1816* (Krakow, 1895), now also in translation by Herbert Levy (Lanham, Md., 2001); and Solomon Rosanes, *Korot ha-Yehudim be-Turkiah* (Sofia, 1934). Rubashov published a series of early essays on various aspects of the phenomenon, later collected in *Ore Dorot* (Jerusalem, 1971). Klaus Davidowicz offers a useful summary of scholarship on Frank in *Jakob Frank, der Mesias aus dem Ghetto* (Frankfurt, 1998), 23–57. Now, some examples of novels and journalism: Jakob Wassermann, *Fränkische Erzählungen. Sabbatai Zewi, ein Vorspiel* (Frankfurt, 1925); Lion Feuchtwanger, *Jud Süß* (Munich, 1925); Felix Theilhaber, *Dein Reich komme! Ein chiliastischer Roman aus der Zeit Rembrandts und Spinozas* (Berlin, 1924); Josef Kastein, *Sabbatai Zewi, der Messias von Ismir* (Berlin, 1930); and Esriel Carlebach, *Exotische Juden* (Berlin, 1932). Michael Brenner surveys this material in *The Renaissance of Jewish Culture*, 148–50. David Biale situates it in the context of Jewish fascination with the Orient in "Shabbtai Zvi and the Seductions of Jewish Orientalism," *Jerusalem Studies in Jewish Thought* (2001).

7. This, perhaps, is what Michael Brenner had in mind when he observed that "Sabbatai Sevi made his literary journey from Izmir to Weimar" at just about the time Gershom Scholem undertook his physical and spiritual journey from Berlin to Jerusalem. Brenner, *The Renaissance of Jewish Culture*, 149.

8. See, for example, the work of Shai Ish-Hurwitz (1860–1922), an eastern European turned Berliner. The heretic was for him a test: in the heretic inhered the limit case of the Zionist bid to negate the exile. "If Judaism is not to be asphyxiated by the fumes of its own breath, it must keep an open corridor to let in a fresh breeze from outside," he wrote. "It is upon us to grant the right of citizenship in Judaism to all the foreign thoughts that have come to reside among us, and to judaize them. All the 'others,' " at once a locution for the alien in the Jewish and a rabbinic reference to heretics, "must find a stance for themselves within Judaism." Shai Ish-Hurwitz, *Me-ayin u-Le-ayin? Kobetz Ma'amarim be-Inyenei ha-Yehudim ve-ha-Yahadut* (Berlin, 1914), 84, cited also in part in Biale, *Gershom Scholem*, 49, but with translation slightly altered. Hurwitz's term for heretics, *aherim* (literally, "others") refers to R. Elisha Ben-Abuya, known also as *Aher* ("other"), who according to legend was one of four to enter paradise, but with the intent of "cutting the saplings," presumably a euphemism for defamation of God and Torah. On Ben-Abuya, see Alon Goshen-Gottstein, *The Sinner and the Amnesiac: The Rabbinic Invention of Elisha ben Abuya and Eleazar ben Arach* (Stanford, 2000). On Hurwitz, see the discussion in Biale, *Gershom Scholem*, 47–49, and Stanley Nash, *In Search of Hebraism: Shai Hurwitz and His Polemics in the Hebrew Press* (Leiden, 1980).

9. Zalman Shazar, *Mivhar Ketavim: Sipurei Zichronot* (Tel-Aviv, 1972), 25–29.

10. Theodor Herzl, *Old New Land*, trans. Lotta Levensohn (Princeton, 1997), 95; Theodor Herzl, *The Diaries of Theodor Herzl*, ed. Marvin Lowenthal (New York, 1956), 49.

11. See Biale, *Gershom Scholem*, 33–51.

12. Leopold Zunz, *Gesammelte Schriften* I (Berlin, 1875), 4. For a discussion see Leon Wieseltier, "Etwas Über Die Jüdische Historik: Leopold Zunz and the Inception of Modern Jewish Historiography," *History and Theory* 20, 2 (1981), 148. This view—that Jewish history might be written only at its end—has since been attributed more to Steinschneider than Zunz.

13. His work on Cardozo at the Oxford archives had prompted him to rethink his answer "to the perennial question as to what Judaism was all about." Gershom Scholem, *Walter Benjamin: The Story of a Friendship*, trans. Harry Zohn (New York, 1981), 136.

14. Scholem, "Redemption through Sin," 84–85.

15. Scholem, "Redemption through Sin," 126–41; Scholem, *Du Frankisme au Jacobinisme. La vie de Moses Dobruska, alias Franz Thomas von Schönfeld alias Junius Frey* (Paris, 1981).

16. Graetz, *Frank und die Frankisten*, 2.

17. Scholem, "Redemption through Sin," 126; Scholem, "Der Nihilismus als Religiöses Phänomen," *Eranos Jahrbuch* 43 (1974), 35.

18. *Book of the Words of the Lord*, no. 1157, cited in Scholem, "Redemption through Sin," 129.

19. As he wrote to his wife, in Rahel and Zalman Shazar, *Ha-Hofim ha-Shnayim. Michtavim*, 1909–1963 (Jerusalem, 1999), 37–38. Scholem recalled those years in a eulogy delivered in Rubashov's honor, republished in Scholem, *Devarim Be-Go* (Tel-Aviv, 1975), 472–76.

20. He published the essay first under the title "Ikvot Achim Ovdim" in *Ha'adama* 6 (1920), and then independently in book form (with corrections and pictures, including one of Frank's skull) as *Al Tile Beit Frank* (Berlin, 1923), here at 1, 4, 23. See also the discussion in Biale, *Gershom Scholem*, 49–51.

21. Scholem met Rubashov in 1917, when they lived adjacent to one another in a Berlin pension. Scholem chalked up the direction of his later research to his encounters with him there. Gershom Scholem, "Al Toldot ha-Mechkar ha-Shabta'i," in Scholem, *Mechkere Shabta'ut*, ed. Avraham Shapira (Tel-Aviv, 1991), 742–46.

22. Scholem, "Al Toldot ha-Mechkar ha-Shabta'i," 743.

23. The various essays are collected in Scholem, *Mechkere Shabta'ut*. The Hebrew biography appeared as *Shabtai Tsvi ve-ha-Tenu'ah ha-Shabta'it be-Yemei Chayyav* (Tel-Aviv, 1957) and the English revision as *Sabbatai Sevi: the Mystical Messiah* (Princeton, 1973). See also Scholem, "Al Toldot ha-Mechkar ha-Shabta'i," 745.

24. Some of these have been taken up by Scholem's students and colleagues. See in particular Isaiah Tishby, *Netivei Emunah u-Minut* (Tel-Aviv, 1964); Yehuda Liebes, *Sod ha-Emuna ha-Shabta'it* (Jerusalem, 1995); and Ya'akov Barnai, *Shabta'ut* (Jerusalem, 2000).

25. As he wrote in a letter to a critic (R. J. Zwi Werblowsky, who would in fact become the translator of his biography of Sabbatai Sevi), Scholem considered the Sabbatians as Jews to the very end: "In truth I do not believe that the followers of Sabbatai Sevi quit being Jews, just because they had so deeply and insolubly entangled themselves." Gershom Scholem, *Briefe II 1948–1970* (Munich, 1995), 41.

26. Others have also situated Scholem's essay in its interwar context. Jeffrey Mehlman likens it to Walter Benjamin's polemic against the liberal fetish for "progress" in *Walter Benjamin for Children* (Chicago, 1993), 42–43. Steven Wasserstrom compares it to discussions then raging in Paris among the circle associated with Georges Bataille in *Religion after Religion* (Princeton, 1999), 215–24.

NOTES TO CHAPTER TEN: JEWISH GNOSTICISM

1. Ioan Culianu, "From Gnosticism to the Dangers of Technology: An Interview with Hans Jonas," in *Gnosticismo e pensiero moderno: Hans Jonas* (Rome, 1985), 147.

2. Harold Bloom, Introduction to *Gershom Scholem*, ed. Harold Bloom (New York, 1987), 2, 7; and Bloom, "Scholem: Unhistorical or Jewish Gnosticism," in *Gershom Scholem*, ed. Bloom, 208, 211, 219.

3. This position was advanced by Joseph Dan, one of Scholem's disciples, in an otherwise excellent discussion, "Jewish Gnosticism?" *Jewish Studies Quarterly* 2 (1995), 328.

4. On this count, see Moshe Idel, "Subversive Katalysatoren: Gnosis und Messianismus in Gershom Scholems Verständnis der jüdischen Mystik," in *Gershom Scholem Zwischen den Disziplinen*, ed. Peter Schäfer and Gary Smith (Frankfurt, 1995), 80–121.

5. Gershom Scholem, *Tagebücher nebst Aufsätzen und Entwurfen bis 1923*, 2 vols., ed. Karlfried Gründer and Friedrich Niewöhner (Frankfurt, 1995), here at vol. 1, 116.

6. *Schalem* (adjective), Hebr.: perfect, whole, complete. Scholem, *Tagebücher* I, 120.

7. Scholem, *Tagebücher* I, 115.

8. "I believe in this hour no longer, as I once believed, that I am the Messiah." Scholem, *Tagebücher* I, 158.

9. Scholem, *Tagebücher* I, 52, 403.

10. Scholem, *Tagebücher* I, 397–98.

11. Scholem, *Tagebücher* I, 163–64.

12. Scholem, *Tagebücher* I, 81–82. Orientalist motifs were ubiquitous in German-Jewish thought of the time. See Mendes-Flohr, *Divided Passions*, 77–132.

13. Scholem, *Tagebücher* I, 208–9. See also, Robert Alter, *Necessary Angels* (Cambridge, Mass., 1991), 113–20; and Richard Rorty's discussion of Nietzsche, contingency, and selfhood in *Contingency, Irony, and Solidarity* (Cambridge, Mass., 1989), 23–43.

14. Scholem, *Tagebücher* I, 61–62. On crisis thought, see Allan Megill, *Prophets of Extremity* (Berkeley, 1987), 114–15. On *Bildung*, see Steven Aschheim, "German Jews Beyond Bildung and Liberalism," in *Culture and Catastrophe* (New York, 1996), 32; Sorkin, *The Transformation of German Jewry*; and Aleida Assmann, *Arbeit am nationalen Gedächtnis: eine kurze Geschichte der deutschen Bildungsidee* (Frankfurt, 1993). For Scholem, Chanukah represented the "festival of *Schwärmer* who for the first time ran through the wall with their heads and conquered." For just this reason, Diaspora theorists such as Daniel Boyarin have privileged resistance in the form of Purim's tricksterism over Chanukah's martial force: "Purim and the Cultural Poetics of Judaism—Theorizing Diaspora," *Poetics Today* 15, 1 (Spring 1994), 5. Boyarin's is but one skirmish in a battle rejoined in public for forty years at the University of Chicago: Ruth Cernea, ed., *The Great Latke-Hamentash Debate* (Chicago, 2005).

15. Scholem, *Tagebücher* I, 224.

16. Scholem, *Tagebücher* I, 226–27.

17. Scholem, *Tagebücher* I, 327.

18. For those inclined toward a certain critical vocabulary, we might say that the *ger* is the specter of heteronomy that haunts every move toward plenitude, or toward a self that is *schalem*. Denied the attention that is its due, the stranger persists as a persecutor, or an otherness internal to the self. On Scholem and the "stranger," see also Irving Wohlfarth, "*Männer aus der Fremde*: Walter Benjamin and the German-Jewish Parnassus," *New German Critique* 70 (Winter 1997), 23.

19. Nietzsche, *The Use and Abuse of History*, 70.

20. Scholem, *Tagebücher* I, 239.

21. Scholem, *Tagebücher* II, 54, 146, 154, 404, 409.

22. Scholem, *Tagebücher* II, 220, 230–31, 256–57, 409.

23. Scholem, *Tagebücher* II, 245.

24. Scholem, *Tagebücher* II, 245, 246.

25. Scholem, *Tagebücher* II, 128, 147–48. For those steeped in Scholemiana, the terms cannot fail to raise eyebrows. They prefigure by decades the most striking language in one of his most celebrated essays, "Revelation and Tradition as Religious Categories in Judaism," in *The Messianic Idea in Judaism*. The language also recalls—or anticipates—that of Carl Schmitt, who used similar terms to describe the status of the sovereign in a state of political exception, and whose work influenced Benjamin's book on the origins of German tragic drama. Eric Santner points to the affinity of Scholem and Schmitt in *The Psychotheology of Everyday Life*, 40–41. He follows Giorgio Agamben in *Potentialities* (Stanford, 1999). But both come well after Jacob Taubes, whose efforts to peg Scholem and Benjamin as practitioners of a Schmittian "political theology" seem finally to have taken root and flowered, if after his death. See Schmidt, *Der häretische Imperativ*; Gesine Palmer, Christiane Nasse, Renate Haffke and Dorothee C. von Tippelskirch, eds., *Torah/Nomos/Ius. Abendländischer Antinomismus und der Traum vom herrschaftsfreien Raum* (Berlin, 1999); and most recently, Jacob Taubes, *The Political Theology of Paul*.

26. Scholem, *Tagebücher* II, 128, 130, 382, 392.

27. Scholem, *Tagebücher* II, 160, 242, 273.

28. Hans Jonas, "The Gnostic Syndrome: Typology of Its Thought, Imagination and Mood," in Jonas, *Philosophical Essays* (Chicago, 1974), 268, originally published as "Delimitation of the Gnostic Phenomenon—Typological and Historical," in *The Origins of Gnosticism*, ed. Ugo Bianchi (Leiden, 1967).

29. Scholem, *Tagebücher* II, 405. In this passage, Scholem speaks about the relation of *Gericht* to his Zionism; elsewhere he dwells on its theological status.

30. A draft of the letter appears in Scholem, *Tagebücher* II, 248–49. The letter itself (of June 23, 1918) is published in Scholem, *Briefe* I, 161–65.

31. Scholem, *Major Trends*, 34.

32. The continuity in expression is striking. Scholem's 1937 letter to Schocken appears in David Biale, *Gershom Scholem*, 215–16: "An den drei einzigen Autoren, die ich kannte, an Saadja, Maimonides und Hermann Cohen empörte mich, wie sie ihre Hauptaufgabe darin fanden, Antithesen gegen den Mythos und den Pantheismus aufzustellen, sie zu 'widerlegen,' während es sich doch hätte darum handeln müssen, sie zu einer höheren Ordnung aufzuheben. Es gehörte ja nichts zu zeigen, daß Mythos und Pantheismus 'falsch' sind—viel wichtiger schien mir die Bemerkung, die mir zuerst ein frommer Jude machte, dass dennoch etwas dran ist." His citation and embellishment of Benjamin appears in Scholem, *Tagebücher* II, 322: " 'Die Aufgabe ist ja nicht, Antithesen gegen den Mythos oder des Pantheismus zu finden, sondern sie zu annihilieren. Zu zeigen, daß es falsch ist, dazu gehört nichts, aber es ist doch etwas daran.' (Benjamin) Dies ist die

prinzipiell falsche Stellung der jüdischen Religionsphilosophie von Rambam bis Cohen. Sie 'widerlegt.' "

33. Some of his early treatments: "Hans Leisegang, *Die Gnosis* (Leipzig, 1924)," (review) *Kiryat Sefer* 1 (1924/25), 206–7; "H. Raschke, *Die Werkstatt des Markusevangelisten*," (review) *Kiryat Sefer* 1 (1924/25), 198–99; "C. Schmidt, *Pistis Sophia; ein gnostisches Originalwerk des dritten Jahrhunderts, aus dem Koptischen übersetzt* (Leipzig, 1924)," (review) *Kiryat Sefer* 2 (1925/26), 247–48; "*3. Enoch*, ed. Hugo Odeberg (Cambridge, 1928)," (review) *Kiryat Sefer* 6 (1928/ 29), 62–64; *Bibliographia Kabbalistica. Verzeichnis der gedruckten die jüdische Mystik <Gnosis, Kabbala, Sabbatianismus, Frankismus, Chassidismus> behandelnden Bücher und Aufsätze, von Reuchlin bis zur Gegenwart* (Leipzig, 1927); "Kabbalot Reb Ya'akov ve-Reb Yitzhak Bnei Reb Ya'akov Ha-Cohen," *Mada'ei Ha-Yahadut* 2 (1927), 165–293; "Über die Theologie des Sabbatianismus im Lichte Abraham Cardozos," in *Judaica* (Frankfurt, 1963), 122–23, originally in *Der Jude* 9, *Sonderheft* 5 (1928), 123–29. See also Scholem's first public address on the Sabbatian phenomenon, "Zur Theologie des Sabbatianismus," delivered on January 21, 1928, AGS 4°1599/277I.67.

34. For criticisms, see Hans Jonas, "The 'Hymn of the Pearl': Case Study of a Symbol, and the Claims for a Jewish Origin of Gnosticism," in Jonas, *Philosophical Essays*; Joseph Dan, "Jewish Gnosticism?"; Jacob Neusner, ed., "Judaism and Gnosticism," Gershom Scholem Library, Jerusalem, 96.1; David Flusser, "Scholem's Recent Book on Merkabah Literature," *Journal of Jewish Studies* 11 (1960), 57–68; M. Tardieu and J. D. Dubois, *Introduction à la littérature gnostique* (Paris, 1986), 33; Ioan Culiano, *The Tree of Gnosis* (San Francisco, 1992), 12–43; and most recently, Moshe Idel, "Subversive Katalasytoren," 86.

35. Scholem, *Major Trends*, 38.

36. First published as Gershom Scholem, "Reflections on Jewish Theology," *Center Magazine* 7, 2 (March–April 1974), 57–71, later in *On Jews and Judaism in Crisis*, 261–97.

37. Scholem, *Major Trends*, 7–8.

38. Though on at least one occasion, an anonymous kabbalist advanced this distinction along decidedly gnostic lines: as an absolute being, God in himself was by his nature "incapable of becoming the subject of a revelation to others," and so quite simply could not be the God of scripture. Scholem, *Major Trends*, 12–13.

NOTES TO CHAPTER ELEVEN: RAISING PANTHEISM

1. *Defensio Cabalae hebraeorum contra auctores quosdam modernos* (Defense of the Kabbalah of the Jews Against Certain Modern Authors), published in 1702.

2. The original has appeared as Abraham Cohen de Herrera, *Puerta del Cielo*, ed. Kenneth Krabbenhoft (Madrid, 1987).

3. Gershom Scholem, "Die Wachtersche Kontroverse über den Spinozismus und ihre Folgen," in *Spinoza in der Frühzeit Seiner Religiösen Wirkung*, ed. K. Gründer and W. Schmidt-Biggemann (Heidelberg, 1984).

4. Moses Mendelssohn, *Morgenstunden oder Vorlesungen über das Daseyn Gottes* (Berlin, 1786), 212; Friedrich Heinrich Jacobi, *Werke* 4, 1 (1819), 217f.

5. See, for example, Israel Misses, "Spinoza und die Kabbala," *Zeitschrift für exakte Philosophie* 8 (1869), 362–64; and David Kahane, "Moshe Cordovero ve-Baruch Shpinoza," *Ha-Shiloach* 2 (1897), 90–92. This tradition in interpretation had been abetted by the ways in which God had been equated with nature. Those interested in advancing the equation relied on the happy coincidence of numerical identity: *elohim*, the sole name for God to appear in the account of creation, has the same *gematria* (or numerical value) as *ha-teva*, nature. This fact earned the attention of Abraham ibn Ezra in his commentary on Ecclesiastes. Abraham Abulafia pushed the equation further, noting that *elohim* and *ha-teva* correspond numerically also to *ha-mugbal*, the finite or limited, which suggests a notion of nature as a limited mode of divinity. Meanwhile, the thirteenth-century kabbalist Asriel of Gerona referred to the *olam mutba*, the natured world, as akin to the last or lower *sefirot*. Scholem took note as early as 1918, and referred to the *olam mutba* as *physis*. On Ibn Ezra and Abulafia, see Moshe Idel, "*Deus sive natura*— the Metamorphosis of a Dictum from Maimonides to Spinoza," in *Maimonides and the Sciences*, ed. R. S. Cohen and H. Levine (London, 2000), 89, 99. Scholem noted the equation in *Tagebücher* II, 380.

6. Stanislaus von Dunin-Borkowski, *Der Junge de Spinoza* (Munster, 1910), 169–90, here at 188.

7. Sigmund Gelbhaus, *Die Metaphysik der Ethik Spinozas im Quellenlichte der Kabbalah* (Vienna, 1917), 12, 108. All this inevitably aroused the forces of reaction. Harvard's Harry Austryn Wolfson, in what was long the standard work on Spinoza's thought, for the most part ignored the prospect of kabbalistic origins. Meanwhile, Heinz Pflaum took aim at the reigning sentiment of the day by arguing for the progressive eradication of the mystical impulse in Spinoza's thought. See Wolfson, *The Philosophy of Spinoza*, vol. 1 (New York, 1934), 17, 394; and Heinz Pflaum, "Rationalismus und Mystik in der Philosophie Spinozas," *Deutsche Vierteljahrsschrift für Literaturwissenschaft* 4, 1 (1926), 127–43. Jonathan Israel takes up the thrust of this argument in his opus on Spinoza and the radical Enlightenment, in which he understands Spinoza as a rationalist par excellence. Jonathan Israel, *The Radical Enlightenment* (New York, 2002).

8. Scholem, *Tagebücher* II, 149.

9. Gershom Scholem, "Die Theologie des Sabbatianismus im Lichte Abraham Cardosos," republished in Scholem, *Judaica* (Frankfurt, 1963), 122–23.

10. Scholem devoted a few lines to Wachter in *Major Trends*, 258, but addressed him at length only in an introduction to an edition and translation of Herrera's *Puerta del Cielo* and in a piece composed much later in life. See Gershom Scholem, "Abraham Cohen Herrera—Leben, Werk und Wirkung," in Abraham Cohen de Herrera, *Das Buch Sha'ar Ha-Shamayim, oder Pforte des Himmels*, trans. Friedrich Häussermann (Frankfurt, 1974), 7–67; and Scholem, "Die Wachtersche Kontroverse."

11. Compare Scholem to Strauss, March 13, 1973, in Strauss GS III, 768: "Whether the Jews will lead the move [to revitalize paganism] or whether they

will go down together with the last of the monotheists, that, my dear Strauss, I unfortunately cannot say. I remain in any event with the Jews."

12. Scholem, *Tagebücher* II, 149, 155. "Ich fühle mich oft als Neuland."

13. For example, Gershom Scholem, "Reste neuplatonischer Spekulation in der Mystik der deutschen Chassidim und ihre Vermittlung durch Abraham bar Chija," *MGWJ* 75 (1931), 172–91; Scholem, *Major Trends*, 109f., 123, 222f., 251f.; Gershom Scholem, "Das Ringen zwischen dem biblischen Gott und dem Gott Plotins in der alten Kabbala," *Eranos Jahrbuch* 33 (1964), 9–50.

14. See also his programmatic writings: Gershom Scholem, "Zehn Unhistorische Sätze über Kabbala," in *Geist und Werk. Zum 75. Geburtstag von Dr. Daniel Brody* (Zürich, 1958), 209–15; and Gershom Scholem, "Reflections on Jewish Theology," *Center Magazine* 7, 2 (March–April 1974), 57–71, later reprinted in Scholem, *On Jews and Judaism in Crisis*, 261–97.

15. Scholem, "Kabbalah and Pantheism," 149.

16. Cited in David Biale, "Gershom Scholem's Ten Unhistorical Aphorisms on Kabbalah," in Bloom, ed., *Gershom Scholem*, 115.

17. Scholem, *Major Trends*, 250.

18. Scholem, "Wachtersche Kontroverse."

19. Scholem, *Major Trends*, 253.

20. Cited in S. A. Horodezky, *Torat ha-Kabbalah shel R. Moshe Cordovero* (Berlin, 1924), 26–27. Scholem's review appeared in *Kiryat Sefer* 1 (1924/25), 203–5, and Horodezky's response and Scholem's response to the response in *Kiryat Sefer* 2 (1925/26), 28–31. The pair clashed again in Gershom Scholem, "Vulliauds Übersetzung des *Sifra Di-Zenutha* aus dem Sohar und andere neuere Literatur zur Geschichte der Kabbala," *MGWJ* 75 (1931), 451–54; and in "Zu Mose Cordovero," *MGWJ* 76 (1932), 167–72. For an account of Cordovero more to Scholem's liking, see the book by his student Joseph Ben-Shlomo, *Torat ha-Elohut shel R. Moshe Cordovero* (Jerusalem, 1965).

21. Scholem, "Vuillauds Übersetzung," 451. But Scholem would write almost exactly as Horodezky did a decade later in *Major Trends*, 252.

22. Scholem, *Major Trends*, 123, 341.

23. Scholem, *Kabbalah*, 148.

24. The analysis by no means ends there. The dialectic comes to no repose, refuses a final synthesis, and insists upon an irreducible moment of nonidentity. See the remarkable passage in Scholem, *Kabbalah*, 149–50.

25. A prominent scholar of the nineteenth century had in fact argued, in futility, that Zoharic kabbalah had not taught emanation, precisely to avoid the pantheist—and hence unpalatable—consequences he suspected would follow. David Joel, *Religionsphilosphie des Zohar* (Berlin, 1923).

26. Scholem sums up the history of post-Lurianic kabbalah as a series of debates on precisely this question, as a battle between those more impressed by the presence of the divine in the world, and those more impressed by his absence. Cf. *Major Trends*, 262.

27. Strauss to Scholem, March 23, 1959, in Strauss, *GS* III, 738.

28. Cited in Biale, "Scholem's Ten Unhistorical Aphorisms," 115–16.

29. Cited in Biale, "Scholem's Ten Unhistorical Aphorisms," 111. Scholem made a similar point fifteen years later, in an essay on the present (1974) task of Jewish theology. "Any living Judaism, no matter what its concept of God," he wrote, "will have to oppose pure naturalism with a definite 'no.' " Scholem, *On Jews and Judaism in Crisis*, 277–78.

30. Moshe Idel, *Kabbalah: New Perspectives* (New Haven, Conn., 1987), 38–41.

31. Scholem, *Major Trends*, 123.

32. Scholem, *Major Trends*, 348.

33. Scholem, "Devekut," 227. Scholem's leading critic, Moshe Idel, has proposed instead a scheme in which union precedes total annihilation in the godhead. Idel also contests the most basic of Scholem's suppositions, that Judaism does not know of mystical union with God. Idel's critique dovetails with his efforts to "de-nationalize" Jewish mysticism, a hallmark of Scholem's thought. Idel, *Kabbalah*, 60.

NOTES TO CHAPTER TWELVE: FROM NIHILISM TO NOTHINGNESS

1. Strauss to Scholem, October 18, 1957. Strauss, *GS* III, 737.

2. Strauss to Scholem, October 18, 1957. Strauss, *GS* III, 737. Gershom Scholem, "Schöpfung aus Nichts und Selbstverschränkung Gottes," *Eranos Jahrbuch* (1956), 87–119.

3. "In any event I am happy to hear that 'Creation From Nothing' speaks to you." Scholem to Strauss, November 21, 1957. Strauss, *GS* III, 737.

4. Strauss to Scholem, August 11, 1960. Strauss, *GS* III, 740.

5. Scholem to Strauss, October 19, 1933, in Strauss, *GS* III, 703. Scholem to Strauss, November 4, 1935, in Strauss *GS* III, 717.

6. Scholem to Strauss, November 4, 1935, in Strauss, *GS* III, 717. A total revision of Jewish history Scholem considered the "actual ratio essendi of the Institute for Jewish Studies at the Jerusalem University."

7. Strauss to Scholem, August 11, 1960, in Strauss, *GS* III, 740.

8. Strauss to Scholem, November 22, 1960. Strauss, *GS* III, 743.

9. Leo Strauss, "German Nihilism," lecture delivered February 26, 1941, at the New School for Social Research. LSP, Box 8, Folder 15.

10. "I frankly confess," Strauss put it to his students, "I do not see how those can resist the voice of that siren who expect the answer to the first and the last question from 'history,' from the future *as such*; who mistake analysis of the present or past or future for philosophy; who believe in a progress toward a goal which is itself progressive and therefore undefinable; who are not guided by a *known* and *stable* standard: by a standard which is stable and not changeable, and which is known and not merely believed. In other words, the lack of resistance to nihilism seems to be due ultimately to the deprecation and the contempt of reason, which is one and unchangeable or it is not." Strauss, "German Nihilism."

11. See among others: Dieter Arndt, ed., *Nihilismus. Die Anfänge von Jacobi bis Nietzsche* (Köln, 1970); Dieter Arndt, ed., *Der Nihilismus als Phänomen der Geistesgeschichte in der wissenschaftlichen Diskussion unseres Jahrhunderts* (Darmstadt, 1974); Karl Löwith, *Martin Heidegger and European Nihilism*, ed. Richard Wolin and trans. Gary Steiner (New York, 1995); Alexander Schwan, *Denken im Schatten des Nihilismus* (Darmstadt, 1975); and Manfred Riedel, "Nihilismus," in Reinhart Koselleck, ed., *Geschichtliche Grundbegriffe* 4 (Stuttgart, 1993), 370–410.

12. Karl Jaspers, *Psychologie der Weltanschauungen* (Berlin, 1919), 261–65. Gershom Scholem, "Der Nihilismus als Religiöses Phänomen," *Eranos Jahrbuch* 43 (1974), 3–4. Like Scholem, recent work locates nihilism's origins not in nineteenth-century thought, but in changing conceptions of God that transpired much earlier. See Michael Allen Gillespie, *Nihilism Before Nietzsche* (Chicago, 1995).

13. Jonas, *Gnosis und spätantiker Geist*, 149–51, cited here in Scholem, "Der Nihilismus," 7.

14. Scholem, "Der Nihilismus," 7–8, 18. This conflation enabled Scholem to describe the gnostics of late antiquity who debased creation and the medieval brothers of the "free spirit" who divinized it as beholden, all of them, to a kind of "pantheist mysticism." (16) Scholem settled on pantheism as a term that more readily calls to mind the absorption (or self-elevation) of man into God. But he more consistently referred to the gnostic and pantheist impulses as competing, but complementary, forms of nihilism.

15. Scholem, "Redemption through Sin," 129.

16. But the Frankist movement had other aspects that ruined the easy parallel and made it more akin to pantheist forms of nihilism. Gnostic nihilism rejected the world in favor of a transcendent beyond; but like the pantheist, Frank destroyed transcendence, urging instead descent into the wild and ungovernable abyss at the heart of the world, the source of what Scholem would call the "anarchic promiscuity of all living things."

17. Jonas, *Gnosis und spätantiker Geist*, 234, cited here in Scholem, "Der Nihilismus," 8. The English translation of the Jonas citation in "Redemption through Sin" obscures the parallel Jonas had intended to draw between gnosticism and dialectical theology. "'Zwischen den Zeiten'" gets rendered merely as "a world in transition." Scholem, "Redemption through Sin," 133.

18. Scholem, *Tagebücher* I, 208–9.

19. Scholem, "Nihilismus," 43–44.

20. Scholem, *Tagebücher* I, 61–62. I do not mean to reduce Scholem's researches to a working out of youthful excess, nor to equate Frank with the *Judenzarathustra*. There are differences. The *Judenzarathustra* argued for overcoming by willful elevation, Frank by willful self-abasement. Nonetheless, both abdicated on the world in which they lived.

21. Scholem maintained a minor correspondence with Blumenberg. See Scholem, *Briefe* III, 77–78. He had engaged with Blumenberg's writings at least as early as 1966, as he wrote in a letter to George Lichtheim. Scholem, *Briefe* II, 216.

22. Scholem, "Redemption through Sin," 127, 128. Scholem's treatment of Frank accords with the terms for the abject hero set out by Julia Kristeva and Michael André Bernstein. Kristeva pronounced tolerable Celine's noxious politics given "the wild beauty of his style." Like Scholem's Frank, Kristeva's Céline speaks the language of *délire*, of a desublimation that moves from self-mastery to heteronomy, from transcendence to carnality. As for Bernstein: despite Céline's failures, he appreciates the novelist's "stunning comic power and literary inventiveness," as well as the stylistic complexity of his work. He replicates Scholem on Frank. Julia Kristeva, *Powers of Horror: An Essay on Abjection*, trans. Leon S. Roudiez (New York, 1982), 174. Michael André Bernstein, *Bitter Carnival: Ressentiment and the Abject Hero* (Princeton, 1992), 122.

23. Strauss, "German Nihilism." On the other hand, nihilism has been mobilized in the service of a this-worldly, progressive politics as well. See Gianni Vattimo, *Nihilism and Emancipation: Ethics, Politics and Law* (New York, 2004).

24. Thomas Kobusch provides an exhaustive review of nothing in the *Historisches Wörterbuch der Philosophie*, Joachim Ritter and Karlfried Gründer, eds., 6 (Basel, 1984), 805–36.

25. So Harry Wolfson argued in a useful resume of the term in "The Meaning of *Ex Nihilo* in the Church Fathers, Arabic and Hebrew Philosophy, and St. Thomas," in *Mediaeval Studies in Honor of Jeremiah Denis Matthias Ford* (Cambridge, Mass., 1948), 355–70, here at 357–58. See also Scholem, "Schöpfung aus Nichts," 97, and A. Schmiedl, *Studien über jüdische, insonders jüdisch-arabische Religionsphilosophie* (Vienna, 1869), 89–128.

26. Scholem, "Schöpfung aus Nichts," 107–8. Asriel of Gerona, for instance, noted that the construction '*eino*, "there is not," used in the passage of the *Sefer Yetzira* to underscore the orthodox interpretation, also means "his nothingness." The transformation of nothingness into being therefore occurs within the divinity itself (Scholem, "Schöpfung aus Nichts," 110). Joseph Gikatilla rearranged the letters of *ayin*, nothingness, to form *ani*, I, in order to argue for a notion of original creation marked by the transformation of God's nothingness into his personality— "surely," Scholem noted, "a remarkable instance of dialectical thought" (Scholem, *Major Trends*, 218). Some years later, the author of the Zohar inverted the meaning of creation from nothing with a marvelous interpretation of the first line of Genesis, *Bereshith bara Elohim*. "We are told that it means *Bereshith*—through the medium of the 'beginning,' . . . —*bara*, created, that is to say, the hidden Nothing which constitutes the [unwritten] grammatical subject of the word *bara*, [he] emanated or unfolded,—*Elohim*, that is to say, its emanation is *Elohim*. It is the object, and not the subject of the sentence. And what is *Elohim*? *Elohim* is the name of God, which guarantees the continued existence of creation insofar as it represents the union of the hidden subject *Mi* and the hidden object *Eleh* (The Hebrew words *Mi* and *Eleh* have the same consonants as the complete word *Elohim*).—In other words, *Elohim* is the name given to God after the disjunction of subject and object has taken place, but in which this gap is continuously bridged or closed. The mystical Nothing which lies before the division of the primary idea into the Knower and the Known is not regarded by the Kabbalist as a true subject." *Major Trends*, 221.

27. Scholem, "Schöpfung aus Nichts," 94.

28. Gershom Scholem, "95 Thesen über Judentum und Zionismus. Teils aus alten teils aus ungeschriebenen Buchern ausgezogen und aufgestellet durch Gerhard Scholem, angeschlagen am 15. Juli 1918 mit 15jähriger Diskussionsfrist," in *Gershom Scholem zwischen den Disziplinen*, reproduced also in Scholem, *Tagebücher* II, 300–307.

29. As Scholem wrote in a draft of his ninety-five theses. Scholem, *Tagebücher* II, 209. It is probably no accident that Cohen frames Scholem's essay of 1957 also, which opens with an explicit nod to Cohen's work on the "miracle of origins" and concludes in similar fashion (even if Cohen goes unnamed the second time around).

30. On originary thinking, see the discussion in Simon Fisher, *Revelatory Positivism? Barth's Earliest Theology and the Marburg School* (Oxford, 1988), 41–42.

31. Peter Gordon, "Rosenzweig Redux: the Reception of German-Jewish Thought," *Jewish Social Studies* 8, 1 (2001), 9.

32. Peter Gordon, "Science, Finitude and Infinity: Neo-Kantianism and the Birth of Existentialism," *Jewish Social Studies* 6, 1 (1999), 41–44; Amos Funkenstein, *Perceptions of Jewish History* (Berkeley, 1993), 270–91.

33. Löwith said so in an essay of 1948, "Heidegger: Problem and Background of Existentialism," *Social Research* 15, 3 (1948), reprinted in Löwith, *Nature, History and Existentialism* (Evanston, Ill., 1966), 39, 44.

34. A translation of the essay appears in Martin Heidegger, *Basic Writings*, ed. David Farell Krell (New York, 1977), 91–112, here at 110.

35. Scholem, *Tagebücher* II, 137.

36. Gordon, "Science, Finitude and Infinity," 41.

37. For a discussion of modern versus Aristotelian notions of privation, see Funkenstein, *Perceptions of Jewish History*, 272–73.

38. Scholem, "Schöpfung aus Nichts," 119.

39. Aristotle, *Categories* 12a30, *Topics* 147b35–148a1, and especially *Metaphysics* 1022b22–32.

40. Scholem, "Schöpfung aus Nichts," 119, italics added.

41. Scholem, *Tagebücher* II, 382. For all Scholem's talk of the divinity that breaks out in the process of life, so too did he speak of the process of life in God. For all his attention to the divinity attached to physis, so too did he attend to the "authentic and deep theosophical teaching of a *physis* of the divinity" as that which distinguished a mystical theology from a rational one (Scholem, "Vuillauds Übersetzung," 452). The kabbalist scheme of *sefirot*, for example, described God as an organism. If the hypostases of Plotinus, those intermediate stages between the one and the phenomenal world, proceeded in a series of emanations, the *sefirot*, by contrast, interacted with one another; they had semi-autonomous status, could ascend and descend, and despite a certain hierarchy, they could occasionally appear elsewhere or otherwise—in other words, "what we have here is something like a real process of life in God." Lurianic kabbalah developed the organological imagery of the Zohar still further by positing the whole of creation as a "gigantic process of inhalation and exhalation." The *shvirat ha-kelim*, or

breaking of the vessels, was likened to the abjection of birth, that "deepest convulsion of the organism which, incidentally, is also accompanied by the externalization of what might be described as waste products." Scholem, *Major Trends*, 225, 263, 267.

42. Scholem, "Schöpfung aus Nichts," 117–18.

43. Isaiah Tishby explores the question in Luria's thought in what began as the first dissertation written under Scholem's guidance: *Torat ha-Ra ve-ha-Kelipah be-Kabbalat ha-Ari* (Jerusalem, 1942).

44. Scholem, *On the Kabbalah and Its Symbolism*, 28–29, italics added. Chapter 1 of the book is an English translation and reworking of the original German essay of 1957. Strauss, to judge by his letter to Scholem, had read both.

45. Jonas, *Gnostic Religion*, 332, 334.

46. Jonas, *Gnostic Religion*, 340.

47. Scholem said as much in 1971, when he spoke to a group of educators from *Hashomer Hatzair* (the Young Guard) about Jewish education for godless communists like themselves: "I will admit that I am a thoroughgoing anti-Canaanite. . . . I do not agree with those who wish to skip over the *Galut*. We all know that there are those among us who preach that there is some inner bridge between those of us (here in Israel) and the biblical period, and that Diaspora is something that we negate. I do not share such views." The transcript from the meeting has been translated and published in Scholem, *On the Possibility of Jewish Mysticism in Our Time*, here at 86.

48. Scholem, *Tagebücher* II, 635.

49. Scholem, *Tagebücher* II, 463.

50. Franz Rosenzweig, *Briefe* (Berlin, 1935), 431. Reproduced here is the translation of the letter that appears in Lawrence Rosenwald, "For and Against Scholem," *Prooftexts* 14, 3 (1994), 296.

NOTES TO CHAPTER THIRTEEN: SCHOLEM'S GOLEM

1. Gershom Scholem, "The Golem of Prague and the Golem of Rehovot," in *The Messianic Idea in Judaism* (New York, 1971), 339.

2. Scholem, *On the Kabbalah and Its Symbolism*, 159.

3. Scholem, *On the Kabbalah and Its Symbolism*, 202.

4. Beate Rosenfeld, *Die Golemsage und ihre Verwertung in der deutschen Literatur* (Breslau, 1934), 41, 47. The golem story apparently did not achieve its "complete" form until the early twentieth century, as Hillel J. Kieval argues in *Languages of Community: The Jewish Experience in the Czech Lands* (Berkeley, 2000).

5. Cited in Scholem, *On the Kabbalah and Its Symbolism*, 180–81.

6. Scholem, "Golem of Prague," 338.

7. The Hebrew original is published in Scholem, *Devarim Be-Go*, here at 396. A full translation appears in Scholem, *On the Possibility of Jewish Mysticism in*

Our Time, 51–71, but the passage presented here has best been translated by David Biale in *Gershom Scholem*, 6.

8. Scholem opposed Hermann Cohen's version of the messianic project for similar reasons; though it affirmed messianism as a project of this world and not the next, it repudiated Jewish self-assertion as a project of Jewish difference.

9. Scholem, *On the Possibility of Jewish Mysticism in Our Time*, 113.

10. Gershom Scholem, "The Threat of Messianism [Interview with David Biale]," *New York Review of Books* (August 14, 1980).

11. Scholem, *On the Possibility of Jewish Mysticism in Our Time*, 116, italics added. The lines reproduce a sentiment he expressed at least as early as 1929. See, for example, his letter to Yehuda Burla in "Al shlosha pishei 'brit shalom'" in Gershom Scholem, *Od Davar* (Tel-Aviv, 1989), 88.

12. Still, this was a thoroughly historical world for Scholem above all in a metaphysical sense, as the relative absence of the Palestinian Arabs from his formulations can attest.

13. Scholem's argument on this count came in for sharp criticism (after his death) from his onetime student and longtime nemesis, Jacob Taubes. See Taubes, *Vom Kult zur Kultur* (Munich, 1996), 43–50.

14. More recently and in German, it is also Christoph Schmidt's. Peter L. Berger, *The Heretical Imperative: Contemporary Possibilities of Religious Affirmation* (New York, 1979); Christoph Schmidt, *Der häretische Imperativ*.

15. The argument also suffers on several counts. For one, to universalize heresy strips the term of its meaning. If every religious choice is heretical, one may just as well say that none of them is. Berger's thesis also homogenizes all that came before as an unconscious and unconflicted living out of tradition in something of an eternal "now." He writes: "For premodern man, heresy is a possibility—usually a rather remote one; for modern man, heresy typically becomes a necessity. Or again, modernity creates a new situation in which picking and choosing becomes an imperative" (28). Berger's scheme also seems ill-suited to the Jewish case, as it underestimates the ambivalence about rabbinic authority in Jewish life before the modern age (to which the Sabbatians, for example, can attest). See, for example, Talya Fishman, *Shaking the Pillars of Exile* (Stanford, 1997).

16. Löwith, *Nature, History and Existentialism*, 32.

17. Scholem, "Redemption through Sin," 112.

18. Scholem, *On the Possibility of Jewish Mysticism in Our Time*, 85.

19. Amnon Raz-Krakotzkin (in *Politik und Religion im Judentum*, ed. Christoph Miething [Tübingen, 1999], 223–38) has used the golem motif to describe the unintended consequences of Scholem's interest in messianism, and to suggest a hidden affinity between Scholem and Rabbi Avraham Yitzhak Ha-Cohen Kook, the first Chief Rabbi of Palestine and the spiritual inspiration for the post-1967 religious settlement movement. Whether Scholem's golem—the Jewish return to history—had to run amok as the sort of counterhistorical messianism underwriting the settlement movement, as Raz-Krakotzkin seems to think, I am not so sure. Still, he may well be right to say that Scholem neglected to leave instructions for tearing the paper from the golem's mouth. Perhaps Scholem did

not do so because he knew that the heretical imperative, once heeded, can be sublimated but not refuted, worked through but not undone.

20. Scholem, *On the Possibility of Jewish Mysticism in Our Time*, 117.

21. Scholem, "The Golem of Prague," 340. The Hebrew original reads: "please don't return the world to the chaos that precedes creation [tohu-va-bohu]." Do not undo, in other words, what God has wrought on our behalf. Scholem, *Devarim Be-Go*, 90.

NOTE TO EPILOGUE

1. Arendt, The *Human Condition*, 2.

Index

19037076R00151

Printed in Great Britain
by Amazon